THE GREAT POLAR FRAUD

Cook, Peary, and Byrd—How Three American Heroes Duped the World into Thinking They Had Reached the North Pole

ANTHONY GALVIN

Skyhorse Publishing

Skyhorse Publishing books may be purchased in bulk at special discounts for sales promotion, corporate gifts, fund-raising, or educational purposes. Special editions can also be created to specifications. For details, contact the Special Sales Department, Skyhorse Publishing, 307 West 36th Street, 11th Floor, New York, NY 10018 or info@skyhorsepublishing.com.

Skyhorse® and Skyhorse Publishing® are registered trademarks of Skyhorse Publishing, Inc.®, a Delaware corporation.

Visit our website at www.skyhorsepublishing.com.

10 9 8 7 6 5 4 3 2 1

Library of Congress Cataloging-in-Publication Data is available on file.

Cover design by Brian Peterson
Cover photo credit Thinkstock

Print ISBN: 978-1-62914-504-4
Ebook ISBN: 978-1-62914-968-4

Printed in the United States of America

CONTENTS

The Arctic trails have their secret tales
That would make your blood run cold.
Robert Service

INTRODUCTION

January 1926, Leavenworth Prison, Kansas

The tall, handsome man walked into the warden's office and sat on the long wooden bench. Though he was getting older and his blond hair was turning gray, he still carried himself well and retained the distinguished look of a prosperous country doctor. His eyes were as piercing as ever. But his face was pale and his body had lost the firmness of his glory days. The years in Leavenworth had done that.

Dr. Frederick Cook was nervous. He got few visitors, not because he was forgotten but because he discouraged them. He did not want people to see him like this. Even his ex-wife, whom he remained close to, was barred. Though he still loved her dearly and she was in his thoughts every day, she would no longer be in his life. Every request for an interview had been turned down. Journalists, old friends, people who had been part of his earlier life when he had been celebrated coast to coast, they were all on the no visit list. But for the man who was on his way to the prison, he had to make an exception. Their lives were entwined in so many ways.

Cook and his guards heard the sound of approaching footsteps, doors clanging open and banging shut, as the visitor made his way to the warden's office. Then the door opened and a guard stepped in. Behind him was a big, ruddy-faced man, dressed well but looking slightly uncomfortable in his fashionable clothes: Roald Amundsen, the famous polar explorer, and the first man to the South Pole. Amundsen stepped around the guard and stood facing Cook, who had risen on his entrance. The two men stared at each other for a moment, then broad smiles broke out on their faces. As if of one mind, each man stepped forward and grasped the other firmly by the hand.

They sat on the wooden bench, side by side. Amundsen did not let go of Cook's hand. He was European, and comfortable with the intimacy.

Cook was glad to feel the warmth of friendly companionship. After an exchange of pleasantries, under the watchful and curious eyes of the warden and a few prison guards, talk turned to the future—specifically to Amundsen's plans to fly to the North Pole.

They avoided the past, as if by a mutual pact. The past was like a ghost in the room, brooding over them. It was one of two ghosts they were both acutely aware of. But they brushed them aside, as Amundsen spoke of the failure of his attempt to fly to the Pole in 1925. The next time, he planned to use an airship. He grew animated as he told Cook about the *Norge*, and his plans for a transpolar flight. He had seen so many features on the ice during the 1925 flight, features which confirmed sightings Cook had made nearly two decades previously. As he listened, Cook got excited. Although he would not say it to the younger man, he knew those sightings could back up his claim, the claim that had both crowned his life's achievements and blighted them.

On April 15, 1909, Cook had arrived in Annoatok, northern Greenland, with a tale of unbelievable survival against the odds. He had disappeared fourteen months earlier with two Eskimo companions, last seen heading north across the frozen polar sea. When he reappeared—long after he was given up for dead—he told a delighted world that he had reached the Pole on April 22, 1908, but the drift of the polar sea had meant that it took him a full year to return to civilization.

Unluckily for Cook, another American explorer had also set his heart on achieving the Pole. Naval Commander Robert Peary had impressive backers; even President Roosevelt had been behind him. Peary set out a year later than Cook, but had not got lost on his return. He reached civilization within five days of Cook, and also claimed to have reached the Pole. He said he got there on April 6, 1909. Cook was happy to share the glory; Peary, less so. The naval commander immediately threw the weight of his considerable circle of friends into a frenzied effort to discredit Cook. The two men, once friends, ended up in an unseemly media war. Bit by bit, all of Cook's previous achievements came under scrutiny. Peary even paid a massive bribe to one man to discredit Cook's claim to have been the first to climb Mount

McKinley, the highest point in North America. It was a campaign of dirty tricks and intense bitterness, and it worked. Within a year, Cook was seen by everyone as a fraud.

The stigma followed him for the rest of his life. Now Peary was long dead, but as Cook languished in Leavenworth Prison, he knew that it was the ghost of Peary that put him there; the judge at his trial had been a personal friend of his rival, and had imposed a sentence far harsher than his offense warranted.

The other ghost that brooded over Cook and Amundsen in the dank visiting room was the elemental spirit of the Pole itself. It had shaped and dominated both their lives. Cook had known from his early twenties that he wanted to reach 90 degrees north; Amundsen had known from his teens, when he had started sleeping naked on top of his sheets, with his windows wide open. The frozen Norwegian air hardened his body for the adventures he dreamed of, and there had been many adventures. Amundsen had spent the first winter in Antarctica with Cook, and had been the first to navigate the Northwest Passage. In 1908 he was ready to make his own dash for the Pole. Then, within a week, he had heard that both his rivals, Cook and Peary, claimed to have snatched the prize.

Devastated, he altered his plans and secretly sailed south, becoming the first man to reach the South Pole, an accomplishment he considered a sort of consolation prize. As he sat with Cook that day in 1926, he must have wondered how things might have turned out if Cook and Peary had not both claimed the main prize. He knew that there were considerable doubts over Cook's claim, and he suspected that there was doubt over Peary's—the brash American had never had a high reputation in Europe. But history had decided, at least then, to accept Peary's claim, and Amundsen had to go along with that verdict.

To Cook, Amundsen appeared pensive and almost depressed that afternoon.

"Our lot has been a hard one," Amundsen said with a sigh. "From the depths of poverty to the heights of glory. From brief spells of hard earned success to the scourge of condemnation. I have wondered for years how you stood it all. I have had the same, with perhaps not so much of the knife in it, but with quite as much of the pain of envy."

After forty-five minutes the warden signaled the end of the visit. As Amundsen turned to go, he said, "I want you to know that even if all the world goes against you, I believe in you as a man."

Amundsen left to continue his lecture tour, a fundraiser for the airship flight over the Pole. If he succeeded he would be the third man to reach the spot, and the first to fly there. But life is never that simple, and he was very aware that he had a rival, a young Navy aviator named Richard Byrd. Although he did not know it at the time, theirs would be a very closely contested race, a race he would lose by hours.

And he would die without ever knowing that Byrd's claim to the Pole was as dubious as Cook's. Eventually, Peary's claim was also discredited. The three American heroes had knowingly and deliberately tried to pull a con on the entire world. Cook got away with it for a couple of months. It took decades before Peary and Bryd were found out. The spirit of the Pole was a dark one, inspiring greed, envy, deceit, and outright fraud. If the race to the South Pole was a tale of courage and self-sacrifice, the race to the North Pole was a sordid tale of great men with great flaws who allowed their soaring ambitions to overcome their ethics and honesty.

As Cook was escorted back to his cell, his step was lighter. The visit had done him a lot of good, and his jaunty air belied his sixty years. Some part of him hoped that Amundsen would find something in the bleak but beautiful polar landscape to back up his own claim to have been the first there. Despite his lengthy incarceration, he could still dream. . . .

SEEKING THE BIG NAIL

Spring, 1908

How far is far enough? It was an impossible question, but one that had been bothering Dr. Frederick Cook for some weeks. He had begun to ponder the problem shortly after leaving the relative safety of Axel Heiberg Island, high in the Canadian Arctic, in early March. Now, after several weeks on the rough and broken sea ice, he thought of little else.

All of his life, since the deaths of his wife and young daughter, had been leading him to these few weeks. He was not just marching across the ice; he was marching toward his destiny. And like all men with a destiny, he had a massive ego. Neither man nor elements—nor facts—was going to deny him his goal.

Cook wanted to be the first man to reach the top of the world, the North Pole. And he was damned if he was going to allow two scared Eskimo to spoil the party.

As he and his two companions—Inuit natives Ahwelah and Etukishook—trudged over the rough ice, the dry crunch of their shuffling feet in the powdery snow was the only sound for miles around—that, the yapping of their dogs, and an occasional sigh from their labored breathing. The sound of their footsteps was like a weak heartbeat, slowing imperceptibly as the days turned to weeks and the cold and hunger bit deeper into their bodies. The puppy fat of civilization was gone, as the three men were living on their reserves. And only one of them was happy with that situation.

The snow stretched before them, behind them, and around them in endless desolation. The horizon was flat, but the ground was broken and rough, making progress slow. The North Pole is on floating frozen sea water, unlike the South Pole. You didn't have to face the high altitude, deep glacial crevasses, and the coldest temperatures on the planet. But sea ice has its own dangers. The waters beneath are constantly moving, and the ice is only a few feet thick. It creaks and buckles alarmingly. Pressure waves build up, leading to rough going. The ground underfoot, buried beneath a few inches of powdery snow, can be as broken as a field of rocks and as dangerous to unwary ankles.

The other danger is leads—spaces of open water revealed when the ice cracks. If you slip and a hand plunges into that water, you will lose the fingers to frostbite. That is not a gamble; it is a stone cold certainty. And if you fall into the lead, it is game over.

Those who have never been to the Arctic have a picture of the region as cold and bleak, like the grainy photos that the explorers brought home. But despite its dangers, nothing could be further from the truth. The Arctic is alive with color. The sun never rises much above the horizon, so the sky is a constant glorious sunset. Sometimes when the cloud cover is dense, the sky can take on a luminous salmon shade that stretches from high overhead down to the horizon. The color becomes reflected in the ice, and the horizon disappears, giving the impression that you are marching disembodied through a pink haze—what Scandinavians call a Pink Moment. At other times the sky seems to be on fire, with red and purple and angry orange hues.

The ice you are trudging through has its own palette of rich blues and greens. And when the conditions are still, particles of moisture crystallize in the air, glittering like diamonds in the sunlight. It is like walking through your own ticker-tape parade.

"I can see the sun lying low above the horizon, which glittered here and there in shafts of light like the tip of a long, circular, silver blade. The globe of fire, veiled occasionally by purplish, silver-shot mists, was tinged with a faint, burning lilac. Through opening cracks in the constantly moving field of ice, cold strata of air rose, deflecting the sun's rays in every direction, and changing the vision of distant ice irregularities which a deceptive perspective, as an oar blade seen in the depth of still water," wrote Cook, some months later.

Attaining the North Pole—or the Big Nail, as the Inuit called it— had been the goal of a generation of explorers, many of whom who lost their lives on the ice. In theory it was simple; just head north until any step you took in any direction was south. But there were complications. So close to the magnetic pole, a compass was useless. It would lead back to the magnetic pole on Ellesmere Island, close to where Cook had left from. So Cook had to use a sextant to keep on track. Observations were complicated, involving mathematical procedures and charts, and could only be taken at noon every day. His two companions couldn't tell time, let alone use a sextant, so all positional questions fell to Cook.

There was another complication: the ice was moving.

You could take your sighting at the beginning of a six-hour march, then cover ten miles. At the end of that drudge you might discover that the ice had moved back three miles, robbing you of a third of your hard-earned gain. Worse, it could drift sideways, meaning you were walking in a perpetual spiral around your final destination. Two steps forward, one step back, and a little jig to the left or right. It is the curse of the Arctic explorer.

However, Cook had one thing going for him. He was pioneering a new style of exploration. He traveled light, and used local knowledge and expertise. Previous generations of explorers had taken large expeditions, with dozens of men and tons of equipment. They were slow and ponderous, and risked being stranded if they did not get clear of the ice before the season turned. Cook brought twenty natives and eight sleighs to the edge of the Arctic Ocean; small by the standards of the time. They killed a supply of fresh meat, then reduced the team to three.

Cook had just two native companions. They were using a team of twenty-six dogs pulling two sleighs, and carrying enough food for eighty days. Living off the land meant killing and feasting on the dogs as the trip progressed; he expected to return with one sleigh and just six dogs. The plan was to move fast, and be gone no more than three months.

Essential supplies included a collapsible canvas boat for the open leads, as well as 805 pounds of beef pemmican (an unpalatable mix of beef and fat), 130 pounds of walrus pemmican, fifty pounds of musk ox tenderloin, and twenty-five pounds of musk ox fat. To wash this down, they packed two pounds of tea and a pound of coffee. They had fuel, matches, a silken tent, and reindeer hide sleeping bags. They also brought two rifles and ammunition, for game hunting and protection against polar bears.

As well as speed and mobility, Cook had another key advantage over earlier explorers. His companions were very experienced in the bleak polar conditions, but they were uneducated savages. They knew they were seeking the Big Nail; at one point the world had been pinned to a great iron spike in the far north. But that nail had fallen in the snow and been lost—which was why iron was so scarce and so valuable. But why the white man wanted to find the nail, they did not know. They could not read his shiny instruments, so they had to trust him when he said they had arrived.

Cook knew his companions could keep him alive in the far north, and could not contradict his story when he made it back to civilization. It was Mount McKinley all over again. Once he got close enough, a bit of flim-flam would convince the world he had achieved his goal. That is why the question of "how far is 'far enough'" was so important.

It was not that Cook needed to cheat. He had serious credentials as an explorer. He had been to the Antarctic twice, and was part of the first team to spend a winter in the far south. He had also opened up the Rockies in Alaska, and was credited with the first ascent of North America's highest mountain, Mount McKinley. He was a founding member of the Polar Club and the Explorers Club. But his experience on McKinley—where he had climbed a minor, neighboring peak and claimed the main prize—showed him that a good story, convincingly told, would be good enough if things turned bad.

Still, he had to make it look genuine, so he pushed north, grittily gaining a few more miles with each forced march. From Axel Heiberg Island to the Pole was just 520 miles, and if conditions were right he would achieve his goal for real.

For three weeks he took his sextant readings faithfully every noon. Every night they made camp on the ice. Every morning they broke camp and pushed farther into the unknown. But Ahwelah and Etukishook were getting worried. Inuit do not like being so far from land, and from game. And they did not understand the white man's obsession with the Big Nail. They were only with Cook because he had promised them each a gun and a knife. Riches indeed to nomadic hunters, but not worth their lives. And the dogs were getting restless; polar explorers had learned that dogs did not relish working on sea ice.

After twenty-four days they had advanced 360 miles, more than halfway to the Pole. They were averaging fifteen miles a day, which was less than the experienced polar explorer would have wished. Cook knew enough to realize his expedition was in trouble. At this rate there was no margin for error; they ran a serious risk of their food running out. And it had not been smooth so far.

On April 8 the weather had broken, plunging the three men into five days of misery, as freezing winds made breathing painful. Finally the two Inuit could take no more; they wanted to turn. As Cook wrote: "They were lost in a landless, spiritless world, in which the sky, the weather, the sun, and all was a mystery."

There was a tense stand-off on the ice. The cold and starved Inuit insisted they would not walk a step further. Cook argued and cajoled. He told them of rich and undiscovered hunting grounds farther north. He threatened to deny them their guns and knives if they let him down. Finally he promised them that they were only five days from the Pole. Five more sleeps and they could turn. Reluctantly, they lifted their whips and urged the dogs forward.

Despite the pressure of imminent mutiny, Cook's excitement grew as the sextant revealed day by day how much closer to his goal he was. Soon he would find out how far was far enough.

"Feverish impatience seized me. Cracking our whips, we bounded ahead. The boys sang. The dogs howled. Midnight of April 21 had just passed. Over the sparkling snows the post-midnight sun glowed like at noon. I seemed to be walking in some splendid golden realms of dreamland. As we bounded onward, the ice swam about me in circling rivers of gold.

"Etukishook and Ahwelah, though thin and ragged, had the dignity of the heroes of a battle which had been fought through to success."

At noon on April 21, Cook called a halt. As his companions prepared a simple meal of pemmican and tea, he took another sextant reading. The Inuit knew this was it. For the white man, glory. For them, the chance to turn for home.

"For that moment I was intoxicated," Cook wrote. "I stood alone, apart from my two Eskimo companions, a shifting waste of purple ice on every side, alone in a dead world—a world of angry winds, eternal cold, and desolate for hundreds of miles in every direction as the planet before man was made.

"I felt in my heart that thrill which any man must feel when an almost impossible but dearly desired work is attained—the thrill of accomplishment with which a poet must regard his greatest masterpiece, which a sculptor must feel when he puts the finishing touch to inanimate matter wherein he has expressed consummately a living thought, which a conqueror must feel when he has mastered a formidable alien army."

Jubilant, Cook took a large stars and stripes flag from one of the sleighs, and tied it to a tent pole. He was claiming the top of the world for his ninety million countrymen.

"I felt a pride as I gazed at the white and crimson barred pinion, a pride which the claim of no second victor has ever taken from me."

The men camped overnight. The temperature was -86°F, and the ice was eighteen feet thick beneath their feet. Under the ice, the Arctic Sea stretched a further four thousand feet beneath them. They were on top of the world. And they were over five hundred miles from the safety of land—*if Cook could be believed.* Even if he was exaggerating their distances, they were in a very perilous position. It was time to turn home.

But had he come far enough?

1

PEARY'S EARLY LIFE

"Give me the boy until he is seven, and I will give you the man," is a famous quote from St. Francis Xavier, one of the early luminaries of the Jesuit order. The Jesuits are the special forces of the Catholic Church. Intellectuals and educators, they believe strongly that the early years are vital in forming character. They would have had a field day with Robert Peary.

Peary was a classic mama's boy, raised in the shadow of a domineering and overprotective mother. She was determined to keep her little boy safe, both from other little boys and from the dangers of the world. Their relationship was so close she even came along on the grown Perry's honeymoon, which caused a lot of tension with his new wife.

It is perhaps understandable, because she was widowed early and her darling Robert was all that she had in the world. She doted on him. But there is no doubt that the unnaturally close relationship between mother and son shaped the man, twisting him in ways that made some of his later polar peculiarities more understandable, if not any more forgivable.

Peary came from good sea-faring stock. His roots were both French (on his mother's side) and English (on his father's). His great-great-grandfather, Stephen Peare, had sailed around Cape Horn to the Pacific Ocean. Even today that is a perilous route, and back in the days of sail, only the most experienced of mariners dared the passage. But after Stephen, the family seemed to have settled on land, though they retained their links with the world of shipping. Many of them were in the lumber business.

Charles Peary was a cooper, a highly skilled trade much in demand. He made barrels, which were essential for shipping. There was considerable art in making a perfect barrel. Each stave had to be perfectly cut so that when they curved together and were bound by bands of iron or brass, the seals became watertight. A good cooper never lacked for work, and Charlie built a thriving business. He was based in Cresson, Pennsylvania. This was a long way from the sea, in the center of the stage. The village was situated high in mountainous terrain, and was noted for its natural beauty, its forests, and its pure mineral springs. When the railway arrived it became a popular destination for the rich on vacation.

It was a thriving community and Charles was doing well. He married Mary Wiley, a woman of French descent. Her family were based around Portland, Maine, and Mary had a reputation for gentleness and piety. She was a soft woman, perhaps more suited for city living. The couple settled in the village and their first son, Robert, arrived on May 6, 1856. They were delighted, and spoiled their young charge. It seemed they were destined for a comfortable, if unremarkable, life in small-town America.

But when Robert was just three his father contracted pneumonia. This is a severe lung condition that can swiftly become fatal. A century ago, before antibiotics, a diagnosis of pneumonia was often a death sentence. Although he was just thirty years old and strong, he was unable to fight off the disease, and he died within a few weeks. Mary, not robust herself, was plunged into a deep depression. She was unable to cope with widowhood. Her family rallied around, but her depression settled like a cloud over the family. All the familiar surroundings reminded her of what she had lost. Not for her the conventional route of staying in the locality and maybe starting afresh with a new husband. She knew she had to leave.

Luckily the cooperage was doing very well. Charles's share of the business was worth close to $12,000—quite a fortune in those days. Mary, who got the full share, knew she would be a wealthy woman. She decided to leave almost immediately, packing her most essential belongings, and taking a train back to Portland. She left within a day or two of her husband's death. In fact, she took his body on the train with her, so that it could be buried in Maine, near where she intended to settle. It was all done with unseemly haste.

Robert, barely talking, was thrust from a bustling world of friends and country freedom into a big gloomy house with only a depressed mother for company. She had lost one of the most important men in her life and was determined she would not lose a second. She began to mollycoddle the young boy. She treated him as part doll, part girl, and part pet. She fussed over him and became wildly overprotective. One thing she quickly decided was that he was weak and delicate, and not suitable for the robust play of growing boys. She rarely let him out with the neighboring kids. On the few occasions that she did let him stray, he had to dress up warmly in winter, or wear a bonnet in summer to protect his sensitive skin from the sun. A small child with a lisp, these few extra humiliations were all that were needed to make him stand out as a figure of fun among the tougher boys of the locality. He was teased unmercifully, and subjected to bullying.

What the bullies did not realize was that a lisp was not a sign of physical frailty; just ask any of Mike Tyson's opponents. Peary might have appeared a weakling, but there burned inside him a fierce pride, and a determination to prove himself. Instead of running away when confronted, he boldly struck back. The result was that he got into a lot of fist fights, and ended up coming home battered and bruised. Of course, this reinforced his mother's belief that he was weak and needed protecting. Instead of letting him fight his own battles, she tried to remove him from the battlefield. The vicious cycle continued. Robert Peary was being raised a sissy, even though he had the backbone of a far tougher character.

Throughout his life he rebelled in small ways, while remaining outwardly loyal and devoted to his mother. Perhaps his polar exploits could be seen in that light, as one massive rebellion against an over-restricted upbringing.

He had five years of loving imprisonment before escape beckoned in the form of boarding school. At the tender age of eight he was sent to a boys' academy, where he thrived in the sudden freedom. He wrote home frequently, and couldn't keep his delight out of the missives. He was trying baseball, and playing with the boys in the fields every day after class. He reveled in this newly discovered man's world.

At the age of fourteen he returned home, much to the delight of his mother, and entered Portland High School in 1870. In a new school, among new companions, you can be whoever you like. But Peary was denied that luxury; not long into his first year he was struck by typhoid fever, a very severe bacteriological illness that is fatal in up to a third of cases if untreated. In 1870 there was no treatment except bed rest and plenty of cooling baths to break the fever. Peary was back in the loving clutches of his mother.

The fever took a month to work its way through his body, and then there were a few more weeks of bed rest to recuperate. Ever cautious, Mary would not let him back into the hurly-burly of school until she was sure he was ready. Instead she brought him an endless stream of books to keep him occupied. He developed a fondness for books on natural history, and dreamed of escape to the exotic climes the books described. When he finally got back to school he had to cram to make up the year's work in three months. Already the determination that would mark his later years was evident.

School was an escape from the cloying atmosphere at home, and Peary thrived in high school. He got good grades and was chosen as one of the student speakers at the graduation. He spoke on Nature's Mysteries, a topic that gave him plenty of scope to talk about natural history and far flung locations. At one point he flung out a question— what would man find at the North Pole? Some years later he would set out to answer that very question.

Peary's final grades were enough to win him a scholarship to Bowdoin College. Bowdoin was a small liberal arts college with a friendly atmosphere and a low student to teacher ratio, making the tuition very personal. Among the more famous graduates were Henry Wadsworth Longfellow and Nathanial Hawthorne. Today it is ranked as the fourth best liberal arts college in the United States. The only drawback was that the faculty was located in Brunswick, a small coastal town nearly thirty miles from Portland. Could Mary Peary bear to see her son take such a long journey?

In the end—much to the consternation of her extended family—she decided that she would have to move to Brunswick with her son. Now a grown man about to embark on his college education, she still would not cut the apron strings.

This unnaturally close relationship with his mother stamped Peary's personality permanently. At times he could be confident and sure of himself. But sometimes the insecurities bred by his upbringing would come out. Also, he had the typical entitled attitude of a spoiled child who is always indulged. The closeness bred some very negative personality traits. He was used to having things done for him, and in later life he hired a manservant who accompanied him on all his polar expeditions. He also developed a rebellious streak, which manifested itself in his desire to escape. You couldn't escape much farther away than the Pole.

Although the college had a liberal arts leaning, Peary chose to study civil engineering. He had a natural calling for the subject, which combined precise mathematical work with the ability to organize large projects. These skills would prove very useful when he became an explorer. He did very well in college. Not only did he thrive academically, he also threw himself into student life. He rowed for his year, and was involved in planning social events such as Ivy Day celebrations, an important event in the college calendar. He was a member of two honor societies, Phi Delta Kappa and Kappa Delta Epsilon. When he graduated in 1877, he was ranked second in his class of more than fifty.

At that point Robert Peary was an independent young man. He had good qualifications and could have found work in any of the growing cities along the east coast. Instead he took the path of least resistance, and followed his mother to Fryeburg, a small village on the border of Maine and New Hampshire. In this rural community in the mountains, surrounded by swift rivers and deep forest, Mary Peary was returning to a community not far removed from what she had left when her husband had died eighteen years previously. It was a curious move—and one designed to keep her son in tow; there were not many opportunities for ambitious young civil engineers in the village.

He managed to get work doing a survey of Fryeburg, his first job. But it hardly stretched his skills, or gave him any satisfaction. As the months passed, the exuberance of his college days slowly drained from him, leaving him lethargic and lacking in confidence. He was in the doldrums, drifting to nowhere. His only outlet was long walks in the woods, observing the wildlife. He took a keen interest in nature still, and began stuffing animals as a hobby, gaining a small reputation locally as a taxidermist. He dated a local woman, and they became engaged.

Mediocrity beckoned.

2

COOK'S CHILDHOOD

Some people are born to be explorers. Others have exploration thrust upon them. The latter was certainly the case with Dr. Frederick Cook, a Brooklyn physician who had no childhood ambitions to wander the remote regions of the globe. He was a middle-class boy with a go-ahead attitude and a great future ahead of him. He wanted a good job and a secure income, an escape from the poverty he had risen out of. If tragedy had not blighted his life, he would never have set foot in the Polar Regions—or left his mark on the world stage.

Dr. Cook did not run away to discover the world—he ran away to escape it.

He had come from stout immigrant stock—like most Americans—and grew up in a rural idyll. His father, Dr. Theodore Koch, was from Germany. After receiving his medical degree, he sailed for the new world full of hope. He arrived in 1848 and settled in a quiet spot, Sullivan County in the Catskill Mountains, north of New York City. Upstate New York is a place of rolling hills, swift rivers, and dense forest. Although only a few hours' ride from the city, it was a wilderness abounding in wildlife, like the forests of his native Germany. Every fall

7

the sale to buy a door-to-door milk delivery service—people always needed milk. He was still in his teens, but showed the drive that would characterize the rest of his career.

Door-to-door delivery was a new idea at the time. It would eventually become common throughout much of urban America, until refrigeration made it unnecessary. Cook was in at the start, and quickly built up a solid customer base. In fact, he bought a horse to cope with the growing demand, and recruited his brothers to help. Eventually he had a number of employees and several wagons delivering bottles and picking up the empties. He was still in high school.

Despite his busy schedule, he graduated from Public School No. 37 with sufficient grades to qualify for Columbia University. Like the man who would become a good friend, rival explorer Roald Amundsen, he had no choice in his college course—his mother pushed him into a career in medicine. The big difference was that Cook embraced the opportunity. He threw himself into his studies while he also continued to work on the milk delivery. The hours suited the life of a student. Cook began his deliveries at 1:00 a.m., working through until morning, so that his customers had fresh milk for breakfast. At 10:00 a.m., he would be in the university, where he stayed until 4:00 p.m. That left him some time to eat, study, then catch up on a few hours of sleep before 1:00 a.m. rolled around again and the process began anew.

Cook was a dynamo of energy, requiring only a few hours of sleep each night. This ability to get by on only a few hours of sleep was something he had all through his life. It gave him a few extra hours each day, and would be particularly important in survival situations.

In 1888, two years before he graduated, there was a massive blizzard that brought the entire city to a standstill. Milk delivery was out of the question; roads were impassable. The University closed its doors for a number of days, as commercial life creaked to a halt. The only people doing good business were the coal yards. Everyone wanted fires, and homes were running low. Cook's own family was feeling the chill. Instead of buckling under the strain, Cook saw the opportunity. One of his brothers had built a boat for the summer. Cook put two stout wooden runners under the boat and converted it into a large sleigh. He hitched two horses to it, and he had transport. Not only did he ferry fuel from the coal yard to his mother, he began delivering to the neighbors—but for a price. For a week, Frederick Cook was one of the busiest men in New York, as he kept the team of horses on their toes. Nothing could keep him down.

When the thaw came, he resumed his studies. Columbia University was quite a distance from Brooklyn. He wasted quite a while on the commute, which included a ferry trip. In 1888 the medical department moved, resulting in a thirty block walk on top of his commute. So he switched to New York University to complete his medical training.

The following year was the turning point in Cook's life. He spotted a wonderful young woman at the Methodist church one weekend. His eye was immediately caught by the attractive blonde. Not only was she pretty, she was bright and independent. In an era when women were reared for the matrimonial bed, she had chosen to enter the male dominated profession of stenographer. She worked in the office of a Manhattan shoe factory. Cook was introduced to Libby Forbes at a social event organized by his church, and he was quickly smitten. She in turn was drawn to the eager young doctor. It was love at first sight. After a whirlwind romance they married in 1889. Frederick would not even wait a year until he had finished his studies and gained his doctorate. Caution was not in his makeup.

The young couple set up home together and were blissfully happy. The world seemed to be opening up for them. Cook was earning money from his entrepreneurial activities, and close to qualifying as a doctor. In a society without the rigid class structure of Europe, where a man made his own destiny, they seemed to be on the cusp of the American Dream. Then Libby became pregnant, and their happiness was complete. They worked out the dates, and realized that the baby would arrive in early 1890, within days of the date that Frederick would qualify as a doctor. What could be more perfect?

As the months progressed he continued to work the long hours at the milk route, while also studying every day and attending his lectures. It was a hectic schedule, but at the end of every day he returned to his wife and the promise of the future.

In the spring of 1890 Libby went into labor, but it was a tough labor, and when she finally gave birth to a daughter, the baby was weak. The child survived for a few hours, then died. The ordeal had also taken a lot out of Libby; she had bled a lot, and they struggled to bring the bleeding under control. She lost a lot of strength, and was confined to bed for a number of days. During that confinement an infection set in, and she began running a high fever. Cook abandoned his other duties and stayed with his young wife, offering what comfort he could. But it was an era before antibiotics, and there was little that could be done apart from making her comfortable and hoping for the best.

A few days after their child died, Cook had to tear himself away to face his final exam. He left Brooklyn and hurried to the university, tearing through the test as fast as he could. Then it was a run to the ferry, and back to the side of his ailing wife. She had weakened further in his absence. All that evening and the following day, along with a local doctor, he battled to turn her condition around. As the sky darkened toward evening, there was a knock on the door. He smiled down at her, squeezed her hand, and went to the door, where a messenger handed him an envelope. He tore it open, and looked for the only word that mattered: Passed.

With a grin he ran to Libby's bedroom, and sat on the edge of the bed. He opened the letter and passed it across to her. She read it and smiled at him. They held hands. In that moment he must have believed it would all work out. She had to see the light at the end of the tunnel, and pull through. She squeezed his hand, and they remained side by side as the evening turned into night.

A few hours later, she died in his arms.

Cook felt like he was falling, and there was no ground to catch him. It had all been for nothing. The years of struggle, the hours in the lecture halls and anatomy theaters, the long nights delivering milk, the constant struggle: just when it was all coming right, it had gone so horribly wrong. Two weeks earlier he was looking forward to fatherhood and a new profession. Now he had lost his child and lost his beloved Libby. The medical degree felt like so much dirt beneath his fingernails.

For a while he was in a wilderness, wandering the streets by night and day, as if seeking in the dark corners some consolation for what he had lost. But there was none. His family rallied around, doing their best to support him in his grief. Eventually he agreed to move from his house in Brooklyn, with all its memories, to a new place in Manhattan. His mother went with him, to look after him in his time of need. He had neglected the milk delivery business in his grief, but his brother William had kept it afloat. In fact, just before moving to Manhattan, he sold the business to William. The money from the sale gave him the funds to rent a house at 338 West Fifty-Fifth Street. He converted one room to a surgery, and hung his sign outside the door. He was going through the motions, doing what any newly qualified doctor was expected to do. But his heart was not in it, and any enterprise begun like that was bound to fail. So it was with his medical practice. Over the next few months visitors were rare, and the young doctor found himself sitting alone with his grief in an empty office, looking at the funds dwindling with his hopes. Stirring within him was an ambition to do something, but he had no idea what.

He later described it: "At that time the ambition which beset me was undirected; it was only later that I found, almost by accident, what became its focusing point. I felt (as what young man does not?) that I possessed unusual qualifications and exceptional ability. An office was fitted up, and my anxiety over the disappearing pennies was eased by the conviction that I had but to hang out my shingle and the place would be thronged with patients. Six months passed. There had been about three patients."

About the only thing that kept him sane, and distracted him from his troubles, was reading. He began to read more and more, developing a taste for tales of exploration. He was particularly drawn to Arctic adventures, perhaps because the loneliness and isolation of the pioneers mirrored his own feelings. He avidly read accounts by American explorers such as Elisha Kent Kane, a physician who achieved a farthest North in 1853, and Charles Francis Hall, who led three expeditions to the Arctic and died in 1871 under mysterious circumstances—possibly poisoned by one of his crew.

He also kept up to date with more modern developments.

When Cook spotted an article in the *New York Herald* toward the end of 1891, for the first time in months he felt a glimmer of life returning. He felt his chest tighten and his pulse quicken. A naval engineer, Robert Peary, was planning an expedition, to try and cross the island of Greenland. He was looking for a crew, and he also wanted a surgeon.

"I recall sitting alone one gloomy winter day. Opening a paper, I read that Peary was preparing his 1891 expedition to the Arctic. I cannot explain my sensations. It was as if a door to a prison cell had opened. I felt the first indomitable commanding call of the Northland."

As he laid down the paper, Cook knew what he had to do. He dashed off a letter to the expedition leader, stating his medical qualifications, and volunteering to be part of the team.

"To invade the unknown, to assail the fastness of the white, frozen North—all that was latent in me, the impetus of that ambition born in childhood, perhaps before birth, and which had been stifled and starved, surged up tumultuously within me," he wrote.

3

AMUNDSEN—THE NAPOLEON OF THE NORTH MAKES HIS ENTRANCE

Roald Amundsen was mythologized in his lifetime as the Napoleon of the Polar Regions and the Last of the Vikings. He was lionized as a Norwegian hero, the man who put the nationalistic ambitions of his people on the map—and on the most obscure and extreme portions of the map, at that. For a man of such lofty reputation, his early days were depressingly mundane.

Roald Engelbregt Gravning Amundsen was the fourth and final son of a wealthy ship owner and captain, a self-made man who had ambitions that his offspring would follow in his footsteps and build a business empire. Jens Engebreth Amundsen had made his own way in the world, and hoped his four sons would do the same.

Norway was part of the Scandinavian stronghold that produced the Viking raiders who terrorized southern Europe for hundreds of years. But by the 1850s, it was just a mountainous backwater under the control of neighboring Sweden. There was a small movement for independence, but most people were more concerned about eking out a living from the harsh landscape. The country was cold and barren and agriculture was limited, but it was surrounded by ocean, with hundreds of narrow deep inlets and fjords that provided ideal harborage. The sea was the key to prosperity.

Whaling, sealing, and fishing were important industries, and many ships plied their way up the western coast servicing the needs of the tiny settlements. Jens Amundsen, born in 1820 in Snekotta, Hvaler in southern Norway, came from a family of whalers. He went into that business initially, sailing with his family until he gained his captain's license. Then he began to branch out into less dangerous and more lucrative lines of trade. A careful man, over the years he built up a tidy fortune, which he put toward buying his own boat. There was no point in captaining someone else's investment.

At the age of thirty-four he joined with a partner to buy and refurbish an old wreck. He called the new vessel the *Phoenix* and set sail toward the Black Sea, an inland sea in south eastern Europe, between Russia, the Ukraine, and Turkey. It was a shrewd move; they bought the ship at a scrap auction in 1854, just when the Crimean War was intensifying. The conflict pitted the Russian Empire against Britain, France, and the Ottoman (Turkish) Empire, and would drag on until 1856. Wars were always great for trade, so the Black Sea was the place to be.

When the *Phoenix* docked in Sebastopol, it was immediately pressed into service by the British and converted into winter quarters for their officers. When spring came, it was cleared of officers and began supplying the British cavalry, hauling forage and straw up the lines to the troops. It was a heady and exciting time for the young captain with a shrewd business brain. There was plenty of work and a constant sense of danger, and Jens thrived. When he returned to Norway in 1856 at the end of the war, the foundations for his fortune had been laid.

Fortune favors the brave, and Jens had another lucky break when a change in British trade policy opened the world's waterways to other nations. The Navigation Act was repealed, and anyone with a ship and the spirit to sail it could make money. It helped if you were ruthless and a bit unscrupulous: two qualities Jens possessed, and passed on to his fourth son in due course. Jens would ship anything, no questions asked. He made a lot of money shipping Chinese indentured laborers around the world, a trade not far removed from the slave trade of a century earlier. Jens was careful with his money, investing in more ships. At one point he was owner or part owner of a fleet of thirty ships across the globe.

Jens Amundsen had made the transition from ambitious but poor teenager to rich merchant. He was a highly respected member of the commercial elite. Home from the wars, it was now time to settle and lay down roots. He married a woman sixteen years his junior, Gustava Sahlquist. She was a good catch—young and pretty, and the daughter of a government official. More than attraction went into the making of that match.

He built a house for his wife at Borge, a tiny rural community in the south of the country. But he was a captain as well as a ship owner, and captains sailed with their ships. Gustava led a wandering life for many years; her first son, Jens, was born in China. She did not get much time to enjoy her secluded retreat near the port of Sarpsbord. Over the years, three more sons arrived. First came Gustav, then Leon. Roald was the final one, born on July 16, 1872.

By now Jens was in his fifties, and it was time for a change of pace. No longer a young man, he agreed to his wife's request to move to Christiania, the capital of Norway (now known as Oslo). They made the move when Roald was just three months old. It must have been a blessed relief for her, to escape the drab confines of Borge. But Christiania was hardly the center of the universe. It still had the feel of a small town, dominated by the port. Their new home was a two-story dwelling in the center of the city, but it still backed onto forest. The family had a number of servants, and all the trappings of prosperity.

The children were thrown into a world where urban and rural met. They had the streets to play in, but they could retreat in a minute to the forest. They grew up with the skills of both worlds, becoming worldly men who were comfortable in the great outdoors. And when their father was not at sea, he was very hands-on with the family. Not for him the distant Victorian ideal. He was a stern man, but he had a kindly side, and loved to sit down with his sons around the fire and tell them tales of the exotic regions he had visited. He was always there for them, ready to lend an ear and offer his advice.

His attitude was often pure Viking. He told his sons that he did not want them getting into fights, but if they did get into one, to make sure to get in the first blow, and make it a good one.

In many ways it was a charmed childhood. From age six to nine, Roald attended the local primary school, before moving on to the Gymnasium, where he would remain until he was fifteen and it was time to go to college. The boys were loved, and their spirit of adventure was nurtured by their father's tales, and the proximity to the wild forests and mountains. The big sailing ships in the port were a constant reminder that the world was a wide place, ripe for exploration.

Gustava was less enamoured of the wide world; once she got to Christiania she stayed there, rarely venturing beyond the city limits. During school holidays she remained at home while the boys traveled with their father to visit relatives in more rural parts of Norway. But she was fiercely determined that her boys would get the best possible start in the world, and she pinned her hopes on a good education. That was one of her reasons for moving the family to the capital. She did not want any of her children ending up as provincial hicks. She enrolled the four boys in a private school, where they got the formal education as befitted the sons of a moneyed father. They learned the usual: classics, mathematics, and a smattering of history. But they also learned English, important if they were to make their mark beyond the narrow confines of Norway.

Tragedy struck when Roald was just fourteen. His father Jens was returning from a journey to England when he became ill. He passed away on August 15, 1886. Roald was devastated. He wrote: "It is hard to lose such a father."

Jens Junior had already dropped out of school and gone to sea. Gustav was nearly finished his studies, and would follow his older brother in quick order. Leon also dropped out and began to work. That left only the youngest still at school. Gustava pinned her hopes on Roald; he would stick it out, go to university, and qualify as a doctor, conferring the ultimate respectability on the family. Roald, young and impressionable, was happy to play along. But his heart was never in his studies. He had inherited his father's wanderlust, if not his business acumen.

Perhaps the studies his mother insisted on played a part in eventually turning her son away from her carefully laid plans for him. He began to read English books at the Gymnasium, and found a growing fascination with English history, particularly the history of the navy and the great explorers. One name stood out: John Franklin.

Franklin was a name to stir the imaginings of a young man. He came to prominence with his expedition in 1819, which aimed to cross the Canadian Arctic from Hudson Bay to the mouth of the Coppermine River. Along the way, eleven of his twenty men perished of cold, starvation, and disease. The few survivors of the three year ordeal had to resort to eating lichens, and trying to boil their shoes. This earned Franklin the unfortunate nickname of "the man who ate his boots." There were also disturbing rumours of murder and cannibalism.

Franklin led three arctic expeditions before retiring to govern Van Diemen's Land. But in 1845, at the advanced age of sixty-one, he was persuaded to come out of retirement to lead one last search for the fabled Northwest Passage.

The Northwest Passage was the golden grail of polar exploration and the last remaining challenge, as far as the Victorians were concerned. When Columbus set sail in 1496, he was searching for a way to reach the Spice Islands and the riches of the Orient—America got in his way. For the next few centuries countless explorers lost their lives in the search for a passage across the top of the American continent into the Pacific Ocean. By 1845 the world knew that the frozen polar sea might be breached, but it would never be a practical commercial route. However, it was a matter of national pride that the British Navy should make the first successful passage. In Franklin they opted for experience over youth and vigor.

Franklin's expedition disappeared, both ships and 134 men swallowed up by the ice. When no word came back, there was no panic initially; it was thought that the ships would be trapped in ice over the winter, and would break free when the brief summer thaw set in. It was a trip expected to stretch out over a few years, and no one back home was alarmed. But as the years passed with no word, no sighting of wreckage, and no accounts of the men, Franklin's wife—now a widow, though she did not realize it—began to pester the authorities to launch a rescue. Over the next two decades several expeditions set out, but none was able to shed light on the fate of Franklin and his men. It would take a century before the full story would emerge.

The ships, the *Erebus* and the *Terror*, had become stuck in the ice that first winter, but they had never broken free from the crushing pressure. The men had overwintered on Beechey Island, part of the archipelago of small and large islands in the high Canadian Arctic. Franklin had died in 1847, according to a note later found on the island, but no grave has ever been found. His men, leaderless, had tried to retreat south, living off the land. It was a hopeless task. Starvation, food poisoning from improperly stored supplies, pneumonia, scurvy, and other diseases took their toll. Examination of some of the remains found over the years revealed signs that the men had resorted to cannibalism, just as in Franklin's earlier expedition to the Coppermine River. It was a total defeat, but to the British, in the golden age of heroism, it was a glorious defeat.

Amundsen eagerly bought into the myth, first reading about Franklin when he was fifteen, then gorging himself on the many expeditions that set sail looking for the lost mariner. At one point there were twelve rescue missions criss-crossing the Arctic at the same time. More men were lost in the rescue attempts than were lost on the expedition itself, but the many voyages were finally mapping the high arctic, and drawing the map that would finally reveal the Northwest Passage.

As Amundsen read the overblown accounts of Franklin and his successors while looking out at the windswept Christiania docks, he began to dream that he might one day sail those seas himself. Perhaps he might even be the man who finally forced his way through to the Pacific.

"When I was fifteen years old the works of Sir John Franklin, the great British explorer, fell into my hands. I read them with a fervid fascination which has shaped the whole course of my life," he later wrote in his autobiography, *My Life as an Explorer*. He added: "Of all the brave Britishers who for 400 years had given freely of their treasure, courage, and enterprise to dauntless but unsuccessful attempts to negotiate the Northwest Passage, none was braver than Sir John Franklin. His description of the return from one of his expeditions thrilled me as nothing I had ever read before. He told how for three weeks he and his little band had battled with the ice and storms, with no food to eat except a few bones found at a deserted Indian camp, and how before they finally returned to the outpost of civilization, they were reduced to eating their own boot leather to keep themselves alive.

"Strangely enough the thing in Sir John's narrative that appealed to me most strongly was the sufferings he and his men endured. A strange ambition burned within me to endure those same sufferings . . . Sir John's descriptions decided me upon my career. Secretly, I irretrievably decided to be an arctic explorer."

While he kept those dreams to himself, he dutifully kept up his studies, finishing in the Gymnasium and moving on to college. Unknown to his mother, he began to prepare for the hardships ahead. He needed to harden his body for the cold, and he found a very effective way to do that. Every night he would throw his bedroom windows wide open and sleep naked on top of the bed. As he shivered in the cold moonlight, he dreamed of even deeper cold and the glory that would bring.

"It was part of my hardening process," he wrote. But he told his mother that he liked fresh air.

During school breaks he began pushing himself. In winter he skied and trekked over the hills and mountains around Oslo, improving his skills and building up his stamina. He slept out under the stars, the dancing lights of the aurora borealis glowing eerily overhead.

When he was seventeen, the most famous Norwegian of the time, Fridtjof Nansen, returned to Oslo to a hero's welcome after skiing across the vast frozen interior of Greenland. It was the first successful crossing of that country, and a source of great national pride. There was a festive atmosphere as Nansen sailed up the fjord toward the city, and the streets were thronged with well-wishers.

"With beating heart I walked that day among the banners and cheers and all the dreams of my boyhood woke to storming life," Amundsen recalled. "For the first time I heard, in my secret thoughts, the whisper clear and insistent: If you could do the Northwest Passage!"

A year later, Amundsen took his final exams. He barely passed, but it was enough. In 1890 he pleased his mother by enrolling in the Royal

Frederick University of Christiania. He chose medicine, as she wished. He pursued this course for a number of years. But all the while he was studying, he was also pursuing his own interests. He continued to ski and trek in his spare time, and he continued to read and study the history and techniques of polar exploration. One explorer made a particular impression: Eivind Astrup. Astrup had lectured at the university about his experiences in the Arctic with American explorer Robert Peary. He spoke of dog sleighs and long ski journeys, and the superiority of the local Inuit people when it came to surviving the conditions. Amundsen listened, enthralled. This, rather than anatomy, was his real calling.

Although he was a serious young man, Amundsen could not keep up the pretense; he simply had no interest in medicine. Very quickly he began to skip lectures, and before long he was failing exams. This created a problem: how could he face his mother? She had her heart set on a doctor in the family. Then, in the autumn of 1893, Gustava Amundsen died. Her unexpected death freed Amundsen from the burden of academia.

"It saved her from the sad discovery which she would otherwise have made, that my own ambitions lay in another direction, and that I had made but poor progress in realizing hers."

"With enormous relief," Amundsen dropped out of college shortly after his mother's death. He suddenly found himself free from responsibilities and obligations—and on top of that, he had come into his inheritance. Having a substantial sum in the bank gave him freedom to consider what he wanted out of life, instead of being pushed into what others expected of him. He decided to pursue his ambitions to explore the Arctic.

He volunteered for an expedition to Spitzbergen, an island far north of Norway, and one of the starting points for attempts on the North Pole. He even suggested that he would be willing to sail for free. His application was rejected; too much enthusiasm and too little experience. But he threw himself into his new studies with a renewed fury. He trekked, he skied, he read, he studied meteorology and geology, all the disciplines he felt he would need. And he planned his first expedition. With a friend he would cross the wild and desolate plateau of Hardangervidda, in central Norway, to the western mountains, on skis.

The two companions set out on Christmas Day 1893, and took the train as far north as it went. Then they set out on skis, expecting to cover the ground swiftly. But their preparation had consisted of plenty of talk and very little exercise. Blizzards, temperatures of -40°F, and poor equipment took their toll. The pair of intrepid explorers did not even reach the plateau. They got fifty kilometers, and had to give up. They retreated with their tails between their legs.

Amundsen had learned in the sharpest way that exploration could be a deadly business. He was a boy in a man's world, and it was time to stop playing.

In the summer of 1894 Amundsen joined the crew of a sealing ship bound for the edges of the Arctic. It was a beginning; his first real job. It was also an important step along the way. He would begin by working for his master's certificate, which would allow him to become a ship's officer. From there it was only a matter of time before he became a captain. He spent the next several years working on a variety of ships and boats, mainly in the waters around Iceland and Greenland. He found the Arctic to his liking.

He took time off to complete the compulsory part-time military service every young Norwegian faced, then returned to the sea. All his reading had convinced him that becoming a captain was a key element of his long term plan to be a successful explorer. He had to be able to lead on sea and on land. Other expeditions had run into trouble because there was one leader at sea, and a second for the landing party. Not on his exhibitions, he was determined.

He broadened his range of experience at sea, venturing on merchant ships across the Atlantic, and as far south as the west coast of Africa. His family connections came in handy when it came to finding berths. On May 1, 1895, his persistence paid off when he was awarded his Mate's Certificate.

Life was looking good, but he had unfinished business. The Hardangervidda Plateau had defeated him three years previously; in the winter of 1896 he tackled it again, bringing along his brother Leon. This time he was far better prepared. No one had ever traversed the plateau in winter, and he hoped to be the first.

They set out with scant provisions, expecting to cross the plain in two days of hard skiing. But the weather changed, and they ended up sleeping out in the rough for five long nights. Their food ran out, and they had to beat a hasty retreat. They came very close to making the traverse, but in the end it was another defeat. The terrain had the measure of him. He came close to losing fingers to frostbite. Years later, in his autobiography, he looked back on the trip as training for what was to come.

"It was a part of my preliminary training for my polar career. The training proved severer than the experience for which it was a preparation," he joked.

It was the last time he set out into the unknown without extensive preparation work and a plentiful supply of provisions. He did not need to be rapped on the knuckles a third time to learn the lesson.

4

PEARY GETS THE EXPLORATION BUG

It was a chance notice in a post office that saved Robert Peary. Early in 1879, two years into his wilderness exile, Peary spotted an advertisement looking for four positions with the US Coast and Geodetic Survey. The job was for draftsmen, and was based in Washington, DC. Peary had the qualifications needed. He wasn't sure of his chances, so he told no one. But secretly he applied for one of the positions, sending in the survey of Fryeburg with his application as a sample of his work. It was enough. He got one of the four posts, and moved to the capital. At the age of twenty-three, he had finally severed the apron strings.

He settled into his new life quickly, enjoying both the work and the new social opportunities. In fact, within months of the move he had broken his engagement—small-town life would not be for him. He reveled in the idea of his new freedom, but the realities of the job bored him. After a year, he secretly applied for a commission in the US Navy. In 1881 he was accepted to the Navy Corp of Civil Engineers, and posted to the Department of Yards and Docks as a lieutenant. It wasn't the glamorous life of a sailor; it was his engineering background the Navy was interested in. The following three years were spent supervising engineering and construction projects around the country.

He enjoyed this—something about the movement appealed to a restlessness in his spirit.

In 1881 France had begun work on a canal to connect the Atlantic and the Pacific Oceans. It would be a massive project that would benefit the whole world, cutting weeks, sometimes months, off journeys from west coast to east coast. It would revolutionize world trade. Unfortunately the French project would eventually peter out, partly due to the expense, but also because of the high cost in human life. The failed effort had cost $287 million, and twenty-two thousand workers had succumbed to diseases like malaria in the harsh environment of dense fetid jungle. The French had chosen Panama as their site. The Americans knew the value of the project, but wondered if there might be a more suitable location—and could they beat the French across the continent?

In 1884 they had sent several engineers south to examine the problem. Peary was part of the team sent to Nicaragua, which seemed to be a strong candidate. He would spend several months there, then return a year later for another sojourn. It seemed like an ideal spot for the project. Ships could sail from the Caribbean up the San Juan River to Lake Nicaragua. From there it was just seven miles to the Pacific— not a difficult distance for a canal.

Peary was very excited to be sailing south. He wrote to his mother, saying that the trip reminded him of Columbus's. Then he added that: "His fame can be equalled only by him who shall one day stand with 360 degrees of longitude beneath his motionless feet and for whom East and West shall have vanished—the discoverer of the North Pole."

Just like in his graduation presentation in high school, he was dreaming of the frozen wastes.

Peary spent a year in the jungles of Latin America, but in the end the project failed to materialize. The French gave up on the Panama Canal in 1889, and the Americans took over the work in 1904. (The canal is now one of the busiest waterways in the world, but in 2012 the Nicaraguan National Assembly gave permission to a Chinese consortium to build a rival canal on Peary's route. Work will begin shortly, with the canal expected to be ready by 2019.)

When Peary returned from his first stint in the jungle, he was itching for another challenge—and perhaps for another year away from the influence of his mother. He had read extensively about polar exploration, including the succession of failed attempts to cross the vast island of Greenland. The interior could have been the far side of the moon, so little was known about it. Only three serious attempts had been made to cross the vast interior, and all three had failed. Peary's pulse began to quicken. Could this be an opportunity to make his mark?

Making his mark was what it was all about. Peary was quite consciously chasing fame. He needed to stand out from the crowd. So he laid his plans. First, he wrote an article in the spring of 1886 for the American Academy of Sciences, on the problems of crossing Greenland. He discussed two routes. The first was the shorter and easier. An explorer could start from the west coast and trek about four hundred miles to the east coast, bisecting the bottom third of the country. The second route was more ambitious. It began at Whale Sound, at the top of the explored portion of Baffin Bay, then proceeded northwest, to answer the question of whether Greenland was an island, or if it extended all the way across the Arctic.

The article was his statement of intent. A short while later he was granted six months leave from the Navy, and set out to reconnoiter. Borrowing $500 from his mother—he could escape, but only with her help—he boarded a sealer and sailed to Greenland. He arrived in Godhavn, a tiny town on Disko Island, halfway up the west coast, on June 6, 1886. His plan was to hire a sled and a team of dogs, and make a solo dash into the interior. While in Godhavn he met a Danish official, Christian Maigaard, who told him he would perish in the attempt on his own. He agreed to take Maigaard along with him, and the two set out in the height of the brief summer. According to Peary, they managed to travel one hundred miles east across the ice cap before running out of food and having to turn back.

This was only a quarter of the full distance, but if his account was true, it was the second deepest anyone had penetrated into the cold interior of the country. It was a major mark for a man green in the ways of the Arctic. And he had learned a huge amount about the challenges he would face if he came back with a major expedition.

He returned home and made much of his achievements. This was his chance to stand out from the crowd. An American was finally making progress where the best of the Europeans had failed miserably.

Privately, some of those Europeans doubted Peary's claims. They felt he could not have penetrated so far, and they were not happy with the level of documentation he produced to back up his claims. There were already mumblings of disquiet, before he had even launched his first proper Arctic expedition. Dr. Fridtjof Nansen, a Norwegian who would become Peary's biggest rival in Greenland, was one of the doubters. A few years later he wrote: "Peary's longitude was only based, as it seems, on some observations of altitude. These so-called 'simple altitudes' are notoriously uncertain for longitude reckoning. The distance of a hundred miles from the margin of the ice cannot, therefore, be considered as established beyond all doubt."

But Peary did not care. His eye was on the main goal—and it was not geographical knowledge. As he wrote in a letter: "Remember, Mother, I must have fame."

5

GETTING BACK TO GREENLAND

Matthew Alexander Henson, born on August 8, 1866, was an unusual figure in the annals of polar exploration. He was an African American who did not come from the usual privileged background of most polar explorers. It was only chance that brought him north, but he proved to be well suited to the challenge.

Henson was the son of free sharecroppers from Maryland. His mother passed away when he was two years old, and his father a few years later. Henson was sent to live with an uncle in Washington, DC, who paid for a few years' schooling for the young boy. But then his uncle died, casting him out on his own. The boy got a job as a dishwasher at a cafe, but at the age of twelve decided to move to Baltimore, Maryland, in search of more opportunities. He went to sea as cabin boy on a merchant ship, the *Katie Hines*. This was the decisive break in his career. Always affable, he made friends easily. Captain Childs took a shine to his cabin boy, and took Henson under his wing. Over the next number of years he taught the boy to read and write, and encouraged him to learn navigation skills. Henson remained on board the *Katie Hines* for five years, and he saw more of the world than most people even read about. In an age before air travel, he visited China, Japan, the Philippines, France, southern Russia, and many African countries. By his late teens he was a skilled navigator and well-traveled young man.

But Captain Childs passed away in 1883 and once again, young Henson was on his own. He worked as a seaman for a while, then settled in Washington for a period. Opportunities for African Americans, even ones as gifted as Henson, were limited. He ended up working in a clothing store.

Like Robert Peary, he had seen a bit of the world. But unlike Peary, he did not have a wealthy mother backing him, and an understanding Navy giving him time to indulge his passions. The two men could not have been more different. They moved in different orbits. All that changed by chance one afternoon in November 1887.

Peary had been home a year from his first Greenland expedition, and was settled back into life as a naval engineer. He was getting restless, but then he received new orders. He was to return to Nicaragua and resume his survey for a new canal. He was delighted to be on the move again, and quickly began preparing. One thing he knew was that the right equipment was vital in a hostile environment. Every detail, right down to the clothes you wore, had to be precisely planned. Peary knew he needed a good sun hat for the trip, so he left his office and walked to a nearby clothing store to purchase one. The young African American behind the counter was very friendly, and soon the two men were chatting about exotic locations, ignoring the other customers in the store. Peary could be a decisive man; by the time he had paid for his hat, he knew he wanted the energetic and enthusiastic young clerk on his team. So he hired him as his personal assistant.

It was a relationship that would endure until Peary's death. Matthew Henson accompanied him on all his expeditions from that day, and they became close friends. Henson was second in command on the polar trips, and distinguished himself by his ability to master native languages and his skills at negotiating with the people they encountered in the Arctic.

But first there was the small matter of real life—work and home. He had some time at home before the trip began, and that gave him an opportunity to ponder his future. The Navy wanted Peary back in

Nicaragua. He knew he wanted to be an explorer, but that would be a tough path. Getting backing for expeditions would never be easy. He also pondered his domestic future. Should he marry his longtime girlfriend Josephine Diebitsch? In many ways, she was an ideal choice. She was highly educated, full of energy, and had a streak of independence uncommon in those days. They had met at a dance in Washington in 1884, and he had been smitten from the first. She was a graduate of a business college, and had made the valedictorian's speech at the college graduation. She had used that opportunity to express the radical view that women should be treated as equals in the workplace. Following her graduation, she proceeded to put that philosophy into action by beating several men to secure a post at the US Census Bureau. When her father retired from the Smithsonian Institution, she applied for his post and got it. She was working as a linguist at the museum while Peary was courting her. The romance survived Peary's often lengthy absences, first in Nicaragua, then in Greenland. Josephine was always waiting when he returned.

In a letter to his mother he confided: "That she loves me I know, that she can make me happy I think. That she would hamper me less than any woman I have met or am likely to meet I am confident." He was less sure of his love for her, and he was wary of being tied down. He thought of putting off the decision; his second voyage to Central America was the perfect excuse to do nothing for the moment. But in the end, he proposed before he set out and Josephine accepted.

Late in 1887 he returned to the fetid jungle for seven months. Henson traveled as part of Peary's close-knit team of six, surveying the jungles and mountains up to and around Lake Nicaragua. Peary was also supervising forty-five engineers who followed the surveyors. During the trip he was impressed with Henson's seamanship and general usefulness, and when he returned home, he knew that Henson would be part of his next Arctic expedition. It was time to head north again, this time to complete the crossing of Greenland.

His mother was not happy. She had hoped one trip to the Arctic would knock the idea out of her son's head. Miss Diebitsch was happier—she had her fiancé back. In August 1888, the couple were married. For a man used to exotic locations, and drawn to the wilder spots on the globe, he picked a very conventional and dull place for their honeymoon: Seabright, New Jersey. Rather bizarrely, his mother, Mary, accompanied the couple on this first holiday together.

When they returned from the honeymoon, the couple set up home together in Philadelphia, and Peary settled back into provincial life, traveling regularly between the docks there and in New York. He put his exploration dreams on hold, having high hopes that his work in Nicaragua would fast-track him in the Navy. But as time passed, it became obvious that his career would receive no boost. Part of the problem was that most of the credit went to the chief engineer on the project, Aniceto Menocal. But another problem was that the project petered out, because of expense and because of the high human cost of working in the unsanitary conditions.

He began to dream of the North Pole again. In more practical terms, he began to dream of completing his crossing of Greenland. That would gain him a sufficient reputation to organize a later bid for the Pole.

This time he was not planning a solo dash—this would be a proper expedition, organized and stocked before it set off. Peary had tried what mountaineers had called the Alpine approach—a small team, limited gear, and fast movement. Now he was going to revert to the more traditional approach of a well-stocked team with plenty of support. First, he had to put a team in place.

Loving publicity, his first step was to announce his plans to all and sundry. Local papers began to carry accounts of his plans. He was not a major name in exploration circles at that stage, so many ignored the brash young man, but word began to filter out that Peary was looking for a crew. Eager young men responded.

As Peary viewed the letters arriving at his home overlooking Fairmount Park, Philadelphia, he felt a growing sense of contentment. This was his opportunity to break free from the ranks of the drones, and become one of the movers. This was his chance for glory and fame. It didn't take long for the dream to be shattered.

On October 3, 1888, Fridtjof Nansen arrived on Disko Island, Greenland. Unlike Peary, he had not sailed in. He had walked and skied, with a party of six, from the east coast of the massive island, crossing the central plateau in forty-nine days. Six weeks earlier, Peary had held the record for the furthest penetration into that vast unknown. Now Nansen had crossed the entire island, robbing Peary of his goal. He could no longer be the first to achieve that landmark. And if he couldn't entice them with the prospect of a first, who would sponsor his expedition, or pay it any attention afterwards? His plans were in tatters.

He was despondent for a number of days, and furious with Nansen for what he saw as the Norwegian dishonorably slipping in and achieving what Peary felt was his by right. It took him quite a while to rally. His wife noted that he looked like a man who had heard of the death of a friend. Nansen's success had put his plans back by more than a year but eventually Peary came up with a new plan, and the expedition was on again. His new plan was bold; he would sail past Disko Island and the safety of Godhavn, and press as far north as he could. He would land high up on the west coast of Greenland and push north, trying to establish how far north the island stretched. At that period, geographers had no idea of the extent of the island, which was locked in by ice year round at the top. Peary could redraw the map. If he could not be the first to cross Greenland, he could at least push farther north than anyone else before him. The expedition could go ahead, just with a new objective.

But it took a while before he could build up any momentum. He did not have the pedigree to command respect, and it was difficult to get his plans taken seriously. Finally, in 1890 he was invited to lecture at the Brooklyn Institute of Arts and Sciences. His success here led to invitations from the Academy of Natural Sciences of Philadelphia and the American Geographical Society of New York. The Philadelphia Academy agreed to back his plan, as long as he brought a group of them along to carry out scientific research. The trip was on.

Once again he went to the newspapers, and many carried reports of the young naval officer who was planning to explore the Arctic. Again letters began to arrive from young men eager to be part of the gamble. One of the letters came from a young New York doctor, Frederick Cook. It got thrown in the pile with the rest of them. Peary had plenty to choose from, and it would take time. And he still had to raise the $6,000 he estimated the expedition would cost. He also had to put in place the publishing deals that afterwards would, with luck, leave him a rich and well-respected man.

The young men applying to take part included some with impressive qualifications. Langdon Gibson was a huge man, with tremendous physical strength. He had been part of the Brown-Stanton expedition that had surveyed the Grand Canyon for a possible railway, so he was used to the harsh life of an explorer. He was unable to pay for his own kit (estimated at $300) but Peary agreed to overlook this. A young Norwegian, Eivind Astrup, who had recently moved to the USA, was also taken. Astrup was the only man, aside from Peary himself, who had experienced the harsh cold of the Arctic. His expertise on skis would be invaluable to the expedition.

John Verhoeff, a slight and weak amateur meteorologist, had fewer real credentials. His initial letter to Peary was anything but promising: "Would like to accompany you, fully realizing that the chances may be nine out of ten that I would never return." No leader wants to recruit someone with a death wish. But Verhoeff offered to contribute $2,000 toward the costs. This was an offer Peary could not refuse, so Verhoeff was signed on. Had he realized how prophetic the young man's initial letter would prove, he might have reconsidered that decision.

One of the berths went to Peary's manservant, Matthew Henson. And, controversially, Peary was bringing his new wife, Josephine, along. Given the era, the inclusion of both a woman and an African American man was brave. It was very forward-thinking of Peary—even if the two were his wife and his servant.

That left just one berth to fill. It had to be a person with the right expertise to complement those who were already on board. Two months after receiving the letter, Peary finally wrote back to Frederick Cook, inviting him to call to his home in Philadelphia for an interview.

6

PEARY MEETS COOK

Spring warmed the air as Frederick Cook made his way along Fairmount Park, then knocked on the door leading to Robert Peary's apartment. He was nervous. For too long he had languished in the depression that his wife's death had plunged him into. He needed this. But the interview had to be handled carefully—if he was too desperate, he could lose his chance.

He was put at ease immediately when Josephine Peary opened the door and graciously waved him into the presence of the expedition leader, who was waiting in the drawing room at the front of the house. As Peary stood to shake hands, the first impression Cook must have gotten was a good one. At over six foot, there were few people who could look him in the eye without straining, but Peary topped him by an inch. And he was dressed in his full naval uniform. He cut an imposing figure.

Cook knew he had to play his cards right. He had no experience in exploration, and there was nothing to suggest that he was cut out for the role. But he was a doctor; that had to count for something. On a trip into the wilderness, a doctor could be the difference between life and death.

35

The interview began with small talk, as Josephine fussed about and prepared tea for the two men. Then she poured a cup for herself. She was not going to quietly retire to let the men discuss business. Once they were settled, Peary launched into his favorite topic: himself, and his grandiose plans. He explained that he was going to determine the northern limit of Greenland and redraw the map of the North Atlantic and the Arctic. Cook was impressed. He knew all about Nansen's trip, but the Norwegian had stayed well south in his traverse of the country. They really were going to be breaking new ground. The talk continued for a few hours, with Peary moving on to the technicalities of field work. This was an area in which he had a genuine expertise. His work in Nicaragua had prepared him for meticulous surveying. But he knew his limitations; he was not a scientist.

He confided in Cook that he hoped to make up for that deficiency by bringing along experts who could work on meteorology, geology, anthropology, and biology. He wanted to make his survey of northern Greenland as comprehensive as possible. Then he looked directly at Cook.

"With your training in medicine, you could handle some of that scientific work," he suggested.

This was not what Cook had been expecting. He had applied to travel as a physician. He saw his role as keeping the expedition in good health. But he was not going to say "no" rashly. Medical training involved a broad education, and he had covered the basics of science as part of his studies. He thought for a moment, then nodded. He could handle the science. As they discussed the details, Cook's role became clearer: he would be in charge of ethnography. This is a branch of anthropology that focuses on knowledge of individual cultures through contact with them. Peary hoped to encounter the native Eskimo and wanted to learn from them. They were the experts in living near the Poles, and if he wanted to make his mark in those regions, he would need to learn from the best. He asked Cook to compile a library of standard anthropological works, which could be brought on the trip for reference.

As the afternoon wore on, Cook sized up his leader and decided he was a "thoroughly decent fellow, and a strong character." Whether that assessment survived a season on the ice remained to be seen. Cook also decided he liked Josephine, who was a strong and intelligent woman. Near the end of their marathon first meeting Josephine left the two men alone for a few minutes, and the formal business of hiring took place. Peary said that the trip would be tough, with harsh living conditions, and with a chance that some members might not return home to civilization. Cook said he was willing to take his chances, and the two men shook hands. Cook was on board, for full board and a remuneration of fifty dollars, payable on return to America. It was poor recompense for the risks all the expedition members were taking, but Cook left the apartment full of enthusiasm. The overture was done, and the curtain was about to rise on his real life.

The expedition was ready to sail in early June. The SS *Kite*, a fifty-year-old barkentine of 280 tons, had been prepared for the ice. Her hull and bow were iron-clad, and the three-mast sailing ship cut an impressive dash as she sailed up the East River from the pier in Brooklyn. In addition to sail she had a steam engine, so the expedition was not at the mercy of the elements.

A large crowd turned out to see the expedition off. Some of them were there to see the strange sight of a woman explorer. Peary's decision to bring his wife, a "second honeymoon" as he joked to Cook, was regarded as foolhardy by many. But they seemed a harmonious group as they pulled out of New York into the north Atlantic. On board were the seven members of the expedition, along with nine academics from the Philadelphian Academy of Natural Sciences, who would travel as far as Greenland, landing before the expedition pushed to the far north.

Every spare nook on the ship was crammed with equipment and provisions. Boxes and crates crowded the deck, making a simple walk a hazardous obstacle course, and below deck the ship was loaded to capacity. In addition to a huge supply of coal, they were carrying food for a year and a half, including tea, coffee, sugar, milk, preserved vegetables, soup, biscuits (a staple on long voyages, and nothing like the chewable confections we are used to), cocoa, and pemmican. Pemmican was a mix of meat and fat, dried out to preserve it. It was high in calories, and did not spoil easily. But it tasted horrible, and by the end of the voyage everyone would be sick of it.

Fresh meat was less in evidence; they had enough for a few weeks, but hoped to hunt along the way and keep the larder restocked that way. Fresh meat was important because it helped prevent diseases of malnutrition such as scurvy. Fresh fruit would have been even more important, but there was no way of including that in the diet.

The ship was also carrying timber to build a cabin for over-wintering in the far north, and for building sledges. They had skis, guns and ammunition, camera equipment, sealed cans of alcohol for fuel, and supplies of the best snow gear their limited experience could suggest. This was not like Peary's first trip to Greenland: the North Greenland Expedition was properly kitted out and had every chance of success.

It took two weeks to reach Newfoundland, where they encountered the first ice. They chipped blocks off an iceberg to get fresh water, and negotiated the shifting bergs carefully. It took several days to cross the Davis Strait and reach the west coast of Greenland. When the shout of *Land Ho!* went up from the *Kite*'s crew, all the members of the expedition came on deck for their first view of their destination. Forbidding black cliffs rose from an angry gray sea, and the choppy waters were covered in broken ice and small bergs. It was bleak and unwelcoming. The *Kite* sailed north along the coast until they landed briefly in Godhavn, on Disko Island. They spent one night there as guests of the Danish governor, then pushed north to Upernavik, the most northerly Danish settlement. Halfway up the coast, it was their last taste of Europe, and it was not very impressive. There were four wooden houses for the Europeans, and a small church. The settlement also included rough native turf huts built into the windswept hillside. Nearby was a stone with runic carvings, marking the most northerly evidence of the Vikings to be found in Greenland. Once they left Upernavik, they knew they would see no more signs of civilization until their return a year later. The only people they would encounter were native Eskimo.

While other expedition members enjoyed a chance to go duck hunting, Cook found himself suddenly busy. With no doctor for miles around, he had to deal with a number of cases. He even performed minor surgery, removing bone fragments from a badly broken arm. Luckily they were not detained there long; the following morning they boarded the *Kite* and resumed their trip north, pushing into the pack ice at the entrance to Melville Bay. Progress was slow. They were not far from where the pack ice was permanent year round, and they would have to make land. They occupied themselves as best as they could, killing the cold days in preparing for the coming winter. Cook joined others in cutting and shaping the timber that would form their cabin.

Until July 14 everything went as smoothly as could be expected. That day Peary was on deck, watching as the *Kite* slowly butted its way through the pack ice, clearing a passage for itself. He was watching rather than working, and it did not take long before he began to feel the cold. He decided to go below deck and warm up for a few minutes. When he returned to the deck a while later, he stepped behind the wheelhouse to get a better look at the stern and the wake of broken water trailing them. The ship was not using sails; breaking the ice required the fine control only the steam engines gave. Edging slowly forward, slowly backward, feeling for weaknesses in the surrounding ice, they were making slow but steady progress. As Peary looked down, the propellers reversed, drawing the ship back in preparation for a start forward that would crash the reinforced bow through the ice. But as the ship began to move backwards, a chunk of broken ice in the wake banged into the stern, and got caught between the rudder and the ship. The ship lurched to the side, and the jolt wrenched the steering wheel from the hands of the sailor behind it. The spokes of the wheel became a blur as the rudder flipped. The tiller swung with the rudder and there was a sickening thud, as the heavy rod of iron struck Peary hard in the leg.

He gripped the railing, and did not go down. As the sailor wrestled the wheel back under control, Peary stood shakily, his face white. He had heard a sickening snap as the tiller struck him, and immediately knew he was badly injured. But when his wife ran up to him, reaching him before anyone else, he tried to reassure her.

"Don't be frightened. I have hurt my leg," he said.

Now Frederick Cook was about to earn his keep.

The injured Peary was gently removed from the deck, and laid out on a bed below deck. He was suffering from shock, which mercifully numbed the pain. Treatment was rudimentary: he was covered in blankets, and given a shot of whiskey. Then Cook cut the boot off his leg, and tore his trousers up to the knee. The damage was frightening. The lower leg consists of two bones, the tibia and the fibula. Both were broken just below the knee. But the damage could have been worse. It seemed to be a simple break that would be easy to set. The members of the Academy of Sciences, looking on, concurred.

Cook packed the injured leg loosely in cotton, to allow room for the inevitable swelling, then gave Peary a shot of morphine to knock him out until the following day. Eventually he prepared a tight splint to immobilize the limb, and gave his leader the bad news; he would have to remain off the leg for at least a month, and it would take several more months to recover. Those first few weeks were rough; every night he needed strong painkillers just to sleep. But as Cook and Josephine took turns nursing him, he managed to preserve his sense of humor. At one point he asked Josephine to pack his leg in ice, until someone could get around to shooting it.

For two weeks Peary remained in his cabin, with Cook in attendance more often than anyone else. Those weeks could have cemented a firm friendship between the two men, but instead they may have sowed the first seeds of discord, unknown to Cook. Peary was understandably worried about the future of the expedition. Also, in Cook, he saw a possible rival. Of the rest of the expedition members, none was a potential leader. But Cook had the education, the drive, and the intelligence—to say nothing of the personal charm—to make him stand out. Cook had no leadership ambitions, but to Peary, confined to a bed on a heaving ship, with everything out of his hands, the thought niggled. In future years, Cook's help during those dark times was written out of history by Peary. In the official account of his eventual polar conquest, *The North Pole—It's Discovery in 1909 Under the Auspices of the Peary Arctic Club*, Cook is quickly dismissed. In the foreword, *National Geographic* president Gilbert H. Grosvenor wrote: "The assiduous nursing of Mrs. Peary, aided by the bracing air, so speedily restored his strength that at the ensuing Christmas festivities which he arranged for the Eskimo, he outraced on snowshoes all the natives and his own men!"

Not only inaccurate (his recovery was not that rapid or miraculous), but he left out the setting of the bone, the splint, and the pain management provided by Cook.

Peary's injury threw the expedition into jeopardy. Privately, many members wondered about the advisability of continuing with their leader out of action. But Cook was optimistic. He believed that Peary would make a full recovery by the following spring, when the real work of exploration would begin. It would be tough, but the expedition could go on. Needless to say, no one broached their fears with the irascible and imperious Peary. They continued to edge northwards through the summer ice.

Finally, on July 26, they could go no farther. Captain Pike told Peary that the pack ice was unbroken north of their position, and if they did not begin heading south soon, the ship ran the risk of being icebound for the winter. They were level with McCormick Bay and two miles north of Cape Cleveland. They were at the widest point of the island, and well over halfway up the coast. From here on their journey would be over land.

All that day was spent bringing supplies across the ice to the shore. Teams rowed from the boat to rocky land and began setting up camp. Peary should have been leading his men. Instead he found himself being carried, lashed to a plank. It was an undignified arrival. Toward evening, Peary was placed in a tent, with Josephine nursing him, while the men went back to the ship for one final load. But while they were rowing the short distance the weather broke, bringing squalls and lashing rain. The rowers were forced to remain on the ship, leaving Peary and Josephine alone in the tent. Throughout the night the tiny structure was battered, and the rain leaked through the torn canvas. It was a miserable first night, and Josephine spent most of it worrying, needlessly, about polar bears.

But the storm died as quickly as it arose, and the following day the unloading of the boat was completed. The *Kite*, with its team of tourist scientists, turned and headed south. Peary and his six followers were alone at last, several hundred miles north of civilization.

They quickly turned a rough timber frame into a two-room dwelling. The larger room was the men's quarters, with five bunks, a stove, and a table for eating; there was also room for a work bench and some storage space. The second room was smaller, and accommodated a double bed for Peary and his wife. It also held the expedition's small library.

Their surroundings were desolate. Nearby red cliffs swept up from the sea, providing some shelter. McCormick Bay was covered in ice, though it was thin and not safe to walk on. Inland, there was a corridor of land where the snow had melted for the summer, and here they found some vegetation, including flowers and grasses. There were plenty of birds, and some small game. Beyond that corridor the ice cap of the interior rose sharply. Much of the interior of Greenland is covered with a sheet of ice two miles thick. It never melts, not even on the hottest summers. They were at latitude 78 degrees, just seven hundred miles from the North Pole. This was five hundred miles higher than Peary's farthest north on his previous trip—and far higher than Nansen had attained. They had picked a terrible place to over-winter. The plan was to sit out the cold season, then in the spring push as far north as they could, hopefully discovering the uppermost extent of Greenland. Then they would come back to the winter camp, and await the return of the *Kite*, which would bear them home in triumph.

Josephine took over cooking duties, using the landed supplies which the men did their best to supplement by hunting. Life settled into a rhythm, as they consolidated their base and prepared for the next year's work. Peary's plan was to use the locals to help build sledges. They could also help with the hunting and could teach the Americans how to build snow huts, or igloos, from the ice. But that plan depended on one small detail: there had to be locals there to make contact with. And it looked as if the landing party had picked a desolate and uninhabited spot. They were on their own.

They had hoped to trade with the locals for warm furs and for trained dogs. But if they could not get dogs, the men were quite prepared to haul the sledges themselves. Man-hauling was a tradition of Arctic exploration, much favored by the British expeditions that had dominated the early days of searching for the Northwest Passage. It had a nobility, in that it pitted man directly against the elements. But it was hopelessly inefficient. Eventually skis and dogs completely replaced snowshoes and man-hauling. But that would not be for another decade, and all six men on the trip knew they might have to spend weeks or months in the harness, if they failed to win over the local population—or find a local population in the first place.

Cook, as second in command, took over the running of the camp while Peary recuperated. He also led the search for Eskimo. Previous expeditions had dismissed the locals as savages, but both Peary and Cook were of one mind; that sort of imperialist thinking would doom the expedition. There was so much they could learn, and both were eager to do that.

Cook took three of the men—Gibson, Astrup, and Verhoeff—with him in a small boat, pushing up the bay to look for signs of habitation. Josephine and Henson remained with Peary, tending the increasingly difficult patient. The four men rowed and sailed north for twenty-four hours. Tensions in the small boat grew—at one point Astrup threw Verhoeff overboard, and the small man had to be fished out of the water, freezing cold. Eventually they pulled into the shore, and lit a fire to warm up. They slept through the night, until Verhoeff woke up and panicked. He began shouting to the others that there was a bear approaching the camp.

The bear turned out to be an Eskimo, dressed in furs and feathers. He spoke no English, and none of the men could speak his dialect of Eskimo, which was substantially different from the language spoken in southern Greenland. But eventually, through smiles and gestures, a channel of communication was opened. Some of the ducks the men had shot earlier were roasting on the camp fire, and when they shared the fowl, that loosened the tongues even more. Cook desperately tried to match sounds to meanings, and eventually figured out a few phrases, including, "What is your name?" The native man disappeared briefly, returning with his wife and two daughters. The couple agreed to return to Peary's camp the following day.

When the boat was making the return trip, with its extra passengers, the party spotted a group of rough tents on an island. It turned out to be a summer settlement, with about twenty-five people and a hundred dogs. Cook and his group, accompanied by a native family, were quickly accepted by the tribe. They spent a few days getting to know the tribe, and went on a few hunting trips with them. Cook's knowledge of the vocabulary slowly began to expand. Reasoning that one spot in a wilderness is fairly much the same as another, Cook invited the group to follow him back to base, to set up their settlement there. He had hopes they would accept the invitation, but with the language difficulties there was no way of knowing.

The boat was launched again and Cook, with his three expedition mates and the original Eskimo family, sailed across McCormick Bay to Peary's encampment, which they had dubbed Red Cliff House. Peary was delighted; it was a good start. Every day parties went out to hunt with the Eskimo, learning to live off the land. Even Josephine got involved. She used a revolver, and proved to be a good shot. Soon roast venison became a fixture on the menu.

There were some small problems, many caused by cultural differences. The Eskimo had a custom of swapping wives, and were a bit disappointed to learn that Josephine was a strictly one-husband woman. And Josephine was a bit thrown by the casual way that both sexes removed their tops while indoors. The sight of bare-breasted women sitting around the fire was jarring for her. Throughout the summer, Cook and Peary learned more and more about their neighbors, and began what would, for both men, be a lifelong study. They made progress with the language, and both men were highly tolerant, accepting beliefs and customs that were alien to them. Cook, in particular, was eager to learn. He made great progress in mastering the Eskimo language, and delighted in recording their strange customs and ways.

By October, the year had turned. High above the Arctic Circle the sun goes down for weeks or months at a time, leading to a long Arctic night. Early that month the golden orb disappeared below horizon. It would not rise again until March. Temperatures would drop and game would become scarce. They were facing a long winter. McCormick Bay froze solid.

But once the bay froze, Peary was delighted to see the Eskimo on the nearby island trudging across the ice. Soon there was a large native settlement surrounding Red Cliff House. Peary gave gifts to the new arrivals, such as knives for the men and needles for the women. Cooperation between both groups flourished, and Peary soon saw the value of his new neighbors, as hunters returned regularly with seals, walrus, and reindeer. He studied the native techniques for working furs and skins. Skins were not cured in chemicals as in America. Instead, the skins were slowly chewed until they became soft and workable. Peary was fascinated. For him, the expedition was finally underway. By winter he had abandoned the crutches he had needed for so long and was hobbling around on his injured leg, slowly building up his strength. The more mobile he became, the more his spirits lifted. He was finally in charge of his own expedition.

Over the winter some of the work they carried out was faintly ludicrous. Peary took photographs of all the Eskimo, standing them in Red Cliff House while Henson held an oil lamp for illumination. The idea was to have a record so that the Greenlanders could be compared with ethnic communities from other parts of the world. Not very useful for the push north, though. Cook took measurements, and noted that extremities, such as feet, hands, noses, and ears that could be vulnerable to frostbite, were smaller than their American counterparts. The people had adapted to their environment, proof of the still-controversial science of evolution.

Astrup came into his own that winter, teaching the members of the expedition how to ski. Many of the team were content with this, but Cook studied with the Eskimo too, learning how to handle a dog team and how to build igloos. Although he did not realize it, this would prove to be of lifelong benefit to him.

All was not rosy, however. During the long night of winter, Cook began to notice a deterioration in the men's health. It began with anemia, then the washed-out faces took on a greenish tint; it was the early signs of scurvy. At that time the cause of scurvy (a deficiency in vitamin C) was not known. But it was known that the disease affected people on long ocean voyages, and in extreme environments. The British Navy and other navies had made a tentative connection between lack of fresh food and the disease. Lemon and lime juice and preserved fruits such as marmalade (literally "sea sickness," from the French) were used to combat the sickness, which spread after a number of months to the limbs, reopening old wounds and attacking the joints. Nosebleeds and gum disease were symptoms of the advanced stages of the disease.

There was no chance of nipping down to the corner store for a jar of marmalade, so Cook had to look elsewhere for his solution. His first observation was that scurvy was only affecting the seven expedition members; it did not seem to affect the native Greenlanders. The only difference between the conditions both groups were enduring was their diet. As he noted years later in his book, *Hell is a Cold Place*: "White men get scurvy. The Eskimo do not."

Peary acknowledged Cook's insight, but was reluctant to do anything about it. He wanted to learn from the Eskimo in all things— except wife-swapping and diet. To him a mark of civilization was "civilized" food, and he would not tackle raw meat. To Cook, this was the main difference between the American and the native diet. He began to take some raw meat on a regular basis, and he was less affected by the early stages of scurvy than the others in the hut.

By mid-January the sky was lightening for a brief period each afternoon, and tensions in the cramped cabin led to a burning desire to escape. It affected Peary more than most, and in mid-February he decided to make a brief foray out. The purpose of the trip was to test his leg, and to see how well his team could move across the frozen land. It was a mixed success. With Cook and Astrup, he managed to climb two thousand feet above McCormick Bay to assess the extent of the sea ice. They also caught that year's sunrise, a month ahead of the group that remained at the camp. His leg held up well, but the trip was by no means easy. All three men suffered greatly, and found the going exhausting. However, Cook was less worried than the others. He put their decline down to lack of exercise, and predicted that they would soon regain their condition. In this he proved correct.

The next two months were spent preparing for the summer push north. Men trained to work with the dogs they had bartered off the Eskimo, and supplies were packed. In April a team went out onto the ice sheet of the interior, bringing a cache of food and fuel to a point 2,500 feet high, several miles out of the camp.

A few weeks later the group set out on the real trip, full of confidence. Five men were selected, while Verhoeff, the smallest and weakest member, was left at Red Cliff House with Josephine. However, they hit a problem almost immediately; the Eskimo refused to venture into the interior, saying it was the country of the dead. The white men would have to travel alone. Henson, who had frostbite on his heel, also returned to base with them. So four men—Peary, Cook, Astrup, and Gibson—marched forward alone, into a region Cook called "one of the most damnable regions on Earth."

They had three heavy sledges and three dog teams. Peary, as expedition leader, walked in front, while the other three handled a dog team each. Initially the going was tough. Spring brought storms, and the path was all uphill until they reached an elevation of several thousand feet. But as they found their rhythm, they managed to average twenty miles a day. It didn't take the group long to penetrate 130 miles inland. They rested for a night in their igloo, and on the following morning, May 25, got ready for another march. But Peary stopped them and explained that there was a change of plan. From here on, he was returning to the "travel light" approach of his first Greenland expedition. He would take just one man, and try to push as far north as possible with greatest speed.

Immediately Cook stepped forward to volunteer. Gibson and Astrup were not far behind him. But Peary had other plans for Cook. As second in command, his job was to ensure everyone's safety and organize their return to America if Peary perished. Cook was going back to Red Cliff House. He wasn't very surprised; Peary had indicated as much to him the previous night. Peary selected Astrup as his companion; since Astrup had more experience on ice than any of them, and was an expert skier, this was a sensible choice. It also helped that Astrup hero-worshipped his leader, a man of considerable vanity.

There may have been one other factor at play in the choice. Cook was the man Peary had the most in common with. They came from a similar middle class background (even if Cook's was more impoverished), and they shared a good education. He was also physically strong. He was the ideal companion on the dash north. But Cook was the only potential rival Peary had, and by sending him back to base, he was denying him the chance to share in the glory of the farthest north.

In similar circumstances at the opposite end of the world, Robert Falcon Scott made a similar call. In 1902 Scott, Ernest Shackleton, and Edward Wilson achieved a farthest south of 82 degrees, only 530 miles short of the Pole. But Scott and Wilson left Shackleton at the final camp and marched several miles farther south, to deny the Irishman a place in the achievement of that mark. Shackleton was a potential rival for Scott, whereas Wilson was not. History proved the correctness of this assessment, when Shackleton led two major expeditions to Antarctica, a region Scott considered his territory.

Peary and Cook would go on to develop a similar rivalry.

But that was all far in the future. The four men took one final meal together, then both groups split. Cook and Gibson took one team of dogs south, while Peary and Astrup took two teams, each sledge loaded with a thousand pounds of supplies, north. Peary retained thirteen dogs, while Cook, who had provisions for only two weeks, took the final two dogs.

Cook's return was tough but uneventful. A week into the trip one of his two dogs broke free of the harness and ran off ahead into the wilderness. He arrived back at camp three days ahead of the group he had abandoned. Finally, on June 3, Cook and Gibson trudged home with an empty sledge, towed by a single dog. They were tired but strong. Cook took Josephine's two hands in his, and smiled at her.

"When we left him two weeks ago, Robert was in good health and fine spirits, and traveling well," he told her.

It took some weight off her mind, but she knew that it could be another two months before the two men returned. Two questions remained: Would they return at all? And if they did return safely, would they all make it back to Red Cliff House before the end of summer? If they did not, they would miss the return of the *Kite*, and would be forced to spend a second winter at McCormick Bay.

7

PEARY TRAVELS NORTH

Peary and Astrup did not have an easy time on their journey north after they parted from Cook and Gibson at Separation Camp. It was a season of storms, with wind driving the snow to create blizzard conditions on many of the days. But they had pushed on, despite the difficulties.

By that stage, everyone knew the interior of Greenland was a vast sheet of ice. It rose to a height of two miles in the center of the island. Peary was prepared for that; he had been into the interior a few years previously, and had read all about Nansen's crossing. But that had been a lot farther south. Conditions were even worse on the northern portion of the island. The ice sheet behaves as one vast glacier, slowly being forced seawards by the weight of the ice in the center. And in places, depending on the local geography, there were actual glaciers.

Moving ice is a lot more dangerous than static ice. One of the dangers is that the sheet breaks up into crevasses—giant cracks. Some of these cracks can be thirty feet across, and they can drop several hundred feet, tapering as they plunge into the depths. Often a fresh covering of snow will conceal these crevasses. This makes them particularly dangerous. One minute you can be trudging across what looks like fresh snow; the

next moment your dog team disappears into the ground, and if you don't
haul back on the sledge immediately and arrest their fall, all is lost.

This did happen several times to Peary and Astrup. Luckily they
were traveling slowly and though the lead dog disappeared a number
of times, they always managed to stop the team and put the brakes on
the sledge in time. Had they failed, an entire dog team and sledge full
of supplies would have been gone in an instant, making their survival
difficult at best.

Although they managed to avoid that, every time a dog plunged
through the ice, it resulted in a long delay. First, everything had to be
brought to a stop. Then Peary or Astrup had to edge slowly forward,
being careful not to fall on the loose snow, until they reached the
edge. Then the poor dog would be hauled up and his harness straight-
ened. Then they had to reverse away from the crevasse, and find a
place to cross it. Some crevasses stretched for dozens of yards, and
a few minutes would get them back on track. But the larger ones
required a substantial diversion to get around.

Sometimes a crack would open up that could be crossed at a jump.
Often the length of the sledge was enough to make a temporary bridge.
Sometimes there was a snow or an ice bridge that they could gingerly
cross. But every break in the ice resulted in a delay and fewer miles
being made that day.

Both Peary and Astrup took notes on the trip, and both told their
companions about what they encountered when the two men returned
to Red Cliff. Those notes and conversations are the only record of the
trip, and it needs to be borne in mind that Peary was not always the most
reliable of witnesses when it came to his own exploits. Here is what
they claim happened.

After leaving Separation Camp the two men decided to lighten
their load. They ditched their sleeping bags, and slept instead in the
warm fur suits supplied by the Eskimo. They tied the sleeves and
legs with drawstrings to keep the snow out, and found this perfectly
adequate for the weather they encountered on the trip north. As it
was spring, and the Arctic is generally a few degrees warmer than the
Antarctic, this is quite conceivable.

At the end of each day's march the two men would unload a three-sided shelter, which they erected in the snow. This wind block gave them shelter from the wind, and allowed them to operate the stove they needed to prepare drinking water, and to heat up their evening meal. The men found that the screen also gave enough shelter to sleep in, and soon abandoned the practice of building igloos. Igloos are round huts made from blocks of ice, and are well insulated. They are a very efficient way of surviving in the cold, but they are time consuming to construct. By abandoning the use of them, Peary and Astrup gave themselves more time to rest and sleep, and were able to add an hour of marching to the day as well.

Their first few days were easy. After leaving Cook and Gibson, they traveled up the ice cap for fifteen miles. The land was undulating, with the ice massed in enormous dome-shaped hills. Going up was a slog, but coming down the other side was a simple jog and slide. Eventually they reached an altitude of nearly nine thousand feet, the height of the interior ice plateau. The actual rock was several thousand feet below them, buried beneath the ice and compacted snow. From here the surface stretched away in waves of whiteness, blinding in the slanting summer sun. It was an almost featureless desert of snow, a great unknown region where no man had ever set foot.

The Eskimo believed that their dead ancestors roamed this wilderness, which is why they had refused to travel with the exploration party. When Peary returned, he was questioned closely and the locals were very disappointed that he had met none of their departed!

The weather was mixed; on good days the going was glorious, if monotonous. But when the storms kicked up, they often had to limit themselves to short marches. On one occasion they had to camp for three days, and try to make up for lost time when the storm abated.

Toward the end of May, they encountered the head of the Petermann Glacier, which broke up the ice badly. A week or so was spent negotiating the broken, glaciated ice. The Petermann Glacier is a large glacier connecting the ice sheet to the Arctic Ocean. It is more than forty miles long and almost ten miles wide. But once they had crossed this, they found themselves back on the higher ground of the interior, where the going was easier, with less cracks in the surface. They still faced the howling winds, and the blizzard conditions. Each day they marched forward as best they could through the featureless landscape. It was monotonous drudgery. Now Peary was handling a dog team alongside Astrup, so there was no one out front breaking the trail. Dogs like to follow a trail, and once Peary was not out front, they slowed down.

The two men experimented, and one of their solutions was to harness both sledges in a line, with all the dogs pulling both. Astrup was in harness alongside the dogs, while Peary, also in harness, was out front. This gave the dogs their target, and progress was made. However it made conversation impossible, leaving each man alone in his bubble of boredom.

Three days of fog led them to negotiate by compass alone, and they ended up catching another glacier. Nearly two weeks was spent crossing the Ryder Glacier and negotiating the deadly crevasses, losing precious time whenever a dog disappeared into a crack. They eventually regained the smoother ice cap, but then they encountered another problem: there was a range of hills blocking their way. It was not just a question of finding a pass through the hills—mountains meant glaciers, and they did not fancy more crevasses. So they turned due east, trying to go around the hills.

They were a month into their trip. For thirty-three days they had pushed north from Separation Camp. The landscape began to dull their senses. The sheer monotony gave it an air of unreality, making it difficult to judge distances. At times they thought they were getting nowhere; at other times they thought they were on a straight highway to the Pole.

As Astrup wrote later in his book, *With Peary Near the Pole* (1898): "Are we really to live to penetrate farther northward than any other mortal . . . ? But life is full of bitter disappointments. Scarcely were we on the road that evening when . . . we came in sight of land that barred our course."

After nearly a month of travel the two men could see mountains to the north and east. If they continued in that direction their way would be barred. So they turned west, toward the coast, meaning to skirt the mountains. They had found little game that far north, and relied on their store of provisions.

On July 1 the terrain sloped steeply upward, and there was no way to avoid it. So they pulled slowly onward, the weight of the sledges sapping their energy. But when they crested the rise they found themselves on the top of a large cliff. The ground fell away sharply to the sea, more than three thousand feet below. Looking across the sea, they could see in the very far distance some peaks rising up out of the ocean. Peary was certain they were on the cusp of a vast bay, looking across at a distant island. That meant they had reached the top of Greenland, and had determined its northernmost extent. Astrup was less sure; he looked out and judged it to be a vast fjord, cutting through the northern portion of the country. It was possible, he felt, that it might extend right across the island, linking up with Victoria Fjord on the east coast. That would make the distant peaks an island. But it might not cut across the country; what lay ahead could be a peninsula.

Peary insisted he was right. They had arrived at their final destination. He named the distant island Peary Land. Astrup confided his doubts to his diary:

"Nothing sure can be said of its extent westwards or the possibility of its going through to Victoria inlet on the west coast. But one thing is sure; the Greenland inland ice does not extend farther north than to the eighty-second parallel," Astrup wrote. He was not as sure as Peary that they had reached the end, but he thought they were close.

Peary was ready to celebrate. They had proved Greenland was an island. They were five hundred miles north of McCormick Bay, and they had determined the upper limits of the land. It was a major geological discovery.

As leader, he got busy naming the features. He called the sea Independence Bay, and the cliff Navy Cliff. This was their farthest north, and both men made a camp so that they could stay and savor their achievement. They established camp at the point they called Observation Bluff, and built a cairn of rocks to mark the site. Their farthest north called for celebration, and packed among all the other gear were some delicacies they had brought to mark the occasion. In addition to the usual grilled musk ox and the ever-present biscuits, they had a brandy cocktail, and some preserved pears.

A map Peary drew on the first day shows Independence Bay with no hint of the land beyond. He marked their farthest north as 81 degrees 37 minutes 5 seconds North, 34 degrees 5 minutes West.

Later research would prove Astrup right. Independence Bay was indeed a fjord, and it did not reach clear across the country to join with Victoria Fjord. Peary Land was a peninsula at the very tip of Greenland. The men had stopped a little more than a hundred miles—or a week of good going—from the top of the country. They had indeed discovered the northern extent of the country's interior ice sheet; it did not push into Peary Land. What lay ahead of them was exposed land, rather than a territory buried under thousands of feet of ice. But had they pushed on, they would have had to travel inland along the fjord for miles before being able to make any further progress north, and the going would have gotten a lot tougher. Peary did not feel they needed to. He was convinced Peary Land was an island.

The men remained three days at Observation Point. The ice sheet had ended, and they found a rocky landscape. It was bleak, but it did have vegetation. When they looked down from Observation Point they could see herds of musk oxen contentedly grazing the plain below them. The animals had never seen humans before, and did not realize their danger. They were no match for two hungry men with rifles.

They also found small flowers blossoming in the cracks of the rocks, and heard the buzzing of bees. It was a magical place, after so long on the ice cap. They knew they were almost certainly the first humans to have found this place.

Their few days were spent surveying and exploring. Peary wrote: "It was almost impossible for us to believe that we were standing on the northern shore of Greenland as we gazed from the summit of this precipitous cliff with the most brilliant sunshine all about us, with yellow poppies growing between the rocks around our feet, and a herd of musk oxen in the valley behind us. In that valley we had also found the dandelion in bloom, and had heard the heavy drone and seen the bullet-like flight of the humble bee."

But eventually it was time to turn their backs on this Eden and make their way back to Red Cliff, with news of their discovery. With renewed supplies of fresh meat, and sledges lightened by the weight of the provisions they had already eaten, they made quick progress. It helped that they were traveling out of, rather than into, the unknown. They were able to spot familiar landmarks, and avoid the two glaciers by staying inland. Progress was quicker high on the ice cap, and they often made more than twenty miles a day. Sometimes they averaged more than thirty.

Unknown to the explorers, anxiety was growing at Red Cliff. The men were expected to be out on the ice for two months, and every day beyond that led to worry. Cook and Gibson had returned on June 3, and were reunited with Henson and Verhoeff. Verhoeff had enjoyed the time with Josephine, but he did not find it easy to mix, and had taken a violent dislike to both Gibson and Peary himself. With the enlarged camp, Verhoeff found himself once more isolated. He was a disagreeable companion, and never found a way to fit in fully.

As Cook noted: "Verhoeff, the best schooled from a standpoint of book learning, did not do much for himself nor for anyone else. He was by nature of an insurgent type and somehow, though a willing worker, he did not fit into any plan of outdoor endeavor. There was evident in him at all times a kind of supressed bitterness which took the form of a grouch against Peary. This antagonism increased as the time neared to go home. He had already told Gibson and myself in confidence that he would never return in the same ship with Peary. But we did not take this protest seriously, for we all had our own impatient spells of complaining."

Verhoeff joined Cook on some trips to study the Eskimo while they awaited the return of the northern party—and the *Kite*, the ship that would bring them home. He also wandered off on his own on occasion, and did not seem to show much concern for his personal safety. As he noted in his diary on July 11, 1982, he hopped from floe to floe on the ice, a very dangerous practice: "After three quarters of an hour's work, I succeeded in getting from shore to ice by floating floes. After two hours' steady walk I reached our side of the bay and got on a floe, but as it grounded, I waded to shore."

In addition to Verhoeff, tension was caused by a sudden deterioration in the relationship between the Americans and their native neighbors. Cook and Henson got the strong impression that the Eskimo were planning to massacre the whites. It was all due to one Eskimo, a moody and violent man eventually killed by one of the others in the tribe, and it never developed into the battle that they feared.

The expedition was greatly relieved when they heard a ship's whistle sound three times in the bay on July 23. The *Kite* had returned to take the expedition home. On board were letters from home—and the nine members of the Academy of Natural Sciences. The familiar faces provided welcome relief from the tensions at Red Cliff, and life returned to normal for a while. But the arrival of the ship brought a new tension. If Peary and Astrup did not return soon, the ship would have no choice but to abandon them and sail south. The captain would not risk being trapped for a winter in the sea ice. It was a tense wait.

Josephine went to the first food cache and waited there for a few days, hoping to catch them on their return. Even the newly arrived professors got caught up in the worry. Deciding to do something practical, rather than sit around the camp fretting, they decided to head out onto the ice sheet. Led by Professor Angelo Heilprin, they left camp on August 5, and climbed as high as they could, with the intention of placing signal posts at regular intervals to guide the returning explorers home. They spent the day struggling to gain altitude, and it was late evening when they placed the first beacon pole, topped with a red handkerchief. They were about eight miles into the interior, at an elevation of 3,300 feet. Wearily they began to move further inland, to place a second beacon.

As Heilprin wrote in *Scribner's Magazine* in 1893: "A shout burst upon the approaching midnight hour which made everybody's heart throb to its fullest. Far off to the north-westward Entrikin's clear vision had detected a black speck that was foreign to the Greenland ice. There was no need to conjecture what it meant. 'It's a man; it is moving,' broke out almost simultaneously from several lips, and it was immediately realized that the explorers of whom we were in quest were returning victoriously homeward."

Peary and Astrup had made impressively rapid progress on their homeward journey, and toward the end, when they were moving down the ice slope to the coast, they were easily managing treks of well over thirty miles a day. They marched long into the night, as the high latitude meant that they had twenty-four hours of daylight. They were still strong; Peary had actually gained a pound in weight over the long summer. Astrup had lost some condition, but not much. He was a little more than ten pounds lighter than when he had set out—but he was a big man, and may have been carrying excess weight. They had survived their ordeal in remarkable shape. Their appearance impressed Professor Heilprin, who gushed: "Like a veritable giant, clad in a suit of deer and dog skin, and gracefully poised on Canadian snow-shoes, the conqueror from the far north plunged down the mountain slope. Behind him followed his faithful companion, young Astrup, barely more than a lad, yet a tower of strength and endurance."

The explorers were delighted to be met with a reception party. After two months of no company, it was good to make contact with the human race again. Peary was modest and reserved, but Astrup enthusiastically shook everyone on the team by the hand, muttering: "It gives me much pleasure!"

They did not waste time on formalities, but continued straight for Red Cliff. The following morning a small boat rowed Peary out to the *Kite*, where Josephine had spent a restless night.

As she wrote in her *Arctic Journal*, published in 1893: "I was roused by the plash of oars and loud talking, and before I had fully grasped the idea that the professor's party had returned, someone jumped over the rail and on the deck just over my head, and a familiar footstep made its way hurriedly toward the companionway. I knew it was Mr. Peary. He came rushing down the stairs and rattled at my door, calling to me to open it; but I seemed to be paralyzed, and he forced it open and stood before me, well and hearty, safe at last . . . I have been afraid to go to sleep since Mr. Peary's return, for fear I might wake up and find it all a dream."

The lovers reunited, it was time to return home.

If only it was that simple. . . .

The *Kite* was ready to sail. It would only take a few days to pack everything that was returning to America onto the steamer, then break through the early autumn ice and head for the safer waters that lay south. With the help of the nine academics and the Eskimo, it would be quick work. It had taken the Eskimo some time to get used to Peary on his return. At first they had assumed he was a ghost, and when they realized he was not, they were disappointed that he had not met their ancestors in the ghost lands. They had expected news of departed loved ones.

Peary had returned a little later than expected, but not much. There was plenty of time left before departure became impossible. Most of their work was done, but the party were reluctant to leave their home of over a year. Peary proposed one final week of survey work. He would take Henson and Verhoeff with him, and explore the Inglefield Gulf. They were accompanied by five Eskimo, and Josephine also joined them. This was important for a simple reason: he intended to name lots of features on the newly drawn map after various benefactors of the expedition. Keep them happy, and they might dig into their pockets for another excursion. While they were on that survey, the others began to pack the ship.

"It was with a feeling akin to homesickness that I took the pictures and ornaments from the walls of our little room, pulled down the curtains from the windows and bed, had Matt (Henson) pack the books and nail them up, sorted the things on the bed, and packed those I wanted to keep," wrote Josephine.

Peary surveyed the gulf quickly, drawing sketches and filling in the details as best he could. Henson proved an able assistant. The trip almost had the feel of a jaunt. Verhoeff pursued his own geological and meteorological studies. But the small man was uncommunicative and disliked the Pearys, particularly Robert. His presence added a tension to the party that should not have been there. When he suggested to Peary that he return to the camp a little early, so that he could do some of his own research along the way, the commander agreed. He gave Verhoeff three pounds of pemmican, a revolver, and fifty rounds.

On August 11 Verhoeff came across Gibson and two Eskimo. He had taken a wrong turn and was miles out of his way, and was glad to meet his companions, who pointed him in the right direction. He stayed a night with them at their camp and ate a huge meal, and slept for a long time. He set off alone on the morning of August 12. He told Gibson he was going to visit an Eskimo village to collect mineral samples, and would return on August 14. A few hours later he came back to the camp, and told Gibson he had changed his plans. He would remain out longer, and asked that a rowboat pick him up on August 16, at Five Glacier Valley. From there it would be a short crossing to Red Cliff.

That was the last anyone saw of him.

When Gibson arrived at Five Glacier Valley on the appointed day, Verhoeff was not there. He waited a day, and then returned to Red Cliff. No one had news of the little man who had partly financed the expedition. A search party was immediately organized. One thing struck everyone as soon as they realized Verhoeff was missing: he had hidden all his possessions in nooks and crannies around the base camp, as if he intended they not be placed on the ship. A suspicion began to grow that maybe he never intended to return on the *Kite*.

Five days of fruitless search found no sign of him. All that was found were some footprints in the snow heading toward a glacier, some mineral specimens on a flat rock, and the label from a tin of corned beef. Eventually Captain Richard Pike of the *Kite* called off the search. The weather had deteriorated, and if the ship did not sail soon, it ran the risk of being beset.

On August 23 Peary left a note at Redcliff House.

"Dear Sir,

"Every effort has been made to find you during the past week by the entire party, without success. On the bare possibility that you may still come out all right, I have cached at Cairn Point just north of the Cairns, a year's supplies.

"All the Eskimo will look after your comfort to the best of their ability and will take you to Cape York next spring, where a whaler will stop for you. You had better plan to get to Cape York not later than June 1."

Peary's treatment of Verhoeff seems callous at this remove, but at the time it was necessary. He could not remain the winter on the ice just in case a man, possibly dead, was actually hiding from him in the interior. It would have put everyone in danger, and they all understood that. But Peary covered his back, by getting Cook to write a letter stating the facts of the case, and that they had carried out a thorough search for the missing man. At the time, Cook was happy to do this, but he later wrote, after his relationship with Peary had become severely dented: "He had paid $2,000 toward the fund of the expedition. Verhoeff was young and enthusiastic. He gave his time, his money, and he risked his life for Peary. He was treated with the same consideration as that accorded the Eskimo dogs. When I last saw him in camp, he was in tears, telling of Peary's injustice. Mrs. Peary—I advert to this with all possible reluctance—had done much to make his life bitter, and over this he talked for days. Finally he said: 'I will never go home in the same ship with that man and that woman.' It was the last sentence he uttered in my hearing. He did not go home in that ship. Instead, he wandered off over the glacier, where he left his body in the blue depths of a crevasse."

Peary's treatment of Astrup on their next expedition, and his treatment of Dr. Dedrick on a later expedition, also came under scrutiny. Taken individually, the incidents can be brushed away. Taken together, they paint a picture of a man so obsessed with his own grand visions that he ignores and steps on those beneath him.

Peary had traveled more than a thousand miles across an unexplored wilderness, and had discovered the top of Greenland. It should have been a triumphant moment. But it was a sad and pensive group, haunted by the specter of Verhoeff, that steamed out of McCormick Bay and headed south toward Godhavn and civilization.

8

HOME FROM GREENLAND

Peary had achieved all his objectives. By any standard the expedition was a remarkable success. He had managed to trek a thousand miles, averaging fourteen miles a day. He had spent eighty-five days in the unknown and had returned in good health. But the strange loss of Verhoeff had tainted the trip. And a second concern was that not everyone would accept his geological findings.

It was a worried commander who sailed from Greenland. Though "spin" is a modern term, it is not a modern concept. Peary knew he would have to spin the truth carefully in the coming months. It began in the St. John's, Newfoundland, telegraph office, on September 11, when he gave the waiting world the news: "US Navy claims highest discoveries on Greenland east coast. Independence Bay, discovered July 4, 1892. Greenland ice cap ends south of Victoria inlet."

This was duly published by the *New York Times* two days later.

Ten days later, the *Kite* entered Delaware Bay and berthed in Philadelphia. Among the throng of well-wishers was one woman who was not celebrating the safe return of the expedition. John Verhoeff's sister was in belligerent mood, demanding to know what Peary had done with her brother. He tried to brush her off, saying that he was not on board, and he had nothing more to say on the matter at that point. Not a diplomatic reply, and when they met again later that day, he failed to satisfy her. She felt that her brother had been used as a paid companion for Josephine Peary, rather than being given the chance to fulfill his scientific potential, then had been abandoned on the ice after an inadequate search.

It gave the press something to focus on. Within a fortnight of announcing his geographical discoveries, the *New York Times* was speculating that Verhoeff had chosen to remain with the Eskimo, and subtly condemning Peary for not being more open about the fate of the young man:

> "In speaking of the fate of Verhoeff, Lieut. Peary said he had no right to indulge in surmises, but he gave the impression that he believed Verhoeff was dead.
>
> "But little information could be gained from Lieut. Peary, Mrs. Peary, or any of the members of the expedition in regard to the scientific results of their journey. Lieut. Peary and his wife are both under contract to newspapers to give them first the results of the expedition, and the other members of the expedition are pledged to silence."

Controlling the media is a double-edged sword. Those outlets that you are not feeding have a tendency to put a negative spin on whatever little information they can glean. At heart, Peary was an autocrat: he appeared affable to men like Cook on the Greenland trip, but when his own interests were threatened, a different side to him emerged. Cook was to find this out over the coming months.

Peary had three objectives on his return to civilization. First, he had to convince the world that he had achieved his objective of discovering the most northerly extent of Finland. Second, he had to convince the Navy to give him more extended leave to organize a follow-up expedition; he could not sit on his laurels. Third, he had to make some money from the next trip.

America was quick to believe the dashing Naval commander. There was no hint of doubt in all the news reports. It was accepted immediately and without question that he had achieved what he said he achieved. Not so in the rest of the world. The big question was the land that Peary and Astrup had spotted across the sea from Greenland. They had not done a proper exploration of the region to determine what that land was. Peary maintained that it was an archipelago of islands north of the country, and it may well have been. But it could just as easily have been a continuation of Greenland itself. Nothing Peary had done could definitively have answered that question. To prove that Greenland ended where he said it ended, he would have had to trek east to link up with Victoria Fjord. Time and resources had not permitted this, and had they, he would have realized he had made a serious mistake. The land to the north was part of Greenland. His declaration that Greenland ended where he said it ended was based on firm belief rather than real evidence. Astrup admitted his doubts, in a report he wrote for a Norwegian publication, *Norsk Geografisk Tidsskrift*. He said that no definite conclusion could be drawn about what lay north. It was enough for the European media. Publications declared Peary's conclusions as rash, and *Nouvelles Geographiques* (January 1894) went so far as to suggest that Peary exaggerated the distances he had traveled, like he had (they alleged) on his previous Greenland expedition.

Still, at home he was accepted as a hero. And home was where the opportunities lay. Peary petitioned the Secretary of the Navy for leave to mount another expedition to follow up on his valuable work. He knew that he now had a pedigree—between the work in Nicaragua and Greenland, he was building up a reputation as a good surveyor and explorer. But he was also building up petty jealousies. He was turned down, and assigned to return to his civil engineering work at the Norfolk docklands. It was a huge come-down, and a slap in the face. But after lobbying from the American Geographical Society, there was an official change of mind, and Peary was granted the leave he wanted. He would sail again in the spring of 1893.

Now he had to raise the funds for his third expedition. Public lectures were the way. In the days before television and cinema, public lectures drew large crowds. In January 1892, Peary began a series of public lectures that would occupy him for nearly four months.

He opened at the Academy of Music in Philadelphia, and crossed the country, bringing Matthew Henson (in Eskimo furs) and his team of five dogs to add razzmatazz to the tour. He did 165 lectures in 103 days, a draining schedule. The tour netted $18,000, but Peary was disappointed; he estimated the cost of his next trip at $80,000. There was a considerable shortfall. The tour also placed a strain on his marriage, when Josephine refused to travel with him.

But Peary pressed on. He loved being the center of attention. As he wrote to his mother: "I have been meeting all sorts of noted men in the last few weeks, and have invariably been the guest of honor among them."

He was paid $1,000 by the World Fair in Chicago for various items Cook had collected among the Eskimo. The World Fair, due to be held that summer, would attract hundreds of thousands of people. As Cook had handled the ethnological work, Peary decided that he would be the ideal man to go to Chicago to supervise the exhibit, but Cook had other ideas. He suggested that he go on his own lecture tour instead, hitting the towns and cities that Peary did not have the time to stop at, and raising more funds for the next expedition. He would give Peary 50 percent of the proceeds.

This suggestion was the wedge that eventually drove the friends apart. Peary had been a huge supporter of Cook, praising his work at every opportunity, and singling him out as one of the outstanding members of the party. He wanted him as the surgeon on the next trip, valuing his intelligence, his coolness, and his loyalty. But he was unwilling to share the spotlight with him. He told Cook to stick to the original plan, and take a booth at the World Fair. Lectures there would be enough of a contribution. Cook, who had been to the site of the World Fair, and knew that it was hopelessly behind schedule, did not think this was the best use of his time, and he declined to go to Chicago. He did agree, however, to be part of the next expedition. That is how matters stood for a few months.

Cook had his own problems. His medical practice had never thrived, perhaps because his heart was not in it after the death of his wife and his child. But he needed to support himself, so he found himself back in Brooklyn, with his shingle up outside his door, looking for patients.

He hoped that the little bit of fame that came from his exploits in Greenland would give his practice a boost. So he got into the habit of talking about his trip to anyone who would listen. He enjoyed recounting his experiences, and even began to prepare a lecture. Peary had made everyone sign a contract saying that they would not publish anything about the expedition until after the publication of his own book—an understandable precaution, and one Cook had no intention of defying. But surely there was no harm in a lecture?

Then, in April, Cook made a serious error of judgement. He spoke to an acquaintance of his, Herbert Bridgman, business manager of a Brooklyn newspaper, the *Standard Union*. Over lunch he told tales of the far north, keeping the other man spellbound for two hours. He was not being interviewed by the paper; he was just chatting to an acquaintance. But Bridgman was so enthralled that he decided he had to write an account of their meeting. In an effort to be fair to both men, he sought the permission of Cook and Peary before he published the article. He wrote to Peary. But before Peary had a chance to reply, the paper had gone ahead and published the article without permission. Bridgman wrote a second letter, apologizing. He said that the editor had been so fascinated by Cook's account that he had insisted it be published immediately.

Peary was not pleased.

A few weeks later, Cook read a paper before the King's County Medical Society in Brooklyn—his first independent lecture. He dealt with the peculiarities of the Eskimo people, and how they were culturally and physiologically adapted to life in the far north. He concluded: "With all our civilization there were indeed few points that we could suggest to them to make them more comfortable in their cold and icy homes, but they, on the other hand, taught us how to make ourselves comfortable and brave the arctic storms. We are indebted to them largely for the good health and success of the Peary Expedition." The talk was reprinted in the *New York Medical Examiner*.

Many of those in attendance urged Cook to write a book about the tribe and their ways. It was an interesting idea—and could not cross Peary's plan to write a book about the expedition and its geographic discoveries. Cook would not touch on that topic. There was no clash.

He decided to visit Peary, hoping to obtain permission to use the photographs of the Eskimo that they had taken over the long winter at Red Cliff. Peary was in the dockyard in Brooklyn at that time, so Cook called on him there.

Peary, perhaps smarting still from the article in the *Standard Union*, was less than encouraging. His own efforts to find a publisher had been unsuccessful to date, and the lack of a book deal was another financial blow to his next expedition. He reminded Cook that all the members of the expedition had signed a contract, and could not publish any details of the expedition for a full year after Peary's account went on sale. He would insist on that being followed to the letter. The contract also called for all records and other materials to be the property of Peary for that time, no matter who had produced them. In other words, Cook could not even use his own observations and notebooks during that time.

Cook was stunned. He thought that he had an open and trusting relationship with his commander, and was surprised and hurt by Peary's reaction.

"I was entirely unprepared for this sudden outburst of selfish autocracy," he wrote later.

Peary must have seen that he had gone too far. He softened his tone a bit, and explained that if he let Cook publish, it would be setting a precedent that others would follow. He had to maintain the discipline of the expedition. The two men parted cordially enough, but within a week Cook had written to Peary, withdrawing from the next expedition.

"I have decided not to go on the next expedition. I regret that I have left this to such a late day but trust that it will not seriously inconvenience you."

He ended the letter by promising to lend his support in any way he could—but not on the ice.

The letter of resignation was followed a day later by another letter to Peary from Bridgman of the *Standard Union*. He had written another article about Cook, and he wanted Peary's permission to publish. He was not going to go behind his back again. Peary immediately fired off a telegram forbidding publication, saying: "If you consider the matter, you will see at once that the matter touches directly on the narrative that

I am now at work upon. Dr. Cook is under agreement not to publish anything in regard to the expedition within a year after the appearance of the official narrative . . . I cannot, in justice to myself, consent."

Peary replied graciously to Cook's resignation, saying that while he was sorry to learn of the decision, it would not inconvenience him in any way beyond personal disappointment. He even suggested meeting up when he was in New York over the weekend. They did meet, and Peary was glad to accept Cook's medical advice on diet and what provisions to order. Both men were making desperate attempts to plaster over the cracks in their friendship. Perhaps there was still time for one or the other to reach out and breach the divide. Cook certainly wanted to return to the Arctic, and when he heard that Astrup was eager to join up, he felt a twinge of nostalgia. But he felt he had been badly treated. Peary did feel regret over the way things had gone, writing to Cook: "I am sorry that you are not going with us."

But events overtook the chance of reconciliation. Peary appointed another doctor, so Cook's berth was gone. On July 1, 1893, Cook visited Peary on the *Falcon*, his new ship, which was packed with well-wishers. As a last-minute fundraising effort, the ship had been opened to the public. Pay a small fee and you could board and see off the Arctic party. They had made four stops (Philadelphia, New York, Boston, and Portland) and over a thousand people had taken up the offer in each port, swelling the coffers nicely before departure. All was ready for sail. There were provisions for at least a year (they hoped to be away two years, but hunting game would supplement their supplies). The wintering party had expanded to fourteen, but still included Henson, Astrup, and Josephine. She had come close to withdrawing, as she was pregnant. But she decided in the end to accompany her husband. Cook, although he was not the expedition's surgeon, agreed to Peary's request that he give the entire team a thorough physical. Peary still trusted Cook completely.

The following day, Peary pulled out of dock and sailed into the Atlantic, bound for Greenland. Cook was regretful, but not as regretful as he might have feared: he was also soon to head north, and this time he would be leading his own expedition.

9

BYRD'S EARLY STEPS

While his rivals were making their first tentative steps on the ice, Richard Byrd was not even ready for his first tentative toddler steps.

But if he was late for the race, it never bothered Byrd. He was a man with a sense of privilege and destiny. His very lineage was bound up in the history of America.

Richard Byrd—whom his parents teasingly called "Dickie Byrd"—came from one of the so-called "first families" of Virginia. America may have been a new nation, thrusting aggressively into the future, but its roots were in a colonial past. And the descendants of the colonists tended to hold on to the power and wealth, for centuries dominating public life and politics. The first families were not the families of the earliest settlers, but the socially prominent families who descended from colonists who arrived in the seventeenth century from England. Most arrived during the English civil war and the turbulent years that followed it. They settled in the colony of Virginia, around Jamestown and Williamsburg, and along the James River. They brought their British traditions of class and aristocracy with them. Although the Revolution in 1776 cut the ties with the Crown, in many of the eastern states, including Virginia, the change meant little on the ground. The sense of privilege prevailed.

The first families tended to intermarry, preserving the British tradition of staying within a social class. William Byrd, the original father of the line, arrived in Virginia in 1669. The son of a wealthy London goldsmith, he was granted twelve hundred acres along the James River. He married an English woman, established a tobacco plantation, and was active in Virginia politics.

The other side the line was even more illustrious, descending from Colonel Robert Bolling, another London born settler. Bolling arrived in Virginia in 1660 at the age of fourteen, and used his connections to establish himself in the colony. He married twice, producing fifteen children. His descendants include two First Ladies, Edith Bolling Wilson and Nancy Reagan, as well as presidential candidate John McCain. The Bush dynasty is also related. The bloodlines of the first families run deep.

In the early years of the colony, Virginians made great efforts to get along with the native Indian population. Relations between both races were strained, but it was not the outright warfare it became in other areas and at other times. But there were frequent skirmishes.

In 1613, the teenage daughter of an important local chief was captured and held for ransom. But the girl, Pocahontas, was treated well by her captors, and eventually chose to remain with the English, converting to Christianity and marrying settler John Rolfe. This was the first interracial marriage in North American history. Through Rolfe's descendants, the blood of Pocahontas was introduced into the first families of Virginia. So not only was Richard Byrd descended from European high society, he was also descended from Native American nobility.

He was born into all the privileges that heritage entailed.

His parents were proud of an ancestry that included the founder of Richmond, and a colonial governor. Snobbery and class distinction almost defined the society they lived in. Richard Byrd Senior had studied at the University of Virginia, before finishing in the Maryland School of Law in Baltimore. So when he returned to Winchester in the Shenandoah Valley, he set up practice as a lawyer. He married Eleanor

Bolling Flood, a local beauty—a very well-connected local beauty—and they settled into their comfortable position near the top of the social ladder. It was a happy union. Both were energetic and ambitious people, well suited for the social swirl of Southern life. Eleanor was described by those who knew her as a very energetic woman, "full of pep," and always supportive of her children and her family. As the years went on, the elder Byrd cemented his position in the community by becoming a judge, then the speaker in the Virginia House of Representatives, representing the Democratic Party. But that was many years into the future.

The couple had a son, Harry, on June 10, 1887. He eventually followed in his father's footsteps, entering politics and becoming a US Senator and Governor of Virginia. A year later, their second son arrived. Richard Evelyn Byrd Junior was born on October 25, 1888, in Winchester, Virginia. From the beginning he was underweight, and throughout his childhood years he was sickly and thin, unlike his older brother. A year later, a third son, Tom, was born.

Richard Byrd Senior tried to cultivate an affable appearance, as befitted a budding politician. He insisted that people call him Dick, and had a large circle of friends. But he could be prickly if crossed, as many an opposing lawyer found to his cost. He had a short fuse, and once he threw an inkwell across the town courthouse, striking an opposing lawyer on the head. As the bleeding lawyer was led from the court, there was a clamor to have Byrd arrested. Whether this would have dented his reputation in the feisty South is a moot point; he managed to talk his way out of trouble. He was a cross between a civilized Southern gent and a wild frontiersman. He would not back away from a challenge, and once rode alone into a wild region of the Blue Ridge Mountains to impose the law on the feuding families.

"He was the most fearless man I ever saw," observed the president of the Shenandoah National Bank, Gary Williams.

He was also extremely intelligent. He was setting a tough example for his three sons to live up to.

Richard Byrd Junior inherited many of his father's characteristics, including the physical courage, the intelligence—and the prickly personality. His personality was molded as much by what he was not, as by what he was. He was not the robust All-American hero his class-conscious father might have wished for, and at times his father could be a bit distant. So from the beginning, Byrd had to fight for his place in the family.

Their home was a large mansion, with a full complement of black servants. The slaves had been freed after the Civil War, but economic emancipation was nearly a century away. Byrd's father was still "The Master," and the growing boy was saved the chores and hardships endured by many boys his age. He grew up in elegance. The rooms were large, with graceful furniture and high ceilings. Other prominent families were frequently entertained, occasions on which Richard would be expected to dress up and behave with the impeccable manners of a Southern gent. Richard accepted the snobbery of the times, and thrived on it.

At the same time, he desperately wanted his father's approval. He threw himself into sports as a way of proving himself. Not big enough to be a star at football, he chose his discipline carefully. Gymnastics suited him. He was a boy capable of great discipline, able to train hard and push past the pain barrier. He mastered the sport, competing regularly in his teens. He also enjoyed gymnastics as a chance to build up his slim physique. He tended to stand with his shoulders thrown back and his chest thrown out, accentuating his height as much as he was able.

He seemed to have been born with no sense of danger, and would climb anything that presented itself—trees, the roof of the house, whatever appeared the most exciting. He was a young daredevil, with a mischievous sense of fun, and often in trouble. But he was polite and had a charm that saved him on occasion.

By the time Byrd hit his teens he was a popular, well-adjusted young man, but he had a discipline and ambition uncommon in boys his age, coupled with a sense of privilege and entitlement. By the time he entered high school, his future Arctic rivals were already making great strides into the unknown, pushing closer and closer to the Pole. The race north was drawing some media attention, but the quest for the South Pole, dominated by explorers from Britain, was drawing even more attention. The stoic Robert Falcon Scott was the model of an Edwardian hero. The expedition he led to Antarctica between 1901 and 1904 gripped the world. Young boys all over America followed his exploits. Although he was forced to turn back several hundred miles short of the South Pole, it was obvious that Scott would make it someday. Then there was his flamboyant Irish companion, Ernest Shackleton. Would he beat his mentor to the Pole?

Back in the days before radio, before television, before Internet, information disseminated much more slowly. It took weeks or months for reports from the far-flung portions of the globe to reach the American papers. But this just added to the mystique. In the absence of verified facts, imagination quickly takes over. Schoolboys across America pictured themselves trudging across frozen wastes in a quixotic quest for glory. They saw the wonders and the strangeness, but few could really conceive the reality; the bitter cold, the near starvation, the torturous monotony.

Byrd was no different. He read the scanty accounts of Scott's failed attempt in Antarctica, and dreamed of becoming an explorer. Convinced that the South Pole would fall before he came of age, he set his sights on the North Pole. He even scribbled a note to a school companion, a girl called Maria, explaining how he would be the first to reach the top of the world. Like Amundsen, who was convinced from a young age of his destiny, Byrd was throwing out a challenge to the universe. From a young age he knew what he wanted to do.

When he was almost fourteen, Byrd traveled with a friend of the family to the Philippines, where he remained for a number of months, staying with his godfather Adam Carson, a judge. While Peary was losing toes in Greenland, and Cook sailing to his rescue, the teenage Byrd was having his own adventures, seeing exotic parts of the world, and enduring terrible storms at sea. Years later, Byrd would change the details of that great adventure. He claimed that he was only twelve, and that he traveled alone. He had a tendency to exaggerate for effect that would follow him through life.

But the truth was impressive enough. After six months abroad, he returned to Virginia with the restless spirit of an explorer. But before he could make his mark on the world, he had to first negotiate high school and college.

10

MIXED FORTUNES ON THE ICE

Cook took time out to see off friend and rival Peary, but really he did not have the time for such luxuries. Unknown to the other man, Cook had his own trip north to prepare for. This time, he was leading an expedition. While Peary's trips were to get bigger and more elaborate (and more expensive) as the years rolled on, Cook liked smaller and more intimate affairs, which were easier to get backing for. Sometimes the opportunities just fell his way.

In the spring, after his resignation from Peary's Third Greenland Expedition, Cook had given his first proper public lecture. The one for the Brooklyn doctors, which had sparked his dispute with Peary, was just a professional engagement, with no fee involved. But this time he was addressing the public at Yale, one of the great academic centers of the new world. And he was paid for doing it. It was the start of a lecture career that would prove every bit as profitable and successful as Peary's. The two had completely contrasting styles. Peary was the showman, loud and expansive. He used gimmicks to bring his lecture alive, including having Henson appear in full Eskimo furs, baking under the stage lights, and having full teams of dogs howling at the crowd. He even let children pet the dogs afterwards. In contrast, Cook was more softly spoken and modest. But he had a very pleasing manner and a dry sense of humor that leavened his presentations. It would be fair to say that the public loved Peary's show, but they loved Cook himself. He was the warmer personality.

The talk at Yale was a great success. In the days before cinema, the populace yearned for live entertainment. Variety shows, traveling plays, and public lectures drew crowds unimaginable today. And they were family affairs. Cook was not addressing the academics of Yale, but the men, women, and children who wanted to be entertained, to be lifted out of their ordinary world and offered a glimpse of the exotic. One of the young men in the audience that night was the son of a college professor. Ben Hoppin was mildly retarded, but a physically vigorous young man. He loved the picture that Cook painted of the Arctic regions. He began pestering his father, fine arts professor James Hoppin, to let him get on a boat heading north.

Hoppin did not know how to respond, so he wrote to Cook for advice. Cook remembered the eager young man, and suggested that there was no harm in indulging him. He would be safe enough if they chose the right vessel for him. Hoppin wrote back, suggesting that if he secured a vessel, Cook might agree to lead the trip. Cook could not believe his luck. He was already tiring of his medical practice, and was eager for a new challenge to replace the Peary trip he had pulled out of. He immediately took the train back to New Haven. It only took a few hours to work out the details with the enthusiastic professor, then Cook began the preparation.

The *Zeta*, a seventy-eight-foot fishing schooner, was refitted for the trip, and Professor Hoppin put up the $10,000 ($250,000 today) needed. It took a month, and the expedition was ready to leave. Cook kept it all secret for two reasons: it was a small, private expedition of no major scientific or geographic significance, and he did not want to antagonize Peary. He had announced that he was not traveling with Peary because of professional engagements, and it would look bad if those professional engagements turned out to be his own expedition.

On July 7—less than a week after Peary set out—Cook took the train to Cape Breton Island, Nova Scotia, in the north of Canada. There he joined his three companions—Ben Hoppin; E. H. Sutherland, who was looking after Hoppin; and Robert Perry, a hunter who had paid $1,000 ($25,000 today) to join them. Cook hoped to travel along the west coast of Greenland to Cape York, where he would continue his Eskimo studies—and bring home a family of the tribe.

The *Zeta* sailed from Halifax, Nova Scotia, on July 10, reaching Upernavik on August 16. Cook wanted to push north as far as he could, hopefully reaching Peary's base to wish the other man luck, and to meet old friends. But he met an insurmountable obstacle—the captain of the *Zeta* refused to go any farther north. So the next few days were spent enjoying the scenery, hunting, and gathering fossils. One of the highlights was a native dance, which went on until two in the morning. Hardly the stuff of epic adventure, but fun nonetheless.

When they returned to the *Zeta* the captain brought them back down the coast to Godhavn. There Cook and Hoppin explored a fjord, while the others went hunting, unsuccessfully. Aside from a few birds, they brought nothing down. Cook did manage to do some trading, securing valuable furs, but his plans for the trip had been thoroughly frustrated by a captain who was afraid to put his ship in any danger. By mid-September they were back in Canada, docked safely in Rigolet, a small port in the northern Labrador territory. Cook knew that Peary was pushing north into the ice pack, hoping to establish a winter base far up the Greenland coast. And here he was, returning from nothing more than a brief holiday. He had been a tourist rather than a traveler, and he knew this trip had been a lost opportunity.

But there was still time to redeem something from the fiasco. He watched a sixteen-year-old native girl dance at Rigolet, and the idea formed—he could bring home this girl, and her young brother, and use them on his lecture tours. They would provide the razzmatazz that his presentation lacked. Henson was just dressing as an Eskimo for Peary; Cook could provide the real thing. The children's father, a dog driver for the Hudson Bay Company, agreed to the two children traveling to New York with the *Zeta*, so long as Cook returned with them the following spring.

The trip home was uneventful. The two children were seasick much of the time—and homesick all of the time. But they arrived in New

York safely, and Cook delivered his human cargo to the home of his brother on Bedford Avenue, Brooklyn, where they would stay for the winter. He told the press that he was delighted with the success of his trip. Like Peary, he was learning to spin his achievements to show them in the best light.

He was inevitably asked about Peary's chances of achieving a farthest north, and possibly reaching the pole. He was diplomatic in his reply to a representative of the *Brooklyn Daily Eagle*: "Whatever he starts in to do will very nearly be done. He is not the sort of man to turn back."

11

PEARY'S THIRD GREENLAND EXPEDITION

Peary's expedition had begun well. The summer was a good one, and they sailed much farther north than on the previous expedition, reaching close to the top of the country. They pulled into a fjord, which Peary had christened Bowdoin Bay after his college. Along the way they had stopped in a number of Greenland ports to take on supplies and hire Eskimo who were willing to make the trip.

By now, Josephine was very heavily pregnant and only months away from her confinement. So the first priority was to construct living quarters. Swiftly a structure went up. It was close to a site where Peary had pitched an emergency tent on the previous expedition to escape a rain storm. That had coincided with his wedding anniversary, so whimsically he decided to call his winter quarters Anniversary Lodge.

While he left workers finishing the building, he set off on the *Falcon* on a hunting expedition into Smith Sound, the narrow strait that separates northern Greenland from Ellesmere Island in the far north of Canada. They shot two dozen walrus and seventeen reindeer when they put to shore. That left them with plenty of meat for the long winter. When they arrived back at camp they found Anniversary Lodge to be a comfortable one-story dwelling, with thick walls for insulation but lots of windows to let in the dwindling summer light. It was surrounded by a veranda. The expedition members settled down for the long wait until the following spring, when they would march north, hopefully toward the Pole. At the very least they would verify Peary's discovery of the most northern extent of the land mass.

On August 20 the *Falcon* returned to America, taking letters from everyone. They would be on their own for the best part of a year before it returned. Josephine had been more successful in finding a publisher for her account of the previous expedition—the prohibition against publication did not extend to her. She sent the final chapter of her book, which would be published that fall, with the *Falcon*. She wrote: "Everything points to the success which Mr. Peary hopes for."

On September 12 Josephine gave birth to a healthy daughter, whom the Eskimo named Anpoomikaninny, or the Snow Baby, because of her pale white complexion. The Peary's chose a different name; Marie Ahnighito Peary. Ahnighito was the name of a native woman who took a shine to the child, and made her a soft fur suit of fox and fawn skins, to protect her against the elements. Though Peary did not realize it, the birth would be the highlight of the trip.

Things began to go wrong on October 31, when a large berg calved off a glacier and plunged into the bay. Everyone heard the huge, extended rumble as the ice cracked and fell, striking the water hard. Any fall like that creates a wave, which quickly dissipates in open water. But the wave traveled up the ever-narrowing fjord, getting bigger and more powerful as it traveled. When the swell, a mini-tsunami, reached the shore it surged forward, passing the high water mark with undiminished force. Two whale boats that had been pulled well up the shore for the winter were suddenly engulfed in water, and smashed against the rocks, destroyed. The water flooded a supply of fuel oil stored in wooden barrels, smashing the barrels open. The precious fuel was lost.

Peary was absent when the drama unfolded. He was twenty miles inland, establishing the first food cache for the next year's march. He was devastated when he heard the news. With their winter supply of fuel gone, they would have to burn walrus blubber and seal oil for heating and cooking. It was less efficient, smelly, and it left them short of their reserves. He could foretell that instantly. He was right; the lodge stank all winter, it was a few degrees colder than was comfortable, and by the spring there were several inches of ice on the interior walls.

It was a tough winter, characterized by frequent blizzards. Peary did his best to trade with local Eskimo communities for dogs and furs, and the team prepared as best they could for the coming summer. Perhaps because of the discomfort, or perhaps because of a natural impatience, Peary could not wait until summer before leaving his smelly and uncomfortable winter quarters. In the previous expedition he had set out early, and turned back. Now he did the same, setting out on March 6, 1894. The sun had reappeared, and there were a few hours of daylight each afternoon, but it was hardly ideal conditions for his team, which consisted of seven expedition members, five Eskimo, and ninety dogs. They were pulling twelve sledges, but the Eskimo were only going as far as the food cache. They still would not venture onto the ice sheet of the interior.

From the beginning there were problems. Several of the dogs fell sick and had to be put down. And conditions were extremely cold. By the time they reached the cache, two of the men had to turn back. One of the two was Eivind Astrup, who had performed so well on the previous expedition. Peary had been relying on his strength, but now the young Norwegian was out of the race, heading back to Anniversary Lodge.

Then the weather worsened, with strong winds and temperatures dropping to minus forty. The wind chill factor made the weather seem even colder. Peary pushed on until the dogs collapsed and forced him to set up camp. But now another expedition member was down, victim of a frozen heel (he eventually had to have part of his foot amputated). Obviously he could not return to Anniversary Lodge on his own. Team physician Dr. Edwin Vincent (Cook's replacement) made the return trip with him. That left Peary with only three expedition members, including Matthew Henson, who had experience in the conditions.

By the time the storm ended the dogs were even weaker—two had frozen to death. The men were suffering too; within days they were only managing a few miles on each march, and two more men had frostbite. Then another storm hit: they lay up for another three days.

It was no longer an expedition. It was more like Napoleon's retreat from Moscow. More dogs were dead, and the men could not face any more. Reluctantly but inevitably, Peary had to turn back to base. Even he was weakened by the ordeal, appearing dazed and with a very red face, showing signs of frostbite.

Peary's Third Greenland Expedition, begun with such hope, had managed to penetrate less than 130 miles. He had managed almost as much on his first expedition, traveling for the first time on the ice as a complete novice. It was a resounding failure; no spin could change that. By April 1894 the expedition was over, and the summer had not even arrived.

12

COOK'S SECOND GREENLAND EXPEDITION

The two Eskimo children had quickly settled in New York, adjusting to strange sights like bridges and street cars. Mikok, the boy, mastered the intricacies of marbles, and quickly won the baubles from other boys in the locality. Kahlahkatak became friendly with other girls in the area, and both seemed happier. Whenever they were out with Cook, they always drew stares from everyone—especially if he also happened to be walking his team of huskies at the time.

For some reason—perhaps to avoid coming into conflict with Peary—Cook began to turn his attention south rather than north. He decided he would explore Antarctica as soon as he could put together the funds for an expedition. It would be expensive—it was a lot more remote than the Arctic. He petitioned the American Geographical Society and other bodies for support. He would need at least $50,000 (approximately $1.2 million today), but at least the papers seemed intrigued with the idea. Cook had backers in the media.

The *Standard Union* carried a piece, written by Herbert Bridgman, saying: "Not since Columbus and his caravels put out four centuries ago, has a voyage fraught with greater or more romantic interest been projected than that which Dr. Cook, our fellow townsman, fully sets forth. The work of unlocking the great mystery of the South, the final problem of the surface and structure of the globe, could be entrusted to no more competent hands than Dr. Cook's."

Major James Pond, the impresario who had backed Peary's lecture tour, agreed to take on Dr. Cook's. Peary was absent, and there was a demand for derring-do in the Arctic. And he loved the fact that Cook would have two genuine Eskimo and a team of dogs for added entertainment. The lecture tour was a great success, both financially and in terms of the profile it was giving Cook and his plans for an Antarctic expedition. He turned down an offer of a position of surgeon on a survey of Ellesmere Island in the northern Canadian archipelago. He was going south; he even had stationary printed with the heading "Official Bureau of the American Antarctic Expedition."

He was far short of his funding target, but he was sure his focus was on the right part of the globe. Meanwhile, he decided to raise some funds by repeating the Greenland trip of the previous summer. But this time he was under no illusions; this was to be a tourist trip, with rich sportsmen and hunters paying for the privilege of traveling to Greenland with the famous explorer. He chartered a rust bucket called the *Miranda*, and fifty-two eager travelers signed up. They included students and academics from Yale, Harvard, the University of Pennsylvania, Chicago University, Bowdoin (Peary's alma mater), Williams, and Oberlin—a "very superior crowd," as one of the tourists put it. There were also eleven Eskimo being returned to Labrador, including the two children who had been such a hit on the lecture circuit.

It was an eventful passage. The captain of the vessel, William Farrell, clashed with Cook about the best route. Cook wanted to hug the Canadian coast to avoid icebergs. Farrell insisted that he could smell the bergs, and would avoid them. Pressing forward at full speed in heavy fog, on the morning of July 17, Cook was disturbed at his breakfast by the engines suddenly going into reverse. Trying not to panic anyone, he ran from the mess to the deck, and was staggered as the ship slid into a huge berg, tearing off twenty-five feet of the railing and bashing in the starboard side. The damage would have been far worse if a pilot employed by Cook had not spotted the berg in time and turned the boat so that it hit sideways instead of colliding head-first.

The crippled ship had to retreat four hundred miles for repairs. The disgruntled passengers nearly mutinied—fourteen abandoned ship and went on a hunting trip through Labrador instead of crossing to Greenland. Eventually the ship got underway again, heading straight across the sea to southern Greenland instead of hugging the Canadian coast, and making a shorter crossing. They did not have time for that scenic route—the summer was swiftly passing. When they reached Greenland they discovered that the ice was farther down than was normal for that season. After his first encounter with a berg—where his nose had let him down—Captain Farrell had become gun shy; he no longer had confidence in his navigation, so he was too timid to land. Their first port of call, Frederickshaab, was abandoned because of bergs and fog, but he did agree to bring the ship into Godhavn.

"Captain is the most timid man I ever saw. Our progress seems to be effectually stopped by his stupidity," Cook complained.

They were still well short of Godhavn when the ship struck a reef and suffered yet more damage. They had to pull into a small port in southern Greenland for more repairs. Despairing of ever getting underway—or getting home—Cook took a small boat and headed up the coast, looking for a schooner to rescue the *Miranda*. He finally came across the *Rigel*, a fishing schooner. For a fee of $4,000 ($90,000 today), and a share of the salvage value of the *Miranda*, Captain William Dixon would get everyone home safe. It was an ignoble retreat from the Arctic. Halfway back to Canada the *Miranda* went under, and everyone—the crew of both boats and all the tourists—ended up stuck on the one schooner, which stank of fish. Once back in Canada, they were distributed on a number of more suitable vessels and made their way back home. Some chose to abandon the sea forever, and took the train home. At least they escaped further drama.

Cook was on the *Portia* with many of the travelers, heading from Halifax to New York. One day out of port there was a thunderous crash. The ship had collided with a yacht, tearing it in two. Four of the five occupants of the yacht drowned. That final disaster could have been a metaphor for the entire venture. Cook had planned an expedition, and from the start it had been an abject failure. It cost him financially, and it cost him in terms of reputation. Who would trust him to explore the unknown southern continent, when he couldn't even be trusted to bring a party of tourists across the sea for a jaunt in the low Arctic? Perhaps he should have swallowed his pride and gone with Peary—or accepted the Ellesmere Island survey job. His own plans were now in tatters.

All that was left was spin. As he told reporters: "A delightful trip, replete with adventures. I have not heard one member of the party that had a complaint to make."

13

PEARY SEARCHES FOR SHOOTING STARS

Peary licked his wounds over a long summer in Anniversary Lodge, as they waited for the return of the *Falcon*. Determined that the trip would not be a complete waste of everyone's time, he surveyed the region around Bowdoin Bay. He also began to quiz the Eskimo about a legend of an Iron Mountain. This had been reported in 1818 by British explorer John Ross. Peary believed, rightly as it turned out, that the iron in question was a massive meteorite. Meteorites are lumps of rock and iron that shoot around the sun in wildly unpredictable orbits. The remnants of broken planets and satellites, they occasionally cross the path of the Earth and come crashing down in fiery balls, smashing deep into the ground. Most small meteorites burn up in the Earth's atmosphere. We know these as shooting stars or falling stars, and occasionally a massive one will strike land.

Large meteorites are extremely rare, with only a handful recovered worldwide. The material throws light on the make-up of interplanetary space, and is worth far more than its weight in gold at today's valuation. But to the Eskimo the iron was priceless. They were a pre-technological society, and they did not have other sources of the precious metal. The iron in the meteorite was their only source of iron for tools and weapons, and they were understandably cautious about revealing its whereabouts.

The site was also sacred. A number of previous expeditions had failed to locate the Iron Mountain, as the locals protected the site carefully.

Peary knew the value of the find. He pushed and cajoled, eventually getting one man to guide him to Iron Mountain in return for a gun. But the man changed his mind mid-march, and they returned empty-handed. Peary had a number of similar false starts, but eventually he located the meteorite when he saw some bluish rock poking out of the snow. He began to dig, and uncovered a huge lump of metallic rock. What he had found was Woman, one of three iron rocks known to the Eskimo. Woman proved to be three metric tons in weight. The locals used to work the metal by beating off bits and shaping them with rocks. It is difficult to work metal without the intense heat of furnaces, and the fact that the Eskimo did not have furnaces is what saved the specimen from much damage.

Peary kept looking, and found a second fragment of the meteorite nearby. This was smaller, weighing four hundred kilos, and was called Dog. He scratched a crude "P" on Woman, claiming it, at least in his head, as his own. Eventually he would uncover the third known fragment, which was the largest of them all. Known as Tent, it weighed a massive 30.9 metric tons. tonnes. While there might be some hope of getting Dog home, it would take a separate expedition to retrieve Woman and Tent.

We now know that the Cape York meteorite, traveling at forty thousand miles per hour mph, struck the Earth around ten thousand years ago, breaking up as it entered the upper atmosphere. A number of large fragments struck the ground around the Cape York area of Greenland. Eight substantial pieces have been recovered, ranging in size from 250 kilos to thirty metric tons. Peary found three, and five have been discovered since, including a fragment of twenty metric tons. Several more of varying sizes—probably from a few kilos up to a few hundred kilos—will be found in the future. Some pieces probably smashed through the ice and are at the bottom of the ocean, while the smaller pieces burnt up in the atmosphere. Brighter than the sun as it burned through the atmosphere, it must have been a spectacular natural fireworks display. It would have struck the ground with the force of a small nuclear bomb.

Locating the fabled Iron Mountain gave Peary some return for a wasted season. At the end of July the *Falcon* returned, on schedule, to bring the party home to America. Peary had been hoping to return a hero, with the Pole conquered. He was not prepared to limp home in disgrace. He announced that he was going to spend a second winter in Greenland, and march for the Pole the following year. He called for volunteers.

It had been an unhappy camp. The men had suffered through a hard winter, after the loss of their fuel. They also resented Peary's imperious manner, and there was a perception that Peary reserved the best food for himself and his wife, leaving the dregs for other members of the expedition. He was not a leader who inspired affection or loyalty, and most of the men wanted to go home. Josephine also wanted to go home. In the end, the party selected for a second winter in the ice were Peary, Henson, and Hugh Lee. Lee had been the first to turn back the previous year, but he agreed to remain with Peary after the latter promised him a government job on his return to America the following year. Lee was appointed a Deputy US Marshal on his return.

On August 26 the *Falcon* headed south, taking everyone but the three in the now vastly reduced party. Everyone was happy to be leaving a troubled camp. As Astrup summed up: "The trouble was with Peary and wife, not the boys."

Peary did not see it that way. As he got older, his autocratic sense of entitlement came more to the fore in his personality. Cook had found him affable and democratic at first, then encountered the controlling dictator by the breakup of their relationship. The other expedition members were about to see this side of his personality. The commander wrote to General I. J. Wistar, the president of the American Geographical Society, complaining that his subordinates had let him down and he had to remain in Greenland to complete his objectives on his own because of their cowardice. He ignored the fact that a tsunami had taken their fuel, and also the fact—his decision —that they had set out far too early in the season, two months before the weather improved enough to make a march safe. Instead he accused his team of desertion. This lack of loyalty on the part of their leader hurt the returning expedition members, and ensured few would have a good word about Peary.

Once at home, Josephine began the furious round of fundraising that would be required to keep her husband on the ice. A second season was something no one had expected, and it would place a severe strain on the expedition. Not only were extra provisions needed, a second ship had to be hired to bring him home the following year. That was a huge expense. She approached a number of potential patrons, with mixed results. One of the people she tried was philanthropist Morris K. Jessup. He was a supporter of a diverse range of Christian and missionary groups, including the YMCA. But he also supported the American Museum of Natural History, so she had some hopes he would be interested in the Arctic quest.

Jessup didn't say yes, but he used a carrot approach. He told her to go away and raise as much as she could, then come back to him. He would top it up so that the rescue ship could be fitted out and dispatched. It was a wonderful incentive—she knew that in the end she had one influential backer who would not let her down. Swiftly she got donations of $1,000 from five bodies; the American Museum of Natural History, the American Geographical Society, Bowdoin College, the Brooklyn Institute of Arts and Sciences, and the Newport Natural History Society.

She then did a run of public lectures for Major Pond, who was very impressed. He felt she had the showmanship and charm to make a permanent career on the stage or platform, but she wasn't interested; it was all about funding the relief ship. At the end of the summer she went back to Jessup—who would go on to become a lifelong backer of Peary—and he was as good as his word, supplying the shortfall to allow her to hire and fit out the *Kite*.

Peary, oblivious to the work that was being done on his behalf, had a second hard winter on the ice. This time conditions were far less cramped, but he must have missed civilization. Just before winter he went out to check on his major food and fuel cache, but was unable to locate it. It had either been plundered by Eskimo or, more likely, simply been buried beneath a blizzard. Once again he would be seriously short on supplies when he set out on the northern trek.

The following spring he was ready to set out again. Before going, he wrote a letter to Josephine. It was a dark and bitter document. He began by complaining of the previous winter.

"The winter has been a nightmare to me. The cold, damp, frost-lined room has made me think of a tomb."

Then he went on to complain that their chances had been badly hit because he could not secure the dogs he wanted from the locals. He blamed Astrup, saying that the Norwegian had told them to hold the dogs over, because he wanted a crack at the Pole himself. This was extremely unlikely. Far more likely was that Peary was looking anywhere but himself for a place to lay the blame.

Peary, with his American companions Henson and Lee and five Eskimo, set out on April 1, three weeks later than the previous year. It might not seem much, but it should have made a good difference. Temperatures would have risen, and there was more daylight. But it was still early in the season. The team had forty-two dogs, and they had substituted reindeer and walrus meat in place of the pemmican they lost in the missing cache. That created its own problem. Pemmican is very dense, high-calorie food, designed for the extreme conditions. It weighed far less than the calorie equivalent amount of meat. From the start the dog teams were under pressure from overloaded sledges.

The Eskimo were getting used to the ways of the white strangers, and this year they did agree to come onto the ice cap, traveling 128 miles. But when Peary failed to find another cache, they had had enough, and they turned for home. That left the three Americans alone. They marched on bravely, finally reaching Navy Cliff. It had taken two seasons, but Peary was now where he had stood a few years earlier with Astrup. He was in a position to begin his real exploration work. Previously Navy Cliff had been the destination; now it was the starting point, and it had taken huge resources to reach it. All but nine of the dogs were dead, and the men were not faring much better. Weakest of all was Lee, who was so bad he had to remain in camp while the other two hunted game to stave off imminent starvation. They came across a herd of musk ox and brought down a number of them, stripping the raw meat from the hot carcasses and devouring it raw. Peary had ignored Cook's dietary advice on their first trip together. Now he was forced by circumstances to go native. Hunger is the best sauce.

They returned to camp and fed Lee, then stashed as much of the game as they could. But they had to face the inevitable. Their supply was too small, and they were too weak, to linger in this bleak spot. They had a five hundred mile trek back to Anniversary Lodge, and a betting man would have taken odds against them making it. They loaded one sledge with provisions for fourteen days, and turned south. It had been a wasted trip. Weeks of hardship, and nothing achieved. No new ground mapped, and no definitive answer on whether Greenland continued north or ended where Peary thought. He could have stayed at home, surveying the Philadelphia and New York docks, for all the good his Third Greenland Expedition achieved.

Hugh Lee's strength gave out first. He had been a strange choice to remain a second season in the Arctic—he had been the first to turn back on the disastrous march of the previous summer. That Peary let him stay on, while stronger men returned home, can only be considered very poor judgement. Days into the march south he was suffering terribly from diarrhea, and barely able to stagger forward. He begged to be left behind to die, but Peary was having none of it. Bad enough that the expedition was an abject failure; he was not going to have a death on his conscience too.

The plan had been to eat the game, and when dogs died, they were to be fed to the other dogs to keep their strength up. Quickly this plan changed. Now when a dog died—and many did —the three men took their share of the meat. Peary took crazy risks on the return trip, particularly when they hit heavily glaciated areas with dangerous crevasses. Lee thought it was a sort of death wish—that his commander would rather perish on the ice than go home in ignominy. The truth is probably more prosaic. Peary rushed because if he didn't rush he would not get to Anniversary Lodge before his supplies ran out. It was a desperate race for life.

On June 25 the party limped painfully into camp. They had abandoned their last sledge, as they were down to one dog, and he was too ill to pull. In fact, the dog wasn't even able to keep up with the sick men, and crawled home behind them. Peary was devastated. It took weeks for the men to recover their strength, and longer to regain their spirits. Peary later wrote about the wait for the relief ship (in *Northward Over the Great Ice*): "I could not go on board and say that I had failed. It would be preferable to remain where I was. At times I even hoped that the ship would not come so that I might make another attempt next spring."

In his condition, this was madness speaking.

In a saner moment, he had a better plan. If he could bring home one of the great meteorites, he would salvage some honor from the fiasco. The relief party on board the *Kite* arrived at Anniversary Lodge in August. Josephine had not traveled this time. She was bitterly disappointed that Peary had elected to spend a second season in Greenland without her, and she felt abandoned by her husband, a feeling that would erode at their marriage. Instead there was a letter, explaining her absence: "When you told me your plan a year ago last April as we sat near the shore of Baby Lake, I felt as if you had put a knife into my heart and left it there for the purpose of giving it a turn from time to time." She had always felt she had second place in her husband's affections, behind his mother. Now she realized she was only a poor third. Exploration and the quest for the Pole was his first love.

Peary read the letter and realized that the cherished reunion was still several weeks away. It must have added to the bitterness he felt, but he did not show it to the men on the *Kite*. He quickly took charge, and loaded two of the meteorites, Woman and Dog, on board. Tent was too big, and would have to wait for another time. Even fetching the two smaller meteorites was a mammoth task, requiring every ounce of manpower and a great deal of ingenuity. They were placed on iron rollers and hauled toward the shore on a platform of wooden planks. After getting a certain distance the planking ran out, and the process had to stop while the planks behind the huge rocks were pulled up and placed in front. It was a sort of primitive man-powered rail line, which was hauled up as quickly as it was laid down. Once they reached the shore, the rocks were wedged onto a large ice floe and floated across to the waiting ship. Huge winches and pulleys brought them on board. It was an impressive feat of engineering, and the only real success of the expedition.

In taking the meteorites Peary was depriving the Eskimo, whom he proclaimed to respect, of their only source of iron. He gave the natives not a thought, his eye being on the bigger picture. And the bigger picture was always, for him, his own self-interest.

The trip home was characterized by a tense atmosphere, and the explorer won himself no friends with his mean-spirited attitude. He was morose, and avoided company. He blamed everyone for his lack of success, putting the failure down to an inadequate supply of men and provisions. But as some pointed out, he had the men and sent them home after the first unsuccessful season, and he could have purchased the provisions. The fault lay with the commander, not with those beneath him.

"I don't think that Peary will try another Arctic expedition. His last expedition was a dismal failure," said Professor L. L. Dyche, one of the relief party. He was a zoologist from Kansas, along to do his own research.

Privately, Peary agreed. He even admitted to the *New York Times* that the dream had died; he would never see the Pole. At thirty-nine, he was far too old now to mount another expedition. His time had come and gone. The prize would be claimed by a younger man.

14

THE DOLDRUMS

The next few seasons—both Cook and Peary had come to think in terms of Arctic seasons rather than years—were poor ones, as interest seemed to dwindle in the race for the North Pole. Cook had proved to be a very poor expedition organizer, and that dented people's confidence in him. Peary had marched for the Pole, and came far short on two attempts. America is not a nation that glorifies defeat, and neither man excited the public. They were capable of giving very entertaining lectures, but they were yesterday's men, unless they could find a way to revitalize their careers.

Cook was forced to reopen his surgery in Brooklyn, where he had more success. At least his notoriety was good for business. He had to take on a partner to handle the extra patients. This was good; it meant his practice could stay open and keep making money at home, the next time he was away for an extended trip. Meanwhile, he had to deal with the mundane problems of enlarged spleens, niggling coughs, childhood illnesses, and hypochondriac patients. He found the health worries of his patients tedious.

Cook suffered from a failing of many great men. He did not have the self-awareness to see his own shortcomings and could not see what everyone else thought they could see: that he was an unsuitable man to lead American hopes in the extreme regions of the world. He felt that, the *Miranda* aside, he was perfect for the job. He knew Peary had an edge in the race for the North Pole. The older man had been so much higher in Greenland, and had made contacts with the Eskimo that would surely get him to the top of the world in the next few seasons. And then there were the Europeans. Fridtjof Nansen had been making steady progress northwards over the past few seasons, and Otto Sverdrup was also beginning to make a name for himself. Both were Norwegians who had grown up on the edge of the Arctic.

Nansen was born in 1861, and grew up with a love of the wild outdoors that surrounded him. He studied zoology because it promised an outdoor life, and fell in love with the Arctic when he was sent on a voyage by his university to study Arctic sea life. Though they didn't have direct contact, his path crossed that of Peary and Cook on a number of occasions. Operating in the same extreme latitudes, he was often in search of the same objectives. Nansen made his first mark with the crossing of Greenland in 1888—the first time he had frustrated the efforts of Peary. The American had been forced to turn his attentions north in direct response to the objective of his Second Greenland Expedition having already been achieved by Nansen before he set out.

After Peary's Third Expedition had ended so dismally, and Cook's tourist venture had been even more disastrous, Nansen announced his own plans. They had been fermenting since 1884, when he read the theory of distinguished Norwegian meteorologist Henrik Mohn. Mohn was convinced there was an ocean current flowing from east to west all the way across the polar sea. Nansen believed that if a strong ship was frozen in the ice high above Siberia, the arctic drift would bring it over or close to the Pole before eventually spewing it out near Greenland. It might involve several seasons iced in, but it gave a real chance of reaching the pole. In 1890 he went public with the idea. He wanted a strong ship with a crew of twelve and provisions for five years.

Old polar hands were skeptical, with Adolphus Greely calling it "an illogical scheme of self-destruction." But the Norwegian parliament offered Nansen partial funding, and the rest was raised through public appeals. The trip was on.

The eventual ship was short and stubby, with tough oak timers and an intricate system of cross beams and braces. It had a rounded hull that could slip upwards out of the grip of the pack ice. Speed was abandoned in favor of warmth and comfort. It was ready by 1892, and was named the *Fram*, Norwegian for "Forward." Then Nansen began the selection of his crew of twelve. Otto Sverdrup was his first choice. Sverdrup had been born in 1854, and had accompanied Nansen in the successful first crossing of Greenland. He was now appointed captain of the *Fram*, and second in command of the overall expedition. Sverdrup went on to have his own successful career as an explorer, discovering many lands in the Arctic, and often naming them before Peary came along and tried to claim the discovery for himself.

The *Fram* set sail from Oslo on June 24, 1893, and would be at sea—and out of contact with civilization—all the time Peary and Cook would be failing miserably at their own endeavors. Nansen brought her up over Norway and east along the coast of Siberia, following the Northeast Passage first navigated by Adolf Nordenskiöld just over a decade previously. Fog and ice made the going difficult. Ten days after crossing the most northerly point of Europe, the *Fram* turned north and became trapped in pack ice over eastern Siberia. The engines were stopped and the rudder pulled up. The drift had begun.

It took until March to drift over 80 degrees north, which was slower progress than they expected. Nansen began to believe it might take the full five years to reach the Pole. Progress was a bare mile a day and Nansen began to consider the possibility of leaving the ship and dashing northward if he got the chance. By November he had settled on this plan. Once the ship passed 83 degrees north, he would take experienced dog handler Hjalmar Johansen with him and make for the Pole. The ship would continue to drift until it emerged into the north Atlantic. Nansen would not try to rejoin the *Fram*, but would make for the nearest land from the Pole and rely on his ice skills to survive. He thought he could reach Franz Josef Land, and from there make for Spitzbergen, where he could catch a whaling ship home.

On January 8, 1895, Fram passed 83°34′N, establishing a new
Farthest North, surpassing the previous mark of American explorer
Adolphus Greely. The illogical scheme of self-destruction was proving very successful. By March they had crossed 84 N, a little over four
hundred miles short of the Pole. Nansen and Johansen left the ship and
began trekking. They planned on fifty days at an average of eight miles
a day. Initially they made quicker progress than this, but then the going
became rougher, and they also noticed a southerly drift of the polar ice,
which was costing them much of their hard-won distance. By April 3
Nansen knew they were in trouble. Their survival depended on crossing
the Pole and heading south to land. But if they fell short of the Pole and
ran out of food, they would be too far from safety to survive. On April 7,
after achieving a farthest north of 86°13.6′N, they made the painful decision to abandon the Pole and turn south, trying to reach Franz Josef Land.

Things went well for a week, then both of their watches stopped.
This was a very serious problem; without knowing the exact time, it was
impossible to calculate longitude. Nansen took a guess at the time, and
they rewound their watches. But from now on, navigation would be guess-
work. They drove the dogs as hard as they could, killing and eating the
weakest as they went. But they were caught by the summer melt before
reaching the safety of land, and ended up on a large ice floe for a month. It
was August before they spotted land. They killed the last dog, had a good
meal, and lashed two kayaks together for the final dash to safety.

Once they reached land, their ordeal was not over. They had to
establish a winter camp in a bleak cove near Cape Felder, on the western edge of Franz Josef Land. There they remained for eight months,
before they resumed their journey south in May of the following year.
In June they crossed the path of British explorer Frederick Jackson,
who was exploring Franz Josef Land, and they were finally rescued.

The *Fram* emerged from the polar ice near Spitzbergen only
days later, and the two explorers were reunited with their shipmates
in Tromsø. Remarkably, both groups of travelers— those on ice and
those on water—arrived in the northerly port within four days of each
other. The *Fram* had drifted roughly as Nansen had predicted, but had
not crossed over the Pole. In fact, it had not even reached the latitude

the two-man team on the ice had achieved. So the waiting world was given the news: all home safe, and Nansen and Johansen were now the possessors of the coveted Farthest North.

It was hard for anyone—even a man as narrow-minded as Peary—to ignore Nansen's success. He was greeted as a conquering hero in every port between Tromsø and Oslo, and in Oslo he was received by the King, in front of the largest crowds the city had ever seen. Tributes flowed in from all over the world. Arctic explorer and mountaineer Edward Whymper, who was the first man up the Matterhorn, wrote that Nansen had made "almost as great an advance as has been accomplished by all other voyages in the nineteenth century put together."

Peary must have fumed as he read the tributes. The Pole was his life's work, and he seemed to be as far from achieving it as ever.

Cook never showed the same jealousy when it came to the successes of others. And he did not believe, at that stage, that he could win the race to the North Pole. But he followed the news avidly, and enjoyed speculating. He wrote to meteorologist Evelyn Briggs Baldwin: "Some enterprising American ought to carry the Stars & Stripes beyond Nansen's Farthest North. Who will be the victor?"

Cook had more pressing matters on his mind. His medical practice was thriving, and he had settled into some semblance of domestic life. His mother-in-law had moved in with him, and was running the house for him. He was still desperately lonely after the death of Libby, but her sisters were frequent visitors, and slowly an attachment grew between himself and Anna Forbes, who was a school teacher. They courted throughout 1896, and at the end of the year they announced their engagement. Perhaps the life that had been interrupted by the death of Libby could be resumed with her sister?

But always, there was the lure of the Poles. Cook read every new book, studied all the new reports, and kept abreast of who was going where, and how far they had managed to get. He was excited when he read reports of Norwegian Carsten Borchgrevink, who claimed to have been the first man to have set foot on the Antarctic mainland. He began to think the time was right for his idea of heading south. He could be the first to the South Pole—less glamorous than the North, but still a target worthy of any explorer. He threw himself enthusiastically into fundraising. Like Peary, he began with rich industrialists with a penchant for philanthropy.

Early in 1897 he secured a meeting with George C. Carnegie, a nephew of steel magnate Andrew Carnegie. The elder Carnegie was a well-known philanthropist, who had poured thousands and thousands into several worthy causes. Cook hoped George would prove as generous. The meeting went well. It was obvious that Carnegie had read up on polar exploration, and knew what he was talking about. He seemed enthusiastic, and a second meeting was arranged for a few days later. Cook prepared thoroughly. He knew his potential benefactor was a hard-nosed businessman, so he approached it as a business meeting, rather than a plea for cash. He spoke rapidly and enthusiastically, and painted a picture of a land ripe for discovery. He didn't talk about achieving the Pole; that was a personal goal. Instead he spoke of the discoveries to be made, the land to be surveyed and explored. He could see the other man being swept up in his enthusiasm.

But at a crucial point, before any firm commitment had been made, Carnegie was called away. When he returned to Cook a while later, his ardor had cooled considerably. Cook feared his chance was slipping away. As Carnegie led him to the door, he said: "Doctor, there is so much to be done in this world nearer by."

The dream was dead.

But no dream ever dies, not fully. Though Cook despaired of mounting his own expedition, he could not stop himself from being drawn to the plans of others. He had turned down the opportunity to survey Ellesmere Island, but he remembered his first break had come when he applied out of the blue to Peary, after reading about his expedition in a newspaper. Now the *New York Sun* was carrying a report of a Belgian Antarctic Expedition about to sail, under the leadership of Adrien de Gerlache. Immediately Cook fired off a letter offering his services. He knew enough about the way the world operates to sweeten the deal. He said that he had Eskimo dogs he was willing to bring with him, and he would also make a financial donation to the expedition.

The reply came almost immediately. The expedition had a full complement, and would not take him on. Now the dream seemed dead.

15

COOK AND AMUNDSEN IN THE ANTARCTIC

On the other side of the Atlantic, Roald Amundsen had just gained his Master's Certificate at the age of twenty-three. He had a number of options—he could have found work on cargo ships, whaling ships, or sealers. Instead he decided it was time to pursue his dream of exploration. Amundsen applied for a position with a new voyage of exploration, a Belgian expedition to Antarctica. It was being led by Adrien de Gerlache, and for once Amundsen was qualified for the expedition he wanted to join. In fact, he was highly qualified in comparison to the other applicants, and was delighted to be appointed first mate. It helped that he once again did not ask for pay.

The trip would involve two years away, and an over-winter on the Antarctic continent, an exploration first. The purpose was to explore the magnetic South Pole. Amundsen was chosen partly for his skills on skis; he had experience that few could match. Many of the expedition were green when it came to snow and ice. This led to a comical situation: de Gerlache wintered in Norway to learn to ski, while Amundsen wintered in Belgium to learn French. Presumably the two men could have worked together to swap skills, but that never occurred to them. Amundsen also studied navigation, essential in the featureless waste of the polar regions.

On August 16, 1897, the *Belgica* sailed out of Antwerp, bound for Antarctica. It would be a two and a half year adventure, and the first real step the young Norwegian had made as a polar explorer.

"The commander was a Belgian sailor. The captain was a Belgian artillery officer who had served in the French navy and who had become a first-rate skipper. The first mate was myself," Amundsen wrote. That should have set alarm bells ringing for him; his study of polar exploration had revealed that when there was a captain to lead on the water and a commander to lead on land, it split the loyalty of the group and led to dissent.

"The first mate was myself. Dr Cook, of later polar fame, was the ship's physician. The chief scientist was a Rumanian. The second scientist was a Pole. Five members of the crew were Norwegians. The rest were Belgians. The expedition was decidedly an international affair."

Cook had not been not the first choice for physician—or the second, or even the third. His application had been firmly rejected, because he had heard about the trip too late. The first choice had been Dr. Massart, who later resigned. De Gerlache replaced him with Dr. Arthur Taquin, who proved to be difficult and pompous. Eventually he was fired, and replaced with a Belgian physician hired on short notice in Antwerp. De Gerlache didn't even bother to record this third man's name. They left Antwerp on August 16, but the ship developed engine problems. They had to put in to Ostend, for repairs. But while they were there the new physician told his leader that he had pressing family matters to deal with, and jumped ship. De Gerlache was desperate.

He had not been interested in Cook's application for two reasons. The first was that the position of physician had been filled. But the second was that he was leading a Belgian expedition, and it was already heavily loaded with non-Belgians, including second-in-command Amundsen. But his hand was forced; he rushed off a telegram to Cook, inviting him to join the expedition.

Back in New York, Cook had given up on the Belgian expedition, and was concentrating, unsuccessfully, on drumming up interest in his own plans. It was late in the evening toward the end of August, and he was home in his study, finishing up for the day, when there came a knock on the door. It was a courier, with the telegram de Gerlache had sent. Cook recognized the name, but the message meant nothing to him; it was written in French. So he had to wait until the following morning to get it translated, by a reporter on the *New York Sun*. It was an offer of the position of physician. He would have to abandon his medical practice immediately, and make his way to Montevideo. Montevideo is the capital of Uruguay, and the most southerly major city in South America. It was a perfect launching place for an Antarctic expedition. The message added that he would not be over-wintering in Antarctica. He immediately replied, accepting the position. He would join the *Belgica* in Rio de Janeiro in September. His partner Dr. Burr would handle the medical practice in his absence. Cook had plenty of polar gear in storage, and did not need to spend any time on preparations. His only concern was his new fiancée, Anna Forbes. She was unwell, and he was worried. But a specialist reassured him there was nothing to be concerned about, so he arranged to set sail on September 3, with Anna and her mother on the dock to wave him off. They waved and waved, but he did not appear. Still concerned over her health, and over her unhappiness with his plans, he had got cold feet, and missed the boat!

Two weeks later, on September 20, he finally left New York. He had mixed feelings, writing: "To consent by cable to cast my lot in a battle against the supposed insurmountable icy barriers of the South, with total strangers, men from another continent, speaking a language strange to me, does indeed seem rash. The Antarctic has always been the dream of my life, and to be on the way to it was then my ideal of happiness."

Despite his delay in departing, Cook arrived in Rio well before the *Belgica*. A Belgian diplomat put him up in his own villa, and he waited the arrival of his crew-mates. They finally made port on October 22, and Cook was not impressed by his first sight of the ship. It was just 110 feet long, and looked tiny among the other great vessels in the harbor. But if the ship made no good impression on Cook, the American doctor did make a good impression on the crew. His luggage seemed perfect—two sleds, snowshoes, fur coats, and the contents of a well-stocked pharmacy. And they warmed immediately to his warm face and friendly manner.

Communication proved to be easier than he feared, as de Gerlache spoke some English, and many of the scientific staff spoke German, a language familiar to Cook. De Gerlache was immediately put at ease over his fears about hiring a doctor unseen, writing: "Guided only by chance, I had a lucky hand. Cook is a charming comrade, helpful, active, and ingenious."

At thirty-two, Cook was the oldest on the expedition. That may have given him an air of confidence. He quickly fitted in, finding endless fascination in his companions. Amundsen struck him immediately as one of the most interesting characters he had ever encountered. He found the Norwegian had a cold and aloof exterior, but was friendly and enthusiastic beneath it.

On October 30 the expedition left Rio, arriving in Montevideo for a brief stop on November 11. A letter was waiting from Anna Forbes, assuring her Fred that she was in good health. Reassured, he faced the journey south with renewed optimism. Heading toward Punta Arenas, and Ushuaia in Tierra del Fuego, he humorously wrote (in *Through the First Antarctic Night*): "At Rio we were done up in good style before we left the ship; dress suits when necessary, the newest things in neckties, and neatly pressed trousers. At Montevideo our garments were crinkled and showed the effects of the sea. At Punta Arenas we did not even try to fix up, but walked about the town as careless of dress as bricklayers; and at Ushuaia, well—the man who dressed and brushed his hair was an outcast; he was not regarded as an explorer."

There was an air of camaraderie as they headed into the southern ocean. But it soon became apparent that the expedition was less professional and less well prepared than it appeared. There was something of the buccaneer about de Gerlache. He was prepared to boldly sail into the unknown, taking a chance on luck over preparation. When that approach goes well, it can go very well.

"I can only admire his audacity. Onwards or bust. I will follow all the way, cheerful and smiling," Amundsen wrote.

But the expedition quickly got into trouble. On January 21, 1898, a storm caught the ship, sweeping unsecured cargo into the raging sea. One sailor attempted to clear the scuppers of loose coal, and was taken by a wave. He clung to a line in the sea, screaming for help. As Cook, one of the first to react to the emergency, began pulling in the line, another sailor jumped overboard to try and rescue his colleague, but had to be pulled back on board. After a long struggle they nearly got the sailor to safety, but at the last moment he lost his grip on the line, and was lost.

"He was a boy with many friends, and his absence was deeply felt in our little party," noted Cook.

The *Belgica* continued to sail south and east, finally reaching the huge ice cliffs of the ice shelf surrounding Antarctica.

On January 31 a small party was set ashore on an island, to explore and carry out important navigational observations. The island was part of the archipelago of islands around Graham Land, the peninsula that juts out of Antarctica, and which separates the Weddell Sea from the waters of the western coast of the continent (Bellingshausen Sea, Amundsen Sea, and Ross Sea). Cook, always eager, was one of the volunteers. So was Amundsen. In all there were five men on the landing party, hauling two sledges with provisions for a fortnight. They hoped to scale a peak on the island, where they could get a view for miles in every direction, giving them a map of their surroundings. Progress was quick for a while, until they met an area of deep crevasses, which stopped them. After a few days of fruitless effort, Cook and Amundsen decided on a bold move. They would get around the crevasses by climbing the wall of rock bounding that section of the glacier. This would be difficult and dangerous, and the two men were roped like mountaineers.

Amundsen quickly came to appreciate Cook's experience, and formed a high opinion of his competence, noting in his diary that it was a long, hard day, in which Cook had led during the difficult portions. He said that it was interesting to see the practical and efficient way in which the American broke the trail. During that long day the two men had plenty of time to chat, and they quickly found they had plenty in common. Amundsen had trained as a doctor, at his mother's insistence, so they shared an educational background. Both had volunteered for the expedition, and were serving without pay, because they were drawn to the Poles. They also discovered a surprising connection, considering they had lived on different continents. They had a friend in common.

Amundsen had gone to school with Eivind Astrup, the explorer who had been with Cook and Peary on the Second Greenland Expedition, and who had spent a year with Peary on the Third Greenland Expedition. Both men had fond memories of the skiing champion, who was friendly and full of enthusiasm for life. Both had been saddened to learn of his sudden death, at the young age of twenty-four. After returning from Greenland for the second time, Astrup was spending time in Norway. During the winter he had made a trip to visit a friend in an isolated part of South Norway. It was a fifty-mile distance, and he took one day's provisions with him. He never arrived. Several weeks later, his body was found. There was some consideration that he might have taken his own life in the wilderness, a reaction to his treatment by Peary and other problems he had faced. More likely he had underestimated the short trip he was going on, and had got lost in a blizzard or trapped by the weather, and had frozen to death.

The two men spent that afternoon unsuccessfully trying to scale the rock wall surrounding the glacier. They filled the tough hours with plenty of talk, and by the end of the day a basis had been laid for a friendship that was to endure until Cook's death.

A few days later, the party succeeded in scaling one of the two peaks on the island, then they returned to the *Belgica*. The ship continued drifting along the edge of the continent, following a path roughly southwest, through the many small islands that dotted the sea in that area. Although chances to land and explore were limited, the men found the passing landscape fascinating.

"There is a glitter in the sea, a sparkle on the ice, and a stillness in the atmosphere, which fascinates the soul but overpowers the mind. There is a solitude and restfulness about the whole scene which can only be felt; it cannot be described," Cook enthused.

At times they had to sail north, away from the continent, to escape the grinding pack ice and the small bergs. When the weather was against them, the *Belgica* took a terrible battering, but de Gerlache was not worried. He believed they could poke and probe their way through the ice to make landfall. Although it was already late in the Antarctic summer, and the chance for real exploration was dwindling, he still thought they could push south, land a small party, and the rest of the crew could return to warmer latitudes for the winter, returning the following year to pick up the landing party. Others on board were less sure.

To escape the storms, de Gerlache sailed deep into the pack ice. He felt it was safer there than on the edge of the pack ice, where bigger bergs could buffet the ship. Soon he ran the risk of being trapped for the winter as the water began to freeze. He consulted the crew about the possibility of allowing the ship to become locked in the ice and drifting for the winter. They were against it. As Cook said: "If our vessel should be lost, no relief could possibly reach us, because it is not definitely known where we may be found. Death by freezing and starvation would be our lot if our trusty ship were disabled."

De Gerlache decided to turn north and head for safe harbor in South America. But a storm on February 28 threw them back into the pack ice. They rode ahead of the storm instead of fighting against it, which is what Amundsen would have done. "The instinct of any navigator accustomed to the polar seas would have been to use every effort to get away to the north and into the open sea. This we could have done," he noted in *My Life as an Explorer*. He was very worried, but the etiquette of the command structure dictated that he should say nothing until asked by his commander. De Gerlache never asked Amundsen's opinion, so he bit his tongue and said nothing. He knew the great danger the expedition was in, but he had no choice except to follow orders and make the best of it.

When the storm subsided the clearest leads, or open water channels in the ice, stretched south, and that is where the expedition leader headed. Unknown to the crew, this had been his intention all along; to become embedded in the winter ice and drift to a Farthest South, as Nansen had drifted to a Farthest North. By March 3 the *Belgica* was locked in solid ice 1,100 miles from the South Pole, and three hundred miles from the nearest known, uninhabited land.

It was the start of a nightmare winter.

"For thirteen months we lay caught in the vise of this ice field. Two of the sailors went insane. Every member of the ship's company was afflicted with scurvy, and all but three of us were prostrated by it," was Cook's bleak summary.

Their first job was to prepare the ship for a long period of immobility, and then to make their quarters as comfortable as possible. Cook traveled across the ice with the Polish naturalist Henryk Arctowski. They found very little evidence of life, but did come across some seals and penguins, which they clubbed to death with their ski poles.

"The calls of science and the dire needs of our stomachs made the deed absolutely necessary," according to Cook.

On May 15 the sun set. It would not rise again for seventy-one days. The long winter had begun.

Stuck in confined quarters—as they would be for more than a year—two things were inevitable: either people would grow to love each other, or hate each other. The friendship between Cook and Amundsen grew, and they spent a lot of time together, sharing their dreams. Cook saw Amundsen as a young man with more sense than most, and well read. Amundsen appreciated the experience, ability, and calmness of the older man. When it came to forays off the ship—for scientific observations, hunting, or just to break the monotony—the two invariably traveled together. Cook eagerly shared his knowledge with the less experienced Amundsen. It was not just a relationship of professional regard; it is quite clear that there were genuine bonds of affection between the two men. Affection and respect.

But once the darkness set in, problems began to mount up. Many on board felt listless, and illness became a concern. The first to die was Lieutenant Emile Danco. He succumbed to cold and heart disease on June 5. Doctor Cook believed the darkness in some way contributed to his decline. He was a popular officer, and his death plunged everyone into a depression—especially as it was followed quickly by the death of the ship's cat.

A few weeks later one of the sailors suffered a psychotic episode, running amok on the deck with a knife, injuring several of the crew. Then he jumped overboard and began staggering across the ice. While Cook attended to the injured, Amundsen set off in pursuit of the crazed man. When he finally caught up with him, the man turned the knife on himself. It was the second funeral among the small party.

Cook tried to rally the spirits at the burial, saying: "Men, we are going through a bad time. I am sure that with enough thought and planning we'll get out of it. But we must maintain level heads. We must be strong."

His natural leadership qualities were coming out again, as they had on the Second Greenland Expedition when Peary had broken his leg. Amundsen followed Cook's speech with a lusty rendition of a Norwegian sea shanty, helping to revive spirits.

But two weeks later there was another funeral, after a sailor fell from a mast to the main deck. It was very obvious that the crew were feeling the effects of severe stress. But Cook could see something else, and it worried him. He noted spongy gums, puffy eyes, and swollen ankles. Complexions took on a pale and oily tone, and many were suffering head-aches, insomnia, and loss of appetite. Diagnosing it as a form of anemia, he recognized it from his time in Greenland. It was a precursor of scurvy.

"We must have fresh meat or die," he said.

Amundsen agreed.

"Both Dr. Cook and I knew from our reading of Arctic travels that scurvy could be avoided by the use of fresh meat. We had, therefore, spent many weary hours, after the day's hard work was done, trave-ling for miles over the ice in search of seals and penguins, and with great labor had killed and brought to the ship a great number of each," he said.

These hunting trips further forged the bonds between them. But the trips served little practical purpose at first; Peary had refused to "go native" when it came to food, and now de Gerlache was the same.

"The commander developed an aversion to the flesh of both that amounted almost to a mania. He was not content only to refuse to eat it himself, but he forbade any of the ship's company to indulge in it. Consequently all of us soon got the scurvy. The commander and the captain were both so prostrated that they took to their beds and made their wills," wrote Amundsen.

Amundsen and Cook had both secretly been indulging in the fresh meat, and their state of health was better than that of their shipmates. With the captain and the commander out of action, Amundsen found himself, as first mate, in command.

"The first thing I did was to get out the few men that were able to work, and dig through the snow to the carcasses of the seals."

The fresh meat quickly brought about an improvement in the crew. Even the commander was persuaded to partake, however reluctantly. Within a week the improvement was obvious. The crisis had been averted. Cook's studies and preparation were showing their value at last.

"It was in this fearful emergency, during these thirteen long months in which almost the certainty of death stared us steadily in the face, that I came to know Dr. Cook intimately, and to form the affection for him and the gratitude to him which nothing in his later career could ever cause me to alter. He was a man of unfaltering courage, unfailing hope, endless cheerfulness, and unwearied kindness."

Cook was equally impressed by Amundsen, writing in *Through the First Antarctic Night*: "He was the biggest, the strongest, the bravest, and generally the best dressed man for sudden emergencies."

Once the sun returned, they worked together perfecting a sledge for the ice. Traditionally sledges were heavy and solid; they designed one that was light and flexible. It was just half the weight of the traditional one, and far easier to maneuver. They also designed a tent that weighed just twelve pounds, went up in minutes, but provided great shelter. The two men, along with Captain Lecointe, took a long trek to a far-off iceberg to test the equipment. During their three-day excursion it proved to work well.

Amundsen noted: "It is a pleasure to make an excursion with the company that I had . . . Cook, the calm and imperturbable, never losing his temper; and in addition, there are the many small things one can learn in the society of such a thoroughly practical polar explorer like Cook. In his contact with the North Greenland Eskimos, and in his profound study of everything concerning polar life, he has greater insight into these matters than most men in the field. He has advice on everything. He gives it in a likeable and tactful manner; not with fuss and noise."

While Amundsen's opinion of the ship's doctor was on the rise, his opinion of his leader was plummeting sharply. Amundsen discovered that not only had de Gerlache made a mistake about the scurvy, he had struck a secret deal with the Belgian members of the crew. If the captain (in charge while the exhibition was at sea) became permanently unable to lead—either through illness, injury, or death—command bypassed the second mate and passed to the third mate, a Belgian. Amundsen was furious when he discovered this. He saw it as a betrayal based on nothing but unthinking nationalism.

It was also a serious breach of the law of the sea. Command always passed to the second mate. Everyone knew that, and it gave sailors a sense of security. Breaking this tradition was a major slap in the face for the young Norwegian. Amundsen was incensed, but his hands were tied. He wrote a furious letter to the expedition leader, saying: "I followed you without pay. It was not a question of money, but honor. That honor you have insulted by denying me my right. As far as I am concerned, there is no longer a Belgian Antarctic expedition, and the *Belgica* is just an ordinary ship locked in the ice. It is my duty to help the men on board. For this reason, captain, I will continue my work as if nothing had happened."

Perhaps Amundsen's decision to knuckle down and do his job had less to do with his sense of duty and more to do with the fact that the ship was beset in the ice. He couldn't walk out, unless he fancied a long swim in very cold water. Tensions were running high as the months turned into a year. Amundsen never forgave de Gerlache. When he wrote his autobiography thirty years later, he would not even refer to him by name.

Summer came, but no thaw. The ship remained trapped. As the months passed, supplies began to run low. Summer passed and autumn came, with still no sign of the break-up of the ice. They began to worry that they faced a second dark winter. Depressed, the crew ignored Christmas. Then Amundsen, on the Crow's Nest, thought he spotted open water in the distance. He and Cook set out to investigate, and returned with the good news; there was a patch of water, which would expand as the surrounding ice melted. It would eventually lead to open water—if they could get the ship to that patch.

Unfortunately, it was half a mile away. Cook proposed a bold plan: they would dig two trenches from the bow and the stern of the ship, both running parallel across the ice to the basin of open water. It sounded crazy, but he believed that once the ice began breaking, it would follow the line of least resistance and break along the trenches, freeing the ship. Amundsen was doubtful, but knew Cook well enough to trust him. He backed the plan.

It took weeks, but the ship finally broke free. The ice split, as Cook predicted, on January 30, 1899, and icy water flooded the man-made trenches. The expedition was afloat again. But the crew were demoralized, supplies were low, and they had already been away as long as they had originally intended. They turned north, making Punta Arenas on March 28. They had nearly two years of news to catch up on—not just personal news, but the world had moved on. The Spanish-American War had broken out, been fought, and America had won in their absence. Scientists had invented the wireless telegraph. They were coming home to a new world.

Cook split from the crew, sailing up to America on his own, and stopping to make anthropological studies of the indigenous South American Indians. The *Belgica* crossed the Atlantic, arriving back in Antwerp on November 5, 1899. Amundsen was not with them. Still feeling the resentment at his treatment by de Gerlache, he had left the ship in Punta Arenas and made his own way back to Norway. He arrived home anonymously on a mail boat, escorting a fellow Norwegian crew member who had gone mad during the years in the Antarctic. It was an inglorious return. The expedition was a failure, and not even a glorious failure at that.

It left Amundsen with a bad taste in his mouth. Several things had gone wrong. The commander had ignored the advice of wiser heads, and put the lives of everyone at risk from scurvy. The chain of command had broken down. The objectives had not been achieved. Chaos reigned. It was not the start he dreamed of. But at least it was a start.

The only positive to come out of it, aside from his handling of the scurvy crisis, was his growing friendship with Frederick Cook. He had learned a lot from talking to the more experienced explorer on their hunting trips, and during the long nights of the polar winter. He had a friend for life. That friendship endured through betrayal, fraud, and disappointment. Their fates had become entwined.

For Cook, the outcome had been a bit more positive. He had finally got to the Antarctic, even if he had not penetrated that mysterious continent like he hoped. He had been part of a European expedition, and now had a reputation of sorts on that continent, which could only give him credibility in future years. He even got decorated by the King of Belgium, Leopold II, making him the only non-Belgian on the crew to be presented with the Order of Leopold. Peary never got that level of respect in Europe.

But on his journey home, Cook got news that made all those honors meaningless: his fiancée, Anna Forbes, had passed away. Shortly after hearing the news he contracted amoebic dysentery, and arrived home weak, bereaved, and depressed. It was time to put the dreams aside, and resume his medical practice. Alone.

16

PEARY AND THE METEORITES

While Cook had been busy trying to excite interest in his Antarctic ambitions, and later on the *Belgica* expedition, Peary had not been letting the grass grow under him. The failure of his Third Greenland Expedition rankled, and the only saving grace had been the recovery of the two large meteorites. To recover the third one would be a real coup— it would be the largest meteorite ever recovered, and a fitting tribute to his work in the North. He also knew exactly where it was, and how to get there. That gave it an edge over the Pole as a destination. Peary put aside his Farthest North ambitions for a while, and decided to mount an expedition he knew he could pull off. He would bring the third meteorite home.

More than anything, it was an engineering challenge. And Peary was an engineer.

His first task was to raise funds, and he decided to become a tour operator, rather like Cook before him. He sold passage on his ship— still not purchased—to academics and others who would travel to Greenland and be dropped off on the coast, to be picked up later when the ship returned with the giant meteorite. He also continued to lecture in the spare time the Navy gave him. It took him a year, but eventually he had his war chest, and could hire a ship.

He had loaned the first two meteorites to the American Museum of Natural History. Woman was the second largest meteorite on display, and museum patron Morris Jessup was grateful. A long-time supporter of Peary, he now used his influence to get the explorer a summer of leave from the ever-patient Navy. The trip was on. Peary left in July 1896, and in August his ship, *Hope*, arrived in Cape York, near the top of Greenland. Peary felt at home; there was no one alive who knew the area better than him.

That year the summer was a good one, and the ice was thin enough in Melville Bay for the *Hope* to break through to the island where Tent was waiting. It could not have been more perfect. The meteorite was at the top of a slope, which ended on a rock ledge. They berthed the boat under the ledge. All they had to do was get the thirty-ton rock down to the ledge, and carefully lower it on board. Peary had brought all the heavy equipment he would need. Quickly his men excavated around the meteorite, freeing it from the ice. They then used heavy hydraulic jacks to mount it on a trolley.

The next part was tricky. They constructed a path using railway sleepers and rails, and they slowly slid the trolley down the path, holding it in check with winches and steel cable. They had it close to the ship when a sudden gale broke up a ridge of small icebergs that had been sheltering their anchorage. The pack ice surrounded the ship, and if they did not leave immediately, they would be wedged in for the winter. That was not part of the plan.

Peary had to return to America empty-handed, leaving the meteorite sitting sentinel on the rock ledge overlooking Cape York. Another failure.

And when he got home, he got the worst possible news: another man's success. When he heard of the new Farthest North achieved by Nansen when he marched from the *Fram*, it completed his misery. Nansen had beaten him across Greenland. Now he was leading the race for the Pole, while Peary wasted his time trying to bring lumps of rock and iron home to put on display in a museum. The Navy had trusted him and given him leave, and once again he had let them down. How many more times would they indulge him?

The best way to respond was to bluster. In January 1897 Peary was presented with an award by the American Geographical Society. He used the occasion to make a dramatic announcement. His next expedition would be for the Pole. It would cost $150,000, and he was prepared to remain as long as five years on the ice, if that was what it would take.

"The Pole is certain to be reached soon; it is only a question of time and money. I know there is not an American man or woman whose heart would not thrill with patriotism to see the realization of this project, and know that it was American money, intelligence, energy, and endurance that had scaled the apex of the Earth, and lighted it with Old Glory," he thundered, to a very appreciative audience. Playing the patriotic card was an old trick of his, and it worked spectacularly. The American Geographical Society immediately got behind his plan.

The Navy didn't. His request for five years' leave was rejected out of hand. In fact, the Navy went further. He was ordered to transfer to the shipyards at Mare Island, California. He would be transferred as far away from his milieu as it was possible for the Navy to arrange. This was not just a rejection of his application. This was the US military telling him, in no uncertain terms, that they had run out of patience with him. If he wanted to draw the salary and get the pension at the end, he would have to knuckle down and do some work.

Peary was devastated at the "determined, concentrated, and bitter" forces he felt were ranged against him. He pulled every string he could. Nothing helped. A chance meeting with political mover Charles A. Moore, a prominent supporter of President McKinley, led to Moore petitioning the Secretary of the Navy on his behalf.

"Anything but that," was the short answer.

Moore was undeterred. He arranged a meeting with the President for that afternoon, and called in some favors. An hour later, he had a letter granting Peary five years' paid leave. He took great delight in going straight to the Secretary of the Navy with the precious document. Peary now had the breathing space he needed.

Before proceeding with his more ambitious plans, there was some unfinished business. He hired a ship and traveled back to Cape York. He was accompanied by his wife and their four-year-old daughter,

Marie Ahnighito. Not only did they retrieve the giant meteorite, Peary also persuaded a Danish official to give him a bill of sale for the three space rocks. Tent joined Woman and Dog in the Museum of Natural History, where it took pride of place in the lobby. Many people assumed that the explorer had donated the rocks. Far from it; they were on loan until he could find a buyer. Peary actually gave the three meteorites to his wife Josephine, who continued to try and shift them. She attempted to sell them to the museum for years, with no luck. Then in February 1910 she found a buyer. The widow of Morris Jessup, a major financial backer of Peary, bought the three space rocks for $40,000 and donated them to the museum, where they are still on display.

In today's terms, Peary had netted over three quarters of a million dollars for the precious treasure of the Eskimo people he claimed to have cared for so much.

He also returned with a more gruesome cargo: a collection of both dead and living Eskimo for the museum. He dug up many bodies and took them without the permission of the tribe, and also brought two of his sledge drivers, the wife of one of them, and their three children. He just delivered them to the museum, and washed his hands of all further responsibility.

Cook had also brought home Eskimo, whom he used on his lecture tour. But he kept them close to him, and looked after them, before returning them to their own land a year later. Peary was not concerned with such niceties. His six Eskimo were housed in the basement of the museum, but were moved to a farm in upstate New York when a heat wave made the basement impossible for them to live in. Despite the move, four died within months of landing in America. The two surviving boys were very bitter for the rest of their lives. One found out that the remains of his father, who had died in America, were on display in the museum. He had attended his father's funeral, not knowing that Peary had replaced the body in the coffin with a log. The body had then been added to the anthropological collection.

None of this concerned Peary. He continued his preparations for a major push on the North Pole. The outbreak of the Spanish-American War in February 1898 did give him reason for concern—he expected his leave to be canceled. Despite his country being at war, he chose not to volunteer for duty. At forty-two, he knew his chances of reaching the Pole were dwindling. This might be his last chance.

On July 4 the *Windward* set sail for Greenland. Peary had his own battle to fight, a battle against the frigid polar ice. While Cook faced a difficult winter in the southern ocean, his great rival was on the cusp of glory in the north.

From the start the expedition seemed doomed. Peary arrived in Greenland in late summer, with plans to push as far north as possible, where he would sit out the long winter. The following season he planned on pushing a further two hundred miles north, where he would establish a base at Fort Conger for the second winter. This was an isolated spot near the top of Ellesmere Island, first used during a surveying expedition in 1881–1883, and since abandoned. It was well above the 80th parallel, and would leave him well placed to establish more northerly food caches and bases. This would not be a quick dash for the Pole, but a slow, steady creep forward.

He thought he had the field to himself, but that first December he got a shock when he came across the camp of Norwegian Otto Sverdrup. Sverdrup had been with Nansen during his polar attempt, and had commanded the *Fram* while Nansen marched north. Now he was engaged in an extensive survey of the top of Greenland, which would keep him in the high Arctic for four years.

Delighted to meet another explorer, Sverdrup welcomed Peary warmly, inviting him to stay for coffee with the team. Peary declined, saying his own camp was only two hours away, and he was anxious to get back there. They chatted for a few minutes, and Sverdrup found the visit a welcome break from the bleak monotony of an Arctic winter. He wrote: "Peary's visit was the event of the day in our tent. We talked of nothing else, and rejoiced at having shaken hands with the bold explorer, even though his visit had been so short that we hardly had time to pull off our mittens."

He asked Peary to take some letters from his men, as it might be years before they got another chance. But Peary was less happy with the encounter and only agreed to take the letters if they made no mention of Sverdrup's work. Peary fumed at this potential fly in the ointment. Always a jealous man, he was not going to carry news of another's successes in the region. What if Sverdrup was lying, and was really planning his own polar dash? He persuaded his companion, Matthew Henson, and expedition physician Dr. Thomas Dedrick, to make a dash north to Fort Conger. They would take four Eskimo and beat Sverdrup there. They had no evidence that the Norwegian had any plans to establish a base at the abandoned settlement (he hadn't), but Peary was paranoid. Henson had doubts because it was a particularly cold and stormy winter, but he followed orders. He later wrote: "During the four years from 1898 to 1902, which were continuously spent in the regions about North Greenland, we had every experience, except death, that had ever fallen to the lot of the explorers who had preceded us, and more than once we looked death squarely in the face."

The trip to Fort Conger was particularly grueling, and two of the Eskimo abandoned the effort. By the time they arrived, on January 6, 1899, Peary was suffering greatly. He had fallen on the ice and damaged his right arm, which was in terrible pain. Worse, he couldn't even feel his legs. As Henson grimly recorded: "In January 1899, Commander Peary froze his feet so badly that all but one of his toes fell off."

An examination revealed that he had suffered extensive frostbite—during the examination, two of his toes just snapped off. After eleven days in Fort Conger, Peary was strapped to a sledge and dragged back 250 miles to the *Windward*, where Dr. Dedrick had to operate, removing all but three of the remaining toes. For the rest of his life Peary would walk with a stiff and unnatural gait and would suffer on long marches.

When the relief ship came that spring it carried Howard Bridgman, now an avid supporter of Peary and a leading member of Peary's Arctic Club, the body the explorer set up to oversee fundraising and look after the logistics of the expeditions, and its members included leading business men, as well as political heavyweights. Bridgman was shocked at the condition of the explorer. The first season had yielded nothing of consequence, and had left Peary seriously compromised. He urged Peary to return home to recuperate. Peary would have none of it. He had scrawled graffiti on the wall at Fort Conger. It was a reworking of a

Latin phrase from Seneca: "I will find a way—or make one." He would not be giving up on his dream.

The second season yielded nothing more, apart from agonizing heartbreak for Josephine Peary. She had given birth to a daughter, Francine, after her husband had set sail. He had never seen his daughter, and she died of cholera at the age of seven months. A heartbroken Josephine sailed north with a relief ship in the summer of 1900, determined to bring her husband back to civilization. But the ice prevented the ship getting as far north as Peary, who was back in Fort Conger. The couple never met that summer—but she did meet an Eskimo woman who claimed to be Peary's wife. Worse, the woman had a two-year-old son whose unmistakable looks proclaimed the truth of her claim. While she had been waiting patiently at home and suffering the loss of their child, her husband had fathered a healthy child with another woman.

Josephine was furious. She did not blame the native woman—in fact, she helped her when she fell ill. Instead she reserved her ire for her husband. When it became obvious that she would not meet him that year, she left him a stinging letter: "You gave me three years of the most exquisite pleasure that can be had; after that the pleasure was pretty evenly divided with the pain, until now it is all pain, except the memory of what has been."

When they eventually met the following year, Peary was unrepentant, and he never saw it as a problem that he had a white wife at home and a native wife on the ice.

At the end of the summer the *Windward* turned south, but became trapped in the pack ice. The ship was iced in for the winter, and Josephine ended up spending yet another winter in Northern Greenland. She was only 250 miles from where her husband was holed in at Fort Conger, but he could have been on the far side of the moon for all anyone knew.

Back home, the members of Peary Arctic Club were seriously worried. There was no word of Peary, and the relief ship failed to come home. In desperation they turned to an old friend. Bridgman contacted Dr. Cook, and explained that Peary was lost in the Arctic. They would fit out a rescue expedition, if Dr. Cook would join. They needed his experience. As a sweetener they told him that Peary's prohibition against publication would be lifted for this trip. Cook agreed to abandon his medical practice once more, to put his rivalry with Peary aside, and come to the rescue.

On August 4 the relief expedition headed by Cook finally located Peary, on board the Windward with his wife and daughter Marie. They were harbored at Foulk Fjord, in the far north of the country, along the channel separating Greenland from Ellesmere Island and the Northern Canadian archipelago. Josephine was delighted to see the rescue ship. Peary seemed more subdued, saying little to Cook during their first dinner together. It was obvious, without him saying much, that he had not achieved a great deal. In 1900 he had reached the most northerly point of the Greenland archipelago—83 degrees 39 minutes north—and named it Cape Morris K. Jessup. He had tried to cross the pack ice from there, but managed only a pathetic twenty-two miles in a week before retreating. The following season he hadn't even reached the polar sea.

There had also been a major falling out between Peary and his physician, Dr. Dedrick.

Cook formed the opinion that Peary was seriously anemic, and in very poor physical condition. Gone was the youthful alertness and enthusiasm of the man he had first sailed with, replaced with stern and icy stubbornness and rigidity. Cook examined Peary privately and was shocked.

"The feet were crippled by old ulcers, the result of repeated frostbites. Eight of his toes had been removed, leaving painful stubs which refused to heal. In the face there was an absence of normal expression, a vacant stare from the eyes, and a morbid cherry-brown in the skin of the face. All outward appearances were those of one affected with some morbid disease."

Cook noted an irregular heartbeat, anemia, and the early signs of scurvy. It reopened an old argument; he told Peary that he would have to eat raw meat, especially liver. The explorer refused. Despite Cook's experience with a similar problem in Antarctica, Peary was determined do to it his own way. Cook recommended he return to America to recuperate, a call Josephine echoed strongly. But Peary was determined. He would remain in the Arctic until he reached the Pole, or his five years' leave was up.

The two ships remained together for a few weeks, hunting and trading for the coming winter. On August 24 Peary called everyone together, and outlined his plans. He would remain in Greenland, but Josephine and Marie would return home. He would send his physician Dr. Dedrick home, and replace him with Dr. Cook. But the relationship between Dedrick and Peary had broken down badly, and it was not so easy to arrange. Dedrick refused to go home, saying that he would not abandon his post while any of the expedition remained in the Arctic. It was a matter of honor with him. And Cook refused the new post while the existing physician was not voluntarily returning home. He felt it would be unethical to step into the other man's shoes against his wishes.

It led to an intense day of negotiation, the end result of which was that Dedrick would not return to America with the *Windward* or the relief ship. Peary simply fired him, and abandoned him on shore. He was allowed to take nothing from the ship, and was warned that he would receive no assistance, no matter how dire his circumstances, and would not be transported home at the end of the expedition. Peary was inflexible on that. The falling out was irrevocable.

Cook and another member of the relief party, industrialist Clarence Wyckoff, did their best by giving Dedrick a gun, ammunition, and food supplies, from their own personal stock. Then they sailed away, leaving Peary and the physician to their strange stand-off. They carried a letter from Peary to Charles Moore, the man who had secured his five-year leave. Peary, ever the optimist, wrote: "My grip is still good, I have a year before me, and I have yet to experience the first feeling of discouragement."

It was a brave face, but it hid the harsh reality, recorded in Peary's diary that winter: ". . . About the worst night I have ever passed . . . Jo and Marie, was I criminally foolish in staying?"

An epidemic of illness passed through the tiny Eskimo settlement around Peary, but he refused to allow Dr. Dedrick to intervene, watching as six adults and a child died. The following spring he set out again, leaving Cape Hecla in the Canadian Arctic in early April and crossing the frozen sea with sledges and teams of dogs. The going was tough. The ground was uneven, and the ocean drift was causing them to lose as much ground as they gained, making each mile very hard won. By April

21, he wrote: "The game is off. My dream of sixteen years is ended. I cannot accomplish the impossible."

That summer he returned home with the relief ship, defeated.

Back in America, Cook had settled into his routine once more. But for once he saw the prospect of happiness open before him. On his thirty-seventh birthday, he married a widow, Marie Hunt, who had a young daughter, Ruth. They followed the wedding with a brief stay in Florida, where he had a lecture tour organized. He mixed lecturing, writing, and medicine, and was quite comfortable. The couple bought a large three-story mansion, and he splurged on a car, quite a rarity at the time. He developed a bit of a reputation as a fast driver, regularly pushing the vehicle beyond ten miles an hour.

Being reunited with the Pearys had been a strange experience for him. He thought he had formed a close bond with Robert on their first expedition together, but subsequent events had caused him to question that. He could see that Peary had changed, becoming more of a megalomaniac as the years of relative failure hardened his attitude. Now he brooked no dissent. His treatment of Dr. Dedrick had disturbing echoes of what happened to John Verhoeff on the Second Greenland Expedition, and Cook knew he would never work with Peary again. He found Josephine aloof and regal, but charming and warm beneath that, and he did try to maintain contact once he returned to America, writing to her regularly, and inviting her to New York to escape the "political degenerates" of Washington.

Peary's return in the fall of 1902 re-ignited interest in the polar regions, with reporters knocking on Cook's door for his views. The feud between Peary and Dr. Dedrick had become public. Dedrick had been brought home by the expedition, but he was not paid for his years of service, and he and Peary did not exchange a single word during the entire voyage from Greenland. Cook refused to get drawn into the conflict, but was very gracious about his rival's achievement in his final season. He had managed a lengthy trip north, reaching his highest latitude yet.

Cook remarked to a reporter from the *New York Times*: "Peary has done great work, and has succeeded in going farther north than any American has ever done before. His trip on sledges was about eight hundred miles each way, and is probably the longest sledge trip ever made."

Peary had still fallen almost three hundred miles short of his target, and privately the Peary Arctic Club thought he was finished. And the row with Dedrick was becoming unseemly. Cook did his best to rise above it, saying: "These three men (Peary, Dedrick, and Henson) had been in the Arctic three long years and passed through three Arctic nights. I have never known men to live together one Arctic night and not feel like kicking each other. The fact is, this affair is simply the ordinary friction of an Arctic expedition."

Dedrick spoke to the press and wrote letters to influential people trying to explain his position. Peary remained silent. When Dedrick was accepted into the Arctic Club, Peary tendered his resignation. In Europe, Dedrick was seen as a hero who had not abandoned his post, even when his commander turned against him. It was less clear-cut in America, but with every expedition he completed, Peary seemed to lose ground with European commentators.

In sharp contrast, Sverdrup returned to Norway with the *Fram* around the same time Peary reached America. His expedition had achieved what it set out to achieve; he had mapped 1,750 miles of coast, and opened out 100,000 square miles of new land. He had done it all without any scandals, fall-outs, or dramatic crises.

Peary tried to put it all behind him, concentrating on his recovery. An operation could not restore his feet, but at least he could walk without a limp, in a curious shuffle. He began to lecture again, and to prepare the way for another attempt on the Pole. Part of his strategy was to name a number of features he had discovered after several of his prominent supporters. The more important the supporter, the bigger the land feature he had named after him.

The fact that Sverdrup had discovered and named these features ahead of Peary in most cases did not bother the American explorer in the slightest.

17

COOK CLIMBS TOWARD THE TOP OF THE CONTINENT

Cook was a happy man. He had a beautiful and well-off young wife, an affectionate stepdaughter, a thriving medical practice, a comfortable income, and one of the first cars in New York. He still had the restlessness of an explorer, but unlike Peary, his wife supported his ambitions. He began to look around for a suitable expedition. It had to be something that could be achieved in a single season, because only a mad man would leave behind the comfortable life Cook had established for himself. So both Poles were out. But that left plenty of other possibilities.

Mount McKinley is a remote point in the Alaskan wilderness. Long known to the natives as Denali (the name it still bears outside the United States), the mountain was first glimpsed by white men in 1794. In 1896 prospector William Dickey came across the range during his search for gold. As a sort of inside joke he named the highest point Mount McKinley after the presidential candidate, who was a strong champion of the Gold Standard. He estimated the mountain at twenty thousand feet, which far surpassed the heights of any of the peaks in the Rockies. If he was right, it would be the highest spot in North America. The location was inaccessible, and the mountain looked virtually unclimbable.

We now know that McKinley is 20,237 feet high. But that statistic is deceiving; it is one of the most impressive mountains on the planet. It begins at a low altitude, and the height from base to peak is eighteen feet, making it the largest of any mountain above sea level (there are bigger mountains in the mid-Atlantic ridge, but they are under water). It is the third most prominent peak in the world, after Everest and Aconcagua. Brutally tough because of its height, location, and weather, it remains to this day a summit only tackled by serious mountaineers.

In the mountaineering fraternity there is a challenge for the very best: the seven summits. This challenge consists of scaling the highest peak on every continent. Some, such as Elbrus in Europe, Aconcagua in South America, and Kilimanjaro in Africa, are relatively easy. Mount Vinson in Antarctica is also easy, apart from issues of accessibility. But Mount McKinley is one of the toughest of the seven summits. Because of its location in the Arctic, it is the coldest of the peaks, with temperatures regularly dropping to extreme levels not even seen on Everest. It is a mountain that separates the weekend warriors from the true climbers.

Few people had even heard of the great mountain in the north until *National Geographic* magazine ran an article on it in January 1903. In the article the authors suggested that there were three possible routes to the summit. Two could be tackled in a single season, while the third was a slow siege, involving a winter embedded in the Alaskan Arctic. Cook read the article and felt the familiar flutter in his heart. Here was an objective worthy of a serious explorer. Could he be the first man to the roof of America?

The expedition had a number of attractions for him. It was to an easily accessible area, rather than sailing into the pack ice around Greenland. It was a definite and achievable objective. And it could be done in one season. He was a family man now, and too happy to contemplate a long sojourn in the wilderness. *National Geographic* authors Alfred Brooks and D. L. Reaburn had even outlined a plan to attack the mountain. It involved a three-and-a-half-month expedition, which would take a month to reach the base of the mountain with a stockpile of provisions.

"Climatic conditions permitting, a month could then be spent in exploring and ascending the mountain."

Although Cook was not a mountaineer he was no stranger to climbing, as he had proved when scaling the wall of the glacier on the island off Graham Land in Antarctica with Amundsen. He was friendly with a number of European climbers, including Matterhorn conqueror Edward Whymper, and he was a founding member of the American Alpine Club. He began to make plans for an expedition to Mount McKinley. He would need six people, and the cost would be less than $5,000. That was easier than trying to get back to the Antarctic.

He felt that a decent reconnoiter would open up a path to the summit. The *National Geographic* had identified three possibilities, but had not been close enough to offer a definite approach. Today we know there is one relatively easy route to the summit that does not involve extensive technical climbing skills. It is a path that can be hiked and scrambled, but that path has only been opened because of a generation of early explorers and their costly mistakes. And even that path is not, in reality, easy. Mainly because of the weather, but also because of the extreme height from base to summit and the altitude, no ascent of McKinley is easy. Cook was tackling the mountain without the benefit of later experience. He was a true trailblazer.

When Peary planned an expedition, he had to deal with a resentful Josephine wondering what he was getting up to behind her back. Cook had a different experience: Marie was fully behind his plans to explore. She knew what she had married, and not only accepted it, but embraced it. He immediately set about planning the expedition. The first thing he had to do was see how many of his skills were transferrable to the new enterprise. Edward Whymper had told Cook that many of his skills would come into play on a mountain. Now Cook needed to know what he brought to the table. The first thing was his approach to expeditions. From the first, he had gone native. The Eskimo depended on mobility to survive. If they could not live off the land and travel light, they died. Cook was not one for the traditional European and American expedition consisting of dozens of men, supported by hundreds of native porters. He favored what in mountaineering is called the Alpine approach; a small team traveling quickly.

Today, a trip to a camping shop will give you all the equipment you need for a quick assault on a mountain. Cook had to invent the equipment. With the help of Marie, a talented seamstress, he began working on innovative tents and sleeping bags. He eventually produced an eight-sided pyramid tent that weighed three pounds and could be folded and put in a big pocket. It had no poles, and was supported on two ice axes. Cook reasoned that climbers would have no other use for an ice axe when they were sleeping. He also worked on an innovative design for a sleeping bag. He created a robe of eiderdown lined with camel hair, which could be worn as a coat during the day. At night, three of the robes were buttoned together to create a sleeping bag.

The theory was that the final team to assault the summit would not be weighed down with heavy equipment. They could travel light, as they were wearing their sleeping quarters rather than carrying them.

When it came to the composition of the team, Cook got a surprise. Not only was Marie behind her husband's obsession, she wanted to share in it. She was behind him to such an extent that she said she would make the trip to Alaska. She might not push to the summit, but at least they would share the adventure. Cook remembered his first time on Greenland when some of the men had resented Josephine Peary, as the only woman. But he had found it no difficulty whatsoever. He was delighted his pretty new wife wanted to be part of something so important to him.

In May 1903 their daughter Ruth was sent to relatives, and Cook once more closed down his medical practice. They joined the other five members of the expedition in Seattle (two of whom had contributed to the costs) and headed into the wilderness. They were well provisioned, with normal supplies for the trip to the mountain and a supply of Arctic rations (pemmican and other high-density food) for the summit push, to keep weight down. A steamer took them up the coast to Alaska, depositing them on the Gulf of Alaska, in a tiny settlement called Tyonek, a row of huts and warehouses on a sand spit. The tiny population was mainly native, with a few whites, and the settlement had no pier. The steamer anchored off-shore, and the horses had to swim through the freezing water for land.

Cook and his wife looked at the rough mountainous terrain surrounding the settlement and blocking them from the mountain one hundred miles farther north. Marie savored the landscape and decided she had had her fill of the Arctic. When the steamer turned south, she got back on board.

For Cook, the real journey was just beginning.

On June 25 they set out, and after a few days the party split into two. Cook and Walter Miller took to a river in a small boat, while the rest led their horses through the forests and foothills, meaning to rendezvous near the mountain. Cook and Miller did not have it easy; either the river was too shallow, or too fast. Going was torturously slow, and they managed an average of twelve miles a day. They got to the rendezvous point days late—but were surprised to find that they had beaten the land party. No one was having an easy time in the Alaskan wilderness. Petty squabbles escalated, and Cook did his best to remain in control. In an effort to motivate the others, he often picked the toughest jobs for himself. But there was no pleasing everyone; one of the members admitted that Cook irritated him because he refused to use tobacco!

But the general consensus was that Cook was a fair man, who would face disaster without a complaint.

As they approached the foothills of the McKinley massif, progress was slow, to preserve the health of the horses. From an initial altitude of two thousand feet the ground began to climb steadily, and soon they were above the treeline. McKinley is blanketed with snow both winter and summer, and soon the mountain dominated their horizon, looming over them like a threat. Cook wrote of the view (in *To the Top of the Continent*): "Behind us was a great waving sea of evergreen forests, in front of us an unknown word of glacial rivers and big mountains."

As they got closer, the shape of the mountain began to be revealed. The final four thousand feet were steep, and the mountain had a double peak—something no earlier surveyor had discovered. By mid-August they were about fifteen miles from the mountain. They looked to be in position for an assault on the summit from the southwest. From here they were in virgin territory, breaking trail. In later years a relatively simple route was found to the summit of McKinley, but that was in 1953, following aerial photography. Cook was literally drawing the map as he went.

It was already three weeks into August, and he had hoped to make a summit attempt at the start of the month. The terrain had proven more difficult than they anticipated. And they needed to rest, so another two precious days were lost. The temperature was already down to 45°F, with heavy torrents of rain swelling the glacial streams they would have to negotiate, but finally they were ready. Taking five horses, they broke camp and began climbing through a high valley. The weather eventually forced them to camp for the night, and when they woke in the morning, the valley was covered in fresh snow; the season was drawing to a close. Winter was approaching and they were still far short of their goal. The next day they abandoned the horses and pushed through the valley and up the far wall onto the ridge of the mountain, gaining a thousand feet. But they met an insurmountable obstacle; a cliff dropping two thousand feet, then rising again the same height on the other side. It was immediately obvious that the chasm could not be crossed, and it took a day of exploration to determine that there was no way around it. The way was blocked.

This chasm had been discovered, unknown to Cook, three months earlier by the first party to attempt the mountain. The leader of that expedition, James Wickersham, was so awed by the obstacle that he gave up on McKinley, declaring that it would take a "flying machine" to reach the top. Cook was less sure. He gave up for the moment, but considered it a temporary setback. The mountain would fall.

The party circled the base, then tried again from a different direction, pitching tent in deep snow at nine thousand feet. The temperature was well below freezing, the Arctic conditions Cook was used to. On August 29 the party set out for a final assault on the summit. They estimated it would take five days to make the top, and two or three more to get back to camp. For safety they carried ten days' worth of provisions. Heavily laden, they found the going tough. The slope was forty to sixty degrees in places, and once, during a rest period, one of the climbers began to slip. Only quick action by Cook prevented him suffering a plunge of several thousand feet to the glacier below.

Cook led the climb, cutting steps in the snow with his ice axe. Torturous work, it reminded him of his time in Antarctica with

Amundsen. Only now he was far higher up, struggling with the thin air. That night they made camp at ninety-five hundred feet. They were less than halfway up. Their second day brought them to eleven thousand feet, which was quite an achievement, as the slope was getting steeper. Cook knew that the climb was taking far longer than expected, and his team was suffering from exhaustion. That night they slept to the raucous music of avalanches. In the morning one of the climbers, Robert Dunn, took a look at the broken ground ahead and turned back for base camp. Cook pressed on, with one companion, to try and find a path through the obstacles. He got through the snowfield, but was stopped by a granite cliff. He thought it was climbable, but beyond it he could see steep slopes of rock stretching several thousand feet into the air. Those slopes were not climbable. He had reached the end. Reluctantly, he turned from the granite face and began to follow his men back to base camp.

The only positive gain from the expedition was that he took a different route home. It proved equally difficult, but with the route in and the route out, Cook had completed the first circumnavigation of McKinley. The party returned to civilization—or what passed for it in those wild frontier regions—on September 25, exhausted, weak, and ragged. But one of the party was unbowed. Cook knew he would be back, and he was sure he had seen a route to the summit.

18

AMUNDSEN ON THE NORTHWEST PASSAGE

The Northwest Passage became big news when Sir John Franklin went missing trying to find his way through the maze of islands to the north of Canada. Sir John Franklin was still missing. He had sailed into the unknown in 1845, and barely a trace of him had been found since. Amundsen knew he was not going to locate Franklin's remains. But perhaps he could complete his task, and find a way through the Northwest Passage. The apprentice was about to become the master. It was time to lead his first proper expedition.

With the backing of veteran Fridtjof Nansen, Norway's most famous explorer, Amundsen began looking for a ship. He had already completed his sea time and qualified as a captain, enabling him to lead in international waters. He also threw himself into studies on geomagnetism, so that he could give a scientific twist to his voyage; he was going to locate the exact position of the North Magnetic Pole. The British Observatory turned down his request to study there, but the Director of Deutsche Seewarte at Hamburg welcomed him. He spent three months in the city, managing his dwindling finances by hiring the cheapest room in the poorer part of the city. But he knew the effort would be worth it.

"My expedition must have a scientific purpose as well as the purpose of exploration. Otherwise I should not get backing," he admitted.

He decided on a small team in a small but sturdy boat. Using a substantial amount of his inheritance he purchased the *Gjøa*, a forty-seven-ton fishing smack, and took it out into the North Atlantic for six months, testing it under all conditions. He then had the hull reinforced with steel, and a small engine put in to supplement the sails.

Then he stocked the boat for a three-year voyage. When searching for equipment he tried his best to follow the lessons learned from previous explorers. One thing he did was to purchase native clothing, furs, and hides. The loose-fitting layers of the Lapps and Inuit were far more suited to the polar regions than the more restrictive clothing of modern society. Never a cultural elitist, Amundsen was not afraid to learn from primitive societies. In fact, he studied those societies with the zeal of an anthropologist.

It took two years to pull it all together. In the autumn of 1902 Amundsen finally got his sea papers, enabling him to captain a ship in international waters. The expedition now had a leader on sea and on land, and unlike earlier expeditions, it was the same leader. The Napoleon of the Polar Regions—a nickname he had earned on the *Belgica* expedition—was now in charge.

He picked a crew of six, offering good wages to keep morale high. Money was no object: he knew that if they were successful they would be returning as heroes, and the funds would flow. Meanwhile he was operating on credit, and scrambling to find sponsors as launch date loomed. His money had run dangerously low, and creditors were beginning to grumble. Amundsen was on the verge of bankruptcy.

When his suppliers got wind of his predicament there was no outpouring of support; instead there were demands for immediate payment of bills. Amundsen did his best to avoid his creditors, but it became increasingly difficult. Finally one man called in the bailiffs. The expedition was about to come to an inglorious end before the *Gjøa* even left port.

The spirit of the Viking surfaced in Amundsen.

"Despair almost overcame me at times because, in spite of everything, sufficient funds were not forthcoming. Some of the more impatient men from whom I had got supplies began pressing me for payment. Finally, on the morning of June 16, 1903, I was confronted with a supreme crisis. The most important of my creditors angrily demanded payment within twenty-four hours, with the threat that he would libel my vessel and cause my arrest for fraud. The ruin of my years of work seemed imminent.

"I grew desperate and I resolved upon a desperate expedient. I summoned my six carefully chosen companions, explained my predicament, and asked if they would cooperate with me in my strategy. They enthusiastically agreed. Therefore, at midnight on June 16, in the midst of a perfect deluge of rain, we seven conspirators made our way to the wharf where the *Gjøa* was tied, went aboard, cast off the hawsers, and turned southward toward the Skagger Rack and the North Sea.

"When dawn arose on our truculent creditor, we were safely out on the open main, seven as light-hearted pirates as ever flew the black flag, disappearing upon a quest that should take us three years and on which we were destined to succeed in an enterprise that had baffled our predecessors for four centuries. The great adventure for which my whole life had been a preparation was underway! The Northwest Passage—that baffling mystery to all the navigators of the past—was at last to be ours!"

Laden so heavily with supplies that the ship was almost submerged to the waterline, and with the decks crammed so high with cargo they looked more like a removal van than a boat, the *Gjøa* sailed to Greenland, making land on Disko Island, a small outpost to the west of the great landmass. There they took on even more supplies. The deck became almost impassable. If you could make your way over the boxes and crates, the snarling dogs would impede your progress. It was chaos, but the chaos of over-preparation rather than the chaos of the *Belgica*.

From Disko Island they headed out across Melville Bay, encountering their first enormous icebergs. These majestic cathedrals of ice awed the men, but Amundsen had a more mundane reaction to the north: "Perhaps as an Arctic traveler, I ought not to admit this, but anyhow, I did feel perishing with cold."

After two weeks they reached Dalrymple Rock, near Cape York, where supplies had been deposited for them by a whaler earlier in the season. They also encountered their first native Inuits, or Eskimo. After a chaotic but enjoyable meeting—a "joyous confusion"—the crew left behind the last vestiges of civilization and crossed Baffin Bay to Lancaster Sound, the eastern edge of the maze-like Arctic Archipelago. They were in Canadian waters now, and at the entrance to the Northwest Passage. The adventure was truly begun.

They stopped on Beechey Island—Franklin's last stand—and took observations, which confirmed that the Magnetic Pole lay on the east coast of Boothia Felix. Then they set off on the great quest and immediately had "three adventures—each one of which threatened to end our careers forever."

First they hit a rock in a deep sound that didn't hole them, but which threw the rudder temporarily out of kilter. Then there was a fire in the engine room, which thankfully was brought under control before the tanks of gasoline ignited. Finally a four-day gale threatened to dash the boat onto the rocky shore of one of the nearby islands.

Finally, by September 9, the adventures were in the past, but winter was setting in. It was time to find a safe spot for their winter quarters, where the boat could be safely encased in ice and not crushed, and the men could hunt game. They had survived a baptism of fire, and knew that the ship, the crew, and the command structure was going to hold. They faced their first winter with optimism. Finding a land-locked bay on the south coast of King William Island, they set up their hut on shore. Many of their crates of supplies were broken up to supply the wood. They also made an observatory for their scientific justification, the magnetic measurements, and kennels for the dogs.

Dogs would pull their sleighs in the snow, providing transport. This was a sharp contrast to the traditional British approach, then still commonplace among polar explorers. Franklin and his men had marched, pulling their supplies. It was the British way—stoic effort and self-reliance. Amundsen was determined to go native, replacing man hauling and forced marches with dog sleighs and skis. He was quite pragmatic. The dogs were tools; when their usefulness was past, he would have no hesitation in killing them and using them as food. In the meanwhile, though, they served another very important purpose. They provided great amusement to the men, who became very attached to the animals. While they were never pets in the modern sense of the word, the presence of the frisky animals on the ice broke up the monotony and made the winter more bearable.

The plan was to stay there for nearly two years, making the magnetic observations that were the scientific justification of the trip. So any distraction would be welcome.

Hunting caribou was a great distraction, as well as stocking the larder. One morning Amundsen and two crew members were on board the *Gjøa* when Amundsen spotted a caribou in the distance. One of his companions, with better eyesight, remarked: "That caribou walks on two legs."

It was an Eskimo, and soon he was joined by others, making their way toward the ship and the settlement. There were five in all, armed with bows and arrows.

"I sent the two boys for their rifles, and then the three of us advanced to meet them," Amundsen wrote.

"I was in the lead and behind me came my little army of two. As the Eskimos neared us we could see they were all armed with bows and arrows. This began to look like a ticklish situation.

"There was nothing to do but meet them face to face. The two parties proceeded to within about fifteen paces and then halted. I turned to my 'army' and instructed them ostentatiously to throw their rifles on the ground. I then turned to the Eskimos. Their leader, seeing this pacific move, imitated it by turning to his followers and uttering a command. They obeyed by throwing their bows and arrows on the ground. I was unarmed and advanced toward them. The Eskimo leader also came out alone.

"It is remarkable how accurately two men can communicate who do not speak a word of a common language, and whose whole experience of life seems utterly separated from each other's."

Many of the great explorers had the instincts of a scientist. Captain Robert Scott, the English man later beaten to the South Pole by Amundsen, was most comfortable in the company of scientists, and tended to socialize with them on expeditions. He was mathematically gifted, and made many useful contributions to the scientific work on his journeys. Had life not pushed him into the Navy, he might well have pursued science. Amundsen was far less gifted academically than Scott, but they shared a scientific curiosity about the world. The difference was that Amundsen's interests tended toward anthropology. He was an instinctive and thorough anthropologist. So the appearance of the Eskimo group filled him with delight.

"I quickly convinced the Eskimo leader that I wished to be his friend, and he reciprocated my wish. Soon we were all friendly and I invited them down to our ship."

That first encounter was filled with thrill and excitement. The Eskimo had never seen white people before, but their ancestors had passed on tales of encounters with British explorers seeking the fabled Northwest Passage. Now the Eskimo were seeing mythical men they had half suspected their ancestors had made up. They marveled at the simplest thing; even a tin was a wonder to them.

But they, and their accoutrements, were an equal wonder to Amundsen, and soon a lively bartering trade sprang up. Trade increased when the Eskimo group asked permission for the rest of their tribe to camp near the white settlement. Soon the hut and outhouses of the *Gjøa* crew were joined by nearly fifty Eskimo huts. Amundsen was in his element.

"This was an opportunity to delight the soul of an anthropologist and ethnographer," he noted.

He built up an impressive collection of native artifacts—including clothing, jewelry, and equipment—which he brought home to Norway at the end of the trip. He also took the opportunity to study the language and customs of his new neighbors. The Eskimo also benefited from the contact, acquiring knives and metal implements which would ease their lives.

"During the two years that we remained at this camp, the Eskimo got from us everything we had that was of use to them, and we, in turn, got our complete collection of their products. It was a perfect example of a good bargain, in which both sides profited."

The only slight cause for concern was that the seven men of the *Gjøa* were severely outnumbered by the more than two hundred Eskimo visitors. Amundsen knew the situation had to be played carefully. Because of their mythology, and the metal tools they saw the white men had, the Eskimo were unlikely to turn hostile. Fear, and respect generated by their stories, would hold them back. But if they did turn, then a display of western arrogance and superiority might keep them in their place. But there was one thing that could destabilize the entire situation.

"The moment the white man yields to his baser passions and takes liberties with the savages' women, he falls in their eyes to the level of mere man, and puts himself at their mercy. I therefore took the first opportunity to have a most serious talk with my companions and urge them not to yield to this kind of temptation," Amundsen recalled.

The message was simple: keep it in your trousers. In his autobiography, *My Life as an Explorer*, Amundsen fails to mention whether his warning was heeded or not. As he didn't mention the outcome, it is fair to assume that his pleas fell on deaf ears. The crew had been at sea for months. They would be in their isolated outpost another two years. And there would be no one—aside from their stern young leader— to see if they strayed. So stray they did.

The Eskimo women were not unattractive, especially after several months away from home. Their attitude toward sex was different from the staid conservatism of Victorian Europe. They were not promiscuous, but there was a tradition among the tribal culture of "loaning" a wife out to honored guests. And the women might have seen the visit of these tall, striking, and intelligent, technologically advanced visitors as a chance of improving the blood stock of the tribe. In addition, Amundsen's men were sailors, used to having a girl in every port—generally a girl they paid for. So some sexual contact was inevitable.

Amundsen could see the attraction, saying of the Eskimo women that: "Some of these women are absolute beauties. They are rather small but shapely." However he had seen the open sores of syphilis on one sick boy, so his exhortation to the crew was not just based on morality, or on the idea of keeping aloof. He also wanted to keep his men healthy.

In public the men did not discuss what went on during those lonely two years. However, there is a lively tradition among the people of Gjoa Haven, the small town that now exists in the spot where Amundsen made his base, which claims the tribe includes descendants of Amundsen's men. Indeed, some of the people claim to be actual descendants of the leader himself. Though DNA testing has disproved this claim, it is possible that some of his men fathered babies during their two years in the bay.

Amundsen himself, it seems, confined his interest in the Eskimo to anthropology. He studied the locals extensively, finding out as much as he could about every aspect of their lives. He was particularly interested in the practicalities of surviving in the harsh environment, and living off the land. These would be skills he would need if he was to make a major mark on polar exploration. He studied their hunting techniques, their clothing, their ways of building shelter, and their ways of traveling. But he was also interested in them in a wider sense, making notes on their language, customs, and even their spirituality. He found them a complex people, and unlike many westerners he did not look down on them. He treated them as his equals, and is fondly remembered in the locality.

His notes on the Eskimo eventually became the most important legacy of his trip. But before he had set out he knew he had to cloak the enterprise with a scientific motive if he expected to attract funding. So he used the two years in Gjoa Haven to make extensive magnetic measurements, fixing definitely the position of the Magnetic North Pole.

In 1831 Captain James Ross had located the Pole at Cape Adelaide on the Boothia Peninsula. Amundsen's measurements also put the Pole on the Boothia Peninsula, but many miles from Cape Adelaide. This provided evidence, since confirmed, that the pole moves due to shifts in the core of the Earth. It is shifting gradually toward Russia from the Canadian Arctic, at the rate of more than thirty miles a year. Going out on long treks to take the magnetic measurements broke up the monotony of the two years on King William Island. So did the hunting expeditions. Both had a secondary purpose; they trained the men, and their leader, in the skills of polar travel. In fact, Amundsen was so keen on improving, he had a hill and a snow slope constructed near their base for ski practice.

But by the summer of 1905 the scientific purpose of the expedition had been well and truly achieved. The measurements had been taken— it would take another two decades for scientists to finish analyzing all the data brought home. Amundsen had collected enough cultural arti- facts for a full museum. It was time to set sail and finish the Northwest Passage. On August 13 Amundsen bid farewell to his Eskimo neighbors and left. It was late in the season, but he was confident they had enough time to reach the Pacific Ocean before the winter freeze set in.

"We set sail through Simpson Strait. Much of this coast had been mapped by earlier explorers who had traveled to it by land from Hudson Bay, but no vessel had ever heretofore troubled these waters or charted their shallows. If they had, we should have had an easier time of it!" he wrote.

It took three weeks to creep through the strait. The *Gjøa* had to inch along, never building up speed because there was never enough depth for a good run.

"But time and again it seemed certain we should be defeated by the shallowness of these tortuous channels. Day after day for three weeks— the longest three weeks of my life—we crept along, sounding our depth with the lead, trying here, there, and everywhere to nose into a channel that would carry us clear through to the known waters to the west. Once we had just an inch of water to spare beneath our keel!"

Amundsen stopped eating. He was too tense. But finally they broke free of the network of narrow channels around the Arctic Archipelago. They spotted a sail in the distance—a whaling vessel that had come up from the west coast of America. They were the first vessel to suc- cessfully navigate the Northwest Passage. The Napoleon of the Polar Regions had won his first campaign.

He celebrated by hacking into the carcass of a caribou and enjoying his first full meal in weeks. He promptly threw up, "feeding the fishes," as he put it. Then he went back for more raw meat, but this time he held it down.

"Soon I was restored to a sense of calm well-being such as I had not known in the three terrible weeks just passed. Those weeks had left their mark upon me in such a way that my age was guessed to be between fifty-nine and seventy-five years, although I was only thirty-three!"

It was August 26, 1905, and the objective had been achieved. But every mountaineer knows that getting to the top is only half the job; you have to get back down safely as well. Amundsen still had to bring the *Gjøa* around the north of Alaska and down the west coast of America to a safe haven. There was plenty more sailing left.

"Little did we imagine that it would take us another year to negotiate this perfectly simple concluding portion of the trip. The ice grew thicker and thicker as we slowly advanced, so that within a week, on September 2, we came to a dead stop of King Point on the north coast of Canada."

Reluctantly the crew selected a sheltered spot behind a grounded ice floe near King Point in the Yukon, and tied up for the long winter ahead. It was not as comfortable as Gjoa Haven, but at least it was safe. They were used to living off the land, and were in no serious danger. In fact, they even had neighbors once more. This time the neighbors were white; a few whaling ships had been iced in between them and Herschel Island, a number of miles away. Their new neighbors were not as friendly as the Eskimo. They saw the small *Gjøa* as a problem. The Norwegians would not be able to fend for themselves over a long winter, because they could not have sufficient provisions on such a small boat. And the whalers were reluctant to share their meager resources.

In the end it was the other way around; Amundsen ended up having to send two metric tons of flour to the starving whalers. They never asked for anything in return, being well able to live off the land.

But Amundsen realized quickly he had one major problem. Funding of his trip had been difficult to organize, and he was sailing home to huge debts. He would have to recoup those debts. One way was to sell the story of the voyage. But to do that he had to get the news out first. Journalism is a fickle business. The man who brought the story out first was the man who would get paid. Amundsen would have slim pickings if word leaked.

In October he heard rumours that one of the whaling captains was planning on hiking south toward civilization with some native Inuit to help him. They were heading toward Eagle City, about five hundred miles south. There was a telegraph station there. The danger was obvious. Amundsen decided he had to join the trip.

So he and Captain William Mogg took one sled, with five dogs, while two Inuit, husband and wife Jimmy and Kappa, took the second sled with seven dogs. Captain Mogg assumed control. A short, fat man of limited fitness, he chose a Western diet with plenty of beans and other non-essentials. Amundsen urged him to consider pemmican, the meat and fat mix that most polar explorers relied upon. It was dense, full of calories, and ideal for the conditions. But it tasted horrible and Mogg would have none of it. Knowing he was facing an arduous journey ill-equipped, Amundsen gritted his teeth and fell in behind the sled.

"I had no fears of the journey itself, but I had considerable apprehensions of making it with Captain Mogg of the *Bonanza*. First of all he had the money and I had none, so he would be in command of our little party. I was sure that he was far less competent for this kind of an expedition than I. In the second place, Captain Mogg was short and fat, so that there was no possibility that he could run with the sledges; but rather the certainty that he would have to ride on one of them and be dragged by one dog team.

"Our course ran up Herschel Island River, over the mountain summit of nine thousand feet elevation, and down the southern slopes to the Yukon River, where we encountered the first trading post at Fort Yukon. Jim ran ahead of one team to break the snow, and I ahead of the other. Physically I was not very hard when we started, but in a few days I got my second wind, and we readily made twenty-five to thirty miles a day through the heavy snow. This was not so bad, but the scantiness of the food at night told heavily on all of us but Captain Mogg. He did no work during the day, as he simply sat on one of the sleds. To the other three of us, however, our little ration of cooked beans was wholly inadequate to replace the drain on our muscles from the exertions of the day."

At Fort Yukon the Inuit couple left, leaving Mogg and Amundsen alone for the final leg of the journey. Now they were closer to civilization, but tensions were running high. There were regular roadhouses situated half a day apart, to facilitate travelers. But Mogg was so insistent on speed he was not willing to stop at these roadhouses for lunch, leaving his hungry companion running on empty.

"I protested strongly against this scheme, reminding him of the difference in the exertions which he and I were making and of my greater need for food. The Captain angrily dismissed my protest and pointed out that, as he was the commander of the expedition and, what was more important, had all the money, his orders would prevail. I said nothing but, like the Irishman's parrot, 'I kept up a devil of a thinking.'"

Amundsen solved the problem in a very practical way; an hour before the next lunch stop he bid goodbye to Captain Mogg and told him he was on his own from now on. Amundsen would head back to where they had stayed the previous night, and Mogg, who owned all the provisions, was welcome to proceed on his own.

"The Captain was dumbfounded and was also frightened almost to death."

The issue was swiftly resolved: Amundsen would get his three meals a day. On December 5 they arrived in Fort Egbert, with the mercury dropping to minus sixty. It was a US army post with a telegraph. He typed a thousand-word account of his three years. Cheekily he sent it collect to Nansen. The elder statesman of Norwegian exploration paid the cost—which ran to the equivalent of more than a thousand dollars in today's money. Amundsen knew he could repay his mentor when he returned in glory. He also sent a message to his brother, who was handling his business affairs. Word was out—the Northwest Passage had been conquered. Norway had a new hero, and Amundsen had made his first significant mark on the world of exploration.

He returned to the *Gjøa*—an easier trip without Mogg. One of his men had succumbed to illness—probably a burst appendix. Aside from that, the rest of the trip went smoothly.

"The ice broke up in July, and without much difficulty we made our way to Point Barrow. Thence we passed through Bering Strait and on down the coast to San Francisco, which we reached in October."

On August 30, as they cleared the Bering Strait—the official end of the Northwest Passage—the men raised a simple glass to toast the occasion. With the conditions, it was all they had time for: "A flag up the mast was out of the question. It was with great joy that we drained our cup. Whatever we might now encounter, we had carried the Norwegian flag through the Northwest Passage on one boat."

Now Amundsen faced two years of public lectures and speaking engagements across Europe and the United States. The proceeds cleared his debts, leaving him free to plan his next trip. He was finally ready to tackle the big one—the North Pole.

19

PEARY'S PENULTIMATE EXPEDITION, 1904–1906

As Amundsen was fundraising for his next trip, and as Cook was turning his attention to climbing, Peary still obsessed over the Pole. But he seemed no nearer his goal than when he returned from his first surveying trip to Nicaragua. All his trips north had ended in failure, and he was a weaker and broken man. How much of the damage could be repaired was his biggest concern. He could worry about rivals later.

The first thing he needed to do was to sort out his feet, or what was left of them. As he looked at the bloodied stumps where his toes had been, he had to acknowledge that Cook might be right; this could be a game-ending injury for a polar explorer. But Peary was a wealthy man, and if money could buy a cure, he was willing to pay. The first step was to get the best doctor in the country. Dr. William Keen of Philadelphia had been good enough to remove a cancerous tumor from President Grover Cleveland, and had performed the first brain tumor operation in the USA.

The doctor was shocked when he saw the condition of Peary's feet. Only two toes remained, the little toe of each foot. And both were frostbitten and damaged. The doctor was limited in his options. He chose to cut off both toes, then he slit the skin at the ball of Peary's foot, and stretched the flap up and over, stitching it to the top of the foot. It provided some sort of a cushion for the tip of Peary's foot, but the explorer would never run for a bus on the stumps. For the rest of his life he was confined to an awkward shuffle. He was able to keep a march up all day with relatively little pain, but he would never again match the pace of younger companions. For the rest of his career as an explorer he would be the slow old man holding the team back—unless he swallowed his pride and took a ride on a sledge.

His leave was finally up—five years with nothing to show for it but the loss of five toes on each foot. He was not a returning hero, just a stranger taking up his official duties in Washington among younger men who had devoted their years to their careers. However, he had seniority, and he passed two promotional examinations, earning him the rank of commander in the Engineers' Corps. In November 1902 he was assigned to the Bureau of Yards and Docks at the Navy Department. He was riding a desk.

As his feet continued to improve, and his weight and strength returned, he found the confines of the job beginning to chafe. He yearned for the open tundra, the ice fields, and the polar seas. There was still a spot on the globe that needed to be adorned with the American flag, and he was damned if he was going to let a Norwegian or—worse—a different American plant that emblem. He began to work his political and industrial contacts and found a strange reluctance on their part to back him. Five years had been a long time to be away. He was yesterday's man. It took all his diplomatic skills to revive any interest in his ambitions. He had to bully and cajole in equal measure, but slowly he began to make progress.

All he required was a new ship, capable of enduring the rigors of the polar ice; top of the range equipment; and money, money, money. He planned on throwing himself into the venture for two years (no more five years in the wilderness) and crowning all past efforts with success. The key thing was the ship. With the right boat he could force his way through the narrow channel between Greenland and Ellesmere Island, deep into the polar sea. If he could break the ice to a higher latitude than any ship before him, it would shorten his dash across the ice to the Pole.

Nansen had built the *Fram* to survive being embedded in the ice, so that it could drift safely for months. Peary wanted to create a heavier ship, with a reinforced prow, and powerful engines. His plan was to smash through the ice, creating artificial leads. But to build such a ship would cost an enormous amount of money. Peary marshalled his supporters, and formalized the unofficial Peary Arctic Club. In April 1904 he incorporated the body, giving it a legal standing, and a charter to "aid and assist" his explorations. Soon the roster of members included some of the leading industrialists of the time. Company presidents and CEOs all clambered to be involved.

But before they could even think of ordering a new ship, or refitting an existing one, the Club had one important task—to alter the public opinion of polar exploration. Fed up by too many failed attempts, America was moving on. It took several months of carefully placed newspaper and magazine articles—several members of the Arctic Club worked in the media—to switch the perception, but at the end of the process America once again believed that their nation should plant Old Glory on top of the world, and Peary should be the man to carry it there.

Even Theodore Roosevelt, the president, backed the campaign. An outdoors man himself, Roosevelt saw Peary as the sort of hero he wanted America to look up to. When he asked that Peary be granted yet more paid leave—three years this time—the bureaucrats had to back down and do as they were told. But they made it clear that this was not to be another ramble around Northern Greenland.

"The attainment of the Pole should be your main objective. Nothing short will suffice," Assistant Secretary of the Navy Charles Darling wrote to Peary.

With the public now behind the trip and Peary's leave secured, the club had to come up with $100,000 for the ship. Morris Jessup gave a quarter of the sum outright to begin the fundraising, and James Colgate gave a generous donation.

Things were looking up for Peary—but he was painfully aware of the rivals snapping at his heels. In September 1904 the Eighth International Geographic Congress was held in New York. The two day event was attended by leading academics in the field from all over the world.

Peary sat in the audience, shaking hands with old acquaintances, and doing his best to revive interest in his plans. But Frederick Cook was on the stage, where he delivered three major papers. One was on the circumnavigation of McKinley, the second was on the *Belgica* expedition, while the third delineated the differences between the Arctic and the Antarctic. Not only was Cook the star, he was the first American, and one of the few in the world, to have explored in both polar regions. For once Peary was in the shadow, watching his once protégé accepting the applause and ovations.

Outwardly the two men remained cordial. Peary had written to Cook the previous winter: "I congratulate you on the work which you did on Mount McKinley, and am sincerely sorry that you did not attain the tip top." But it galled him that he was now seen as the minor player. In a desperate attempt to snatch the attention of the world back on himself, Peary used the occasion of the Geographic Congress to announce his plans for one more push north. Speaking after a dinner at which he had been given an award by the Paris Geographical Society, he declared: "Next summer I shall start north again. Shall I win? God knows. I hope and dream and pray that I may."

By October the keel of the new ship was ready and they were ready to construct the superstructure. By the following spring the shipyard in Bucksport had finished the job. Contributions continued to flow in from the Arctic Club, and the coffers of the explorer, for once, were full. Always a man with an eye to pleasing a patron, Peary christened the ship the *Roosevelt*. She was launched in March 1905 before a cheering crowd. Like the *Fram*, the *Roosevelt* was designed to pop like a cork above the pressure of the ice, riding high and out of danger. Her hull was reinforced with struts, and covered outside with thick steel. In places the hull of the ship was almost three feet thick. She was narrow and stubby for easy maneuverability, and fitted with strong engines and detachable rudder and propellers. This was a battering ram of a ship, the world's first true ice-breaker.

The expedition left New York on July 16, sailing down the Hudson toward the Atlantic. On board were Josephine Peary, their daughter Marie, and their toddler son Robert Junior, as well as several members of the Arctic Club. They enjoyed the mad excitement of the day, as sailing clubs up the coast lined up to give them a guard of honor, and cannon roared from the shore. Finally a tug removed the passengers, Peary waved a fond farewell to his family, and the trip was on in earnest. It took two months to reach Cape Sheridan, on the north coast of Ellesmere Island. The ship had performed magnificently, smashing through the summer ice and breaking the flows to create new leads. The result was that Peary found himself three hundred miles farther north than he had ever been at the start of an expedition. He was just 450 miles from the Pole, and only sixty miles shy of his furthest ever North. It was a dream start.

Of course, there was a lot of work to be done before he could cross that trifling (to his boundlessly optimistic mind) distance. First, they had to survive the harsh winter, a winter that would be even harsher for being so much farther north than other explorers had camped. Peary was following his usual plan of using the local Eskimo population, sending them out on the ice to hunt game so they would have a plentiful larder for the long winter night. Musk oxen, caribou, and hare were stock-piled. This year there was no need to build a lodge, or wait for the return of a boat the following season. *Roosevelt* was iced in, and provided very comfortable quarters for the winter party. Peary had even thought to bring along a primitive record player, and two hundred cylinders of music, as well as a good library.

Come spring, Peary was going to try a new approach to reach the Pole. Previously he had relied on a small party traveling light and fast. It had failed him miserably. Now he was trusting to a major logistical operation, with thirty men and over a hundred dogs. Depots would be established, with teams relaying food and fuel up the line to support the final party. He was sure this was what had been lacking in his previous efforts; a chain of support. His background in engineering made him an ideal man to control such a complex operation, which he christened "the Peary system."

The system was not new or unique, as he well knew. Previous expeditions had pioneered it, including that led by Irish explorer Francis McClintock fifty years earlier, in search of the missing Franklin expedition in the Northwest Passage. McClintock used man-hauling instead of dogs, but aside from that his well-established system of depots was the full Peary system. Once again, the American was showing scant regard for those who came before him, as when he had tried to rename lands discovered in the previous expedition by Otto Sverdrup.

Spring comes late at the high latitudes, but by February there were a few hours of dim light in the middle of the day. Temperatures were still very low, but the first parties went out that month, laying depots. Within twenty miles they were free of the archipelago of islands north of Ellesmere, and were on the frozen polar sea. The plan called for depots every fifty miles. Peary was optimistic, but not unrealistic, in his planning. He believed he could achieve ten miles a day, and at that rate he would reach the Pole and return safely in a little over three months. That left plenty of margin for error. On March 2 Peary set out, a few weeks behind the advance parties, which included his faithful servant and companion Matthew Henson.

"The battle is on at last," he noted exuberantly in his diary that day, before breaking camp and marching resolutely onto the polar sea.

If you regarded the race for the Pole as a track event, Peary's plan was a team relay rather than a straight race. Once the main party caught up with the advance party, the group split into a number of smaller groups. Each group was led by an American, and consisted of a team of dogs and Eskimo. Despite his long years of service and his undoubted ability in the cold, Henson was not considered for the role. To the end, Peary retained an attitude that only whites had the brains, character, and education needed for leadership.

One party would race ahead with supplies, set up a depot, then drop back while another took the lead. The advance party would not break camp at night; instead they left everything in place so that the followers did not have to bother putting up new tents. This made for faster progress, and at the end Peary would race past the depots and dash to the Pole. For his return, he had a fully stocked chain of supplies, making the plan safe and apparently foolproof. That is exactly how it panned out for the first few weeks. But on March 25 the Arctic let them know they were facing elements far more dangerous and challenging than the puny efforts of man could surmount.

That day, somewhere between 84 and 85 degrees north, they came across a wide stretch of open water. Leads—channels in the water—are common in the polar ice. Most of them close and freeze over after a few days. They are generally short enough to walk around if they show no signs of closing by themselves. But the Big Lead they encountered that day was something different. It was longer and wider than any they had encountered before, a break of dark water in the endless whiteness of the ice. It stretched away to both horizons, showing no sign of a crossing point. The advance party reached the lead, and came to a sudden stop. They were perched on a floating crust of ice, only a few feet thick, with four thousand feet of frigid water beneath them. And there was no way forward, because the thin crust of ice had broken ahead of them.

A few hours later the second advance party came to a halt at the same point. Throughout that afternoon all the advance parties arrived at the same spot, stopped their dogs, laid down their loads, and scratched their heads. There was no way forward. Late that evening the main party, with Peary, arrived to find a far bigger camp than they were expecting, and far less forward progress than they had been making for the past several days. It was a potential disaster.

The Big Lead had been observed before, by other explorers. And it would be seen again, both by Peary on his next trip, and by Frederick Cook. It was not a temporary break in the ice caused by the movement of the sea cracking the thin crust; it was a fairly permanent feature, caused by the topography of the sea floor several thousand feet below them. The Big Lead roughly marked the spot where the continental shelf fell in a steep cliff to the floor of the polar sea.

The group could do nothing. Either the lead would close, or the expedition was doomed. They made the best of it, about thirty men, a hundred dogs, and tons of supplies camped on a few feet of ice at the edge of a terrifying plunge into the sea. After a week that seemed to pass like a month, new ice formed over the gap. Once it was solid enough to risk, the groups loaded the sledges and dashed across to the thicker ice on the other side. The race for the Pole was back on.

But a few days later a gale blew up, stopping the group for six days. Their latitude was barely above 85 degrees, and Peary took an observation that showed the pack ice had drifted about seventy miles to the east. This was not proving to be the straightforward romp he had hoped for. But at least they knew where they were, and they knew the speed of the drift. The supply chain was unbroken. Peary sent Henson ahead with supplies for another depot, while he sent two Eskimo south to pick up supplies and ferry them up the line. Within a day the Eskimo returned with bad news: there were a number of big leads to the south, cutting them off from the supplies. The Peary System, after just a month, had collapsed.

This was a major problem. To supply the more northerly caches, supplies had to be relayed from the caches down the line. But cut off from these, with empty sledges and dwindling supplies, Peary was unable to establish the essential northern caches. Despondent, the group came together and marched north as a single party, slowly negotiating through the increasing number of leads they were coming across. At noon on April 12 Peary used a sextant to determine their position. A major flaw of Peary's planning was that he was the only member of the party capable of taking the complex reading. Henson, despite spending several years at sea, was not a navigator, and the Eskimo did not even know what the instruments were. They navigated by landmarks, and were in a featureless desolation of broken ice. So Peary's observations that day are backed up by no one, and the only evidence of their accuracy is his integrity.

The observation had to be taken at noon. The angular height of the sun was measured, then a series of calculations were done which gave latitude. Depending on the environmental conditions, the quality of the sextant, and the steadiness of the man using it, that reading could be off by several miles, but no more. It was reasonably accurate rather than pinpoint accurate. If the sun was obscured by clouds—often the case in the polar sea—the observation could not be taken.

The forenoon on April 20 was clear, and Peary was able to take his measurement. He then sat on a sledge with his pencil and did the necessary calculations. When he looked up he was smiling. He told everyone that they had reached latitude of 86 degrees 6 minutes. The Eskimo looked at him blankly. It meant nothing to them. Henson knew what it meant though; they had broken the record for the farthest North, held by Italian Umberto Cagni. Only by thirty miles, but the record now belonged to Peary.

"We had at last beaten the record, for which I thanked God," he noted in his journal.

It must be noted that Peary kept no record of his sextant measurement that day—and his journal reveals nothing of the three days' march leading up to that observation. No mileages, no other collaboration. He had noted in earlier days the tiredness of the men and dogs, and the rough and broken conditions they had encountered, making progress very slow. His previous sextant observation, taken about three days previously, showed the group ninety miles south of his claimed farthest north. If we are to accept that Peary did achieve a Farthest North that afternoon, we must accept that he covered ninety miles in three days, with a tired team, exhausted supplies, and a morass of leads and broken ice impeding his progress.

Other explorers in similar conditions—such as Nansen—tended to average well under ten miles a day. Could Peary really have achieved more than three times their speed? It seems unlikely, verging on the impossible. Peary produced no evidence to back up his claim, and no collaboration of his measurements. When he returned to civilization, he did not turn his diaries and journals over to respected geographers for analysis. He expected to be taken at his word. Decades after his death, when his papers were finally allowed to be examined, they were found to contain nothing new.

We must conclude that Peary fell far short of his claimed Farthest North. As he was an experienced navigator and surveyor, and as he deliberately kept only a sketchy record of his final few days, we must also conclude that he knew this well, and that it was a deliberate fraud.

The South Pole is located on the Antarctic continent. If you claim to have reached a spot, and you mark that spot, future expeditions can verify that you were there. When Robert Scott reached the South Pole in 1911, he found the tent left by Roald Amundsen. But the North Pole and the area around it are located on the permanently frozen polar sea. Marking a spot with a tent and a flag will not work. The drift of the ice will take your mark miles away within days. Peary knew no future generation could collaborate his claim. The corollary of that was: no one could contradict it. He was safe in his deception.

Wearily, he turned his back on the north and began the difficult march back to his base at the *Roosevelt*. He returned to New York to a hero's welcome.

20

COOK RETURNS TO MCKINLEY

Cook's first attempt at mountaineering was a bit like Peary's early Greenland trips. He had fallen short of his objective, but at least he had come back with something. He had circumnavigated Mount McKinley, and discovered a deep valley that ran through the massif, splitting it east to west. Some honor was salvaged. But he did not have the luxury of a second failure. A mountain is a lot smaller than the Arctic, and there were no secondary objectives left. It was either summit or fail.

For his second attempt three years later, Cook decided to become a travel agent again. Professor Herschel Parker, a physicist from Columbia University, paid $2,000 to be in the party, while the son of a rich industrialist, Henry Disston, agreed to throw in $10,000 as long as Cook arranged for a few weeks of big game hunting in the fall, after the summit attempt. Marie once again enthusiastically got behind her husband's strange obsession—but this time she decided to back him from a distance. They had just had a baby, and she opted to remain at home while he traveled. By May 1, 1906, he was back in Seattle, ready to head north. On May 29 the party of explorers reached Tyonek. They were a few weeks ahead of the last time, and this time they were in familiar territory.

Cook split the party in two, sending a team of pack horses loaded with provisions overland, while he took some of the men by boat. This time it was easier; he had got a power launch with a shallow draught which suited the conditions well. At the rendezvous both parties rejoined, and hiked into the mountain. Although it was easier second time around, it was still brutally tough. By the time they got to eighteen miles from McKinley, Professor Parker was ready to quit. He had proven inadequate for the conditions, being used to a more civilized type of existence. He was so exhausted he needed to be hoisted up onto his horse at the start of each day. He didn't have the strength left to do it himself. The constant rain was getting him down; he declared that the conquest of McKinley was a marine affair, not a matter of mountaineering. But as there was no way of getting back to civilization on his own, he had to remain with the group, his moaning presence a constant reminder that exploration was never easy.

As they approached the mountain the land got increasingly rugged, with high ridges and fast-flowing glacial streams. It soon became obvious that they could not scale the mountain from the direction they were traveling, so Cook ordered everyone to begin skirting the massif toward the coast, hoping to find an easier approach. On August 1, Cook arrived in Susitna Station, a small prospecting outpost. Here he encountered near tragedy. A group of prospectors had tried to run the rapids on one of the glacial streams, and been tossed from their boat, which had been smashed to pieces. The men had been forced to stand on a partially submerged rock for four days, unable to cross the raging torrent. When they were rescued they were in very poor condition, after their legs had been exposed to freezing water for days on end. Despite his own exhaustion, Cook spent most of that day tending the ill, and not resting until he was satisfied they were out of danger.

Miner J. A. MacDonald later wrote: "Although tired and worn and in bad physical condition himself . . . he spent hours working over these men, and did not give himself a thought until they were properly cared for."

The expedition slogged on through the month of August, not achieving much by way of penetrating the towering peaks. The party split, as various groups went off on exploring forays, or hunting.

Roald Amundsen with pilot Oskar Omdahl in Alaska in 1922 during preparation for their first failed polar flight.

Matthew Henson, the first colored polar explorer, who accompanied Peary on all his major expeditions, including the controversial polar trip in 1909.

Robert Peary in the furs he got from the Eskimos of Greenland, looking haggard on his return from his final polar expedition in 1909.

Richard Byrd checking out one of the early planes he learned his craft on.

Robert Peary with Captain Robert Bartlett onboard the *Roosevelt* on their way to Greenland for his final expedition. This picture was taken at Battle Harbour, Labrador, Canada.

Amundsen's great rival Captain Robert Scott and his four companions reach the South Pole—only to discover the Norwegian flag there ahead of them.

Frederick Cook with one of his Eskimo companions outside an igloo they built on the frozen polar sea in 1909, allegedly at the North Pole.

Roald Amundsen, Viking turned aviator. Taken in Svalbard in 1925.

Roald Amundsen missed out on the North Pole, so he turned south, and beat
Captain Scott to the South Pole, where they set up temporary camp.

The Napoleon of the North, Roald Amundsen.

Frederick Cook (left) and Roald Amundsen on their first Antarctic expedition, with the *Belgica*, in 1898.

Cutting a Canal to Release the Belgica

Cook and Amundsen toil with their shipmates to cut a canal to free the *Belgica* in 1899. They were trapped for the winter in the frozen Bellinghausen Sea.

Robert Peary knew the importance of furs. Different items of clothing were made from the furs of different animals to ensure optimum warmth. This picture was taken in 1909, before setting out on his final expedition.

Richard Byrd and Floyd Bennett in their Fokker F-VII setting out for the Pole from Spitzbergen in 1926.

Josephine Peary Diebitsch in Greenland with her husband during an early expedition in 1892.

Frederick Cook looking dapper in 1917, as he tried to put controversy behind him and reinvent himself as an oil tycoon.

Roald Amundsen as the distinguished elder statesman of exploration.

Richard Byrd, the handsom and dashing hero of the jazz age.

Roald Amundsen at the wheel of the *Maud* in 1920.

A rare encounter—Robert Peary (left) and Roald Amundsen
meet at a dinner in 1913.

Robert Peary in his full Naval regalia as Rear Admiral, taken in 1911.

The pole at last. Umberto Nobile looking out the window of the airship *Norge* at the frozen wastes of the Arctic Ocean during the first verifiable attainment of the North Pole, in May 1926.

The faked summit shot Cook claimed proved he had been to the summit of Mount McKinley in 1906.

Professor Parker found a steamer heading downriver, and abandoned the quest entirely. By the end of August they looked to be further away from their objective than they had been three years previously. Like Peary on his Third Greenland Expedition, this was proving a disastrous waste of everyone's time. By the end of the month Cook had decided to use the boat to explore the southern approaches to the mountain, in the hopes of finding a route to the top for the following season. He was close to quitting this season, and knew he had to have everyone ready for home by early October. Time was running out.

Taking Edward Barrill and John Dokkin as his companions, he set off up a river that led to a glacier coming off the massif, which he had named Ruth (in honor of his stepdaughter) on his last expedition. They reached the glacier and began to climb; the route had proved a dead end the previous year, but Cook wanted another look. After a day of climbing Dokkin turned back, but Cook and Barrill continued. Barrill, a black-smith from Hamill, Montana, was a giant of a man who towered inches over everyone, including the tall Cook. Simple and uneducated, he was a tower of strength, but of no use when it came to the practicalities of navigating or taking altitude readings. There were no other witnesses to the events of the next few weeks, once Dokkin turned back.

According to Cook, the two men made great progress after Dokkin left them, and decided to try to get to the top of a twelve-thousand-foot ridge, where they might be able to find a suitable route for the follow-ing year. At that stage it was a purely reconnoitering foray—they had no thoughts of making the summit. But once they got to the top of the ridge, there was a break in the weather, and they decided to push on for as long as they could. The ridge was not the knife-edge they expected, but had a flat top that could be traversed.

From the ridge they struggled up the steep slope of ice, rock, and snow for two days, camping at a height of 14,200 feet. They had been lucky so far, finding paths and nooks that led them to that spot. But it was desolate. They could not find a level spot for a camp that night, so they spent the long hours of darkness sitting side by side on a narrow step they had hacked out of the ice with their axes. The following morn-ing they were too cold and miserable to cook a breakfast, so they set out early. It was a long morning of hacking steps in the slope and using them like the rungs of a ladder. But after several hours of toil they found a flat area where they could make camp and rest.

The following day they resumed the step-cutting. They were aiming for a ridge that connected the two peaks of the mountain. By nightfall they had made the ridge, establishing a camp at the height of eighteen thousand feet. At that altitude the thinness of the air is a serious problem. Breathing can become labored with only the slightest exertion, and food takes longer to boil for the evenings. As a non-smoker, Cook possessed an advantage over many of the climbers of his day, but even for him this was an ordeal. The temperature was eighteen below zero. That was cold, but there was a gale blowing. Factoring in wind chill, Cook reckoned they endured the equivalent of seventy below that night. Even for a seasoned Arctic explorer, that was cold. Neither man slept. The chattering of their teeth and the constant avalanches were noise enough to drive sleep away.

The following morning, September 16, they were almost immobile with the cold. They had to dance on the spot in the pale sunlight to return some circulation to their feet. But they were on the summit ridge, and the end was in sight, just two thousand feet above them. Gamely they pushed on, roped together against the strong winds. After a few hours, according to Cook, they reached the summit.

"We reached the top at ten o'clock. We intended to stay there two hours, but actually stayed only twenty minutes, so great was our suffering. About two hundred or three hundred feet below the peak we left a record of our visit—made out of a pile of stones and an American flag. With this we left the names of our party, the line of march, the date, and the temperature."

That cairn of stones and the flag have never been found.

Cook was hailed as a hero as news of his conquest began to spread. People warmed to the story of the plucky doctor who was only reconnoitering for a future attempt, but took his chances when the weather cleared. It was the stuff of fairy tales. But to one man, it *was* a fairy tale. Professor Parker immediately had doubts, telling the *New York Times* on November 10: "He may have ascended one of the peaks of the range, but I do not believe that he made the ascent of Mount McKinley."

Parker felt that he knew how the expedition was going when he left. He knew they were running out of time, and a summit attempt was not being planned. He also had reservations about the "travel light" approach that Cook had adopted, pointing out that Cook had brought no scientific instruments to the summit with which to measure altitude. This was a serious problem. The only evidence that they had of the summit was Cook's own account. He did provide a photograph. But the photograph Cook produced was one taken from a considerable distance down the ridge, purportedly showing Barrill holding a flag at the summit. Later analysis would suggest that picture was taken at a different point on the massif, a full nineteen miles from the actual summit.

Local climbers in Alaska were immediately skeptical, with Hudson Stuck saying: "Cook is a prig. Moreover I find it hard to contain within myself my vehement suspicion that he is an ass. And a prig and an . . . ass will never climb Mount McKinley."

That was in a private letter, rather than a public pronouncement, but from the start there were doubts about Cook's achievement. There had never been doubts about him before. Peary had always been dogged by questions about whether he was exaggerating his claims, but to this point Cook had been accepted as an honest historian of his own efforts. Now he was on a footing with Peary. He would not be accepted on his word any more.

Modern polar explorer and mountaineer Pat Falvey is one of those who doubt the good doctor. Falvey, who has been up Everest twice, and been to both poles (including a traverse of Antarctica on foot) was kind but damning in his assessment of Cook: "Mountaineering is something you do for yourself. But a hundred years ago reaching the top of Mount McKinley was such a big accolade people probably exaggerated the truth in a way that put them in the situation of having achieved what they set out to achieve. I would like to believe Cook was telling the truth, but I am more prone to believe the evidence that is now actually in front of us, that he didn't get to the top.

"A lot of our achievements are based on honor. It's like the situation today with drugs in sport. When there is such a high reward system, people may go over to the other side. I hate to say it, but I think Cook told a mistruth."

He added: "There probably was enough good climbing gear in 1906 to get up Mount McKinley. It is not a technical mountain. On McKinley there is every possibility that someone could have climbed it back then with the equipment that was available. The equipment is better now and so is the knowledge we have of the mountain, so now it is perceived to be easier. But you still have to endure the same winds and the same cold. It is mental ability that counts, and that was the same back then as now. It's the want, the need, the passion to be in those remote places with fantastic scenery, and to be in a place that few people have ever stood. Cook achieved that, even if he did not get to the top.

"With getting to the top of Mount McKinley, or getting to the North or the South Pole, 95 percent of the achievement is in the trying, and in getting as far as you can go. The problem for claims that prove to be false is that they destroy the reputation of the claimant themselves, and of others in the same field, all for the sake of what is probably only 5 percent of the effort, the final leg."

It is now widely accepted that Cook did not reach the summit of McKinley in 1906. The first assent was not made until 1913, by Hudson Stuck and Henry Karstens. Mountaineering experts who have analyzed Cook's route and his notes feel that his account is fabrication. It is possible that he could have climbed the peak, but his account does not support that view. And the creeping doubt about his mountaineering claim would, as Falvey pointed out, come back to haunt him when he made an even more dramatic claim a few years later.

21

PEARY AND COOK
MEET AGAIN

The reputations of both Peary and Cook were riding high by the end of 1906. Peary had wrested the coveted Farthest North from his European rivals, and was planning his final assault on the Pole. As far as the public knew, Cook had climbed the unclimbable mountain and planted Old Glory on the top of the continent. There were questions about both men, but the questions were asked in private, among a select few men who were experts in the fields of exploration. To the public, America had two heroic explorers to celebrate. And celebrate them they did.

On December 15 of that year the two men were both guests at the National Geographic Society's annual dinner in Washington, DC. Both were seated at the top table, in positions of honor, rubbing shoulders with cabinet ministers, congressmen, senators, foreign dignitaries, industrial giants, and academic heavyweights. Not just rubbing shoulders, but lording it over them. Peary had finally achieved his "fame." Cook, driven more by the desire to succeed and secure his family, had also achieved what he wanted.

There had been tensions between the men in the past, but there had also been a long period where they were firm friends. This evening was an event which emphasized the friendship, and both men greeted each other cordially. With four hundred guests looking on, neither was going to let themselves down. The Italian ambassador was one of those who addressed the gathering. Italy had held the Farthest North record until Peary took it back to America. Peary was magnanimous in victory, replying that the search for the Pole was: "The most manly example of friendly international rivalry that exists."

Frederick Cook was a special guest, and was introduced by one of the most famous men in America, inventor Alexander Graham Bell.

The man behind the telephone acknowledged Peary at the top table, then said: "But in Dr. Cook we have one of the few Americans, if not the only American, who has explored both extremes of the world, the Arctic and the Antarctic regions. And now he had been to the top of the American continent, and therefore to the top of the world."

Cook smiled as the audience burst into applause, then he stood to tell his story. Round one to the Brooklyn doctor. Peary smiled too. He knew that his moment was coming.

Halfway through Cook's exciting tale of climbing Mount McKinley the door of the function room banged open, and all eyes turned. Striding into the hall was a figure familiar to everyone in the room. The usher made his announcement in stentorian tones, but it was unnecessary. Everyone knew the President of the United States, Theodore Roosevelt.

Cook knew his moment had suddenly passed. He stepped aside and sat down, while the President took his place behind the podium to address the room.

"Civilized people usually live under conditions of life so easy that there is a certain tendency to atrophy of the hardier virtues. And it is a relief to pay signal honor to a man who by his achievements makes it evident that in some of the race, at least, there has been no loss of hardier virtues," he said.

The man in question was not Cook, but his rival Peary. The Commander was to be presented with the inaugural Hubbard Medal, to mark his latest polar achievement. And the medal would be presented by none other than the President himself. Peary knew it paid to have powerful friends.

Accepting the honor, Peary said: "Should an American first of all men place the Stars and Stripes at the Pole, there is not an American citizen at home or abroad, and there are millions of us, but what would feel a little better and a little prouder of being an American; and just that added increment of pride and patriotism to millions would of itself be ten times the value of all the cost of attaining the Pole. Tonight the Stars and Stripes stand nearest to the mystery, pointing and beckoning. God willing, I hope that your administration may yet see those Stars and Stripes planted at the Pole itself."

Round two to Peary.

22

COOK PLANS FOR
THE POLE

Cook's focus had switched from the Pole to smaller and more manageable expeditions. So far his life as an explorer had given him a certain fame, and he enjoyed a steady income from lecturing and his books about his adventures. But the expeditions themselves were a logistical nightmare, and always ended up costing him more than he made. Although he had married a wealthy widow, he did not feel this gave him carte blanche to wander the globe, disappearing for years on end like Peary. When he failed to generate interest in an Antarctic expedition, he took the sensible decision that the Pole—either Pole—would be a destination for a younger, better funded man. He was not happy to give up on his ambitions, and felt the confinement of the urban canyons of Brooklyn. Still, he had a loving wife, a wonderful stepdaughter, a new son, and a fast car. He would be content.

But life has a way of delightfully spoiling our plans.

In the spring of 1907, a wealthy member of the Explorers Club came to Cook with a proposal. John Bradley had made a fortune through his gambling empire, and like most gamblers he needed excitement in his life. Horse racing was fine, but what he really loved was big game hunting. And the more exotic the location the better. He had traveled the world in search of animals to fix in the scope of his rifle, and was in Asia bagging tigers and elephants when Cook was climbing Mount McKinley. Both men met in the Explorers Club and swapped war stories. While listening to Cook's descriptions of the Arctic, Bradley began to consider the gaps on his trophy wall. Caribou, polar bear, and walrus would fill those gaps nicely.

He offered to finance an expedition to the Arctic region of Canada if Cook would organize it for him. To Cook it was a great opportunity to continue his ethnological work, at someone else's expense. As Bradley put it: "I had fully made up my mind to go that year, and invited Dr. Cook to go as my guest. He was to photograph Eskimo, and I was to shoot walrus and polar bear."

The pair bought a 111-ton fishing schooner and reinforced the hull with thick steel to withstand the ice. They also fitted an auxiliary engine and loaded enough supplies for two years. Neither man intended to be away so long, but Cook knew enough of the cruel Arctic Ocean to plan for the unexpected. Now that he had a backer with deep pockets, Cook organized the expedition quickly. By June, three months after Bradley had approached him, everything was in place. Both men met for lunch in Manhattan. During the lunch, Cook dropped a bombshell.

"Why not try for the Pole?" he said.

This was something Bradley had not been expecting. No explorer himself, he had no interest in long uncomfortable marches over game-free ice. But he suggested that Cook head for the Pole on his own while he shot walrus. Cook told him that it would involve an additional expense of up to $10,000—small money for the gambling tycoon. Bradley argued with him, but by the end of the lunch he had been infected with the doctor's enthusiasm, and had agreed to finance the mad scheme.

Bradley suggested keeping their plan a secret. If Peary found out, he would leave ahead of them, and hire all the best dogs and men, leaving Cook with the dregs. And Bradley had no interest in a race. He wanted to proceed up the coast at his leisure, with plenty of time to shoot along the way. He was not going to shell out all the money to rush his time in the Arctic. Cook agreed with the secrecy. Before the meal was quite over, Bradley had taken out his checkbook and handed over $10,000 to

Cook. They clinked glasses and downed a celebratory Burgundy. The race was on—even if one of the competitors had not been notified of it.

Cook spent the next three weeks madly racing around, sorting out gear, calling in monies owed, and trying to finish his book about the ascent of McKinley. In the end he did not finish it, leaving it to Marie and his editors to get it ready for print. Marie was not happy to see her husband heading north so soon after his grueling mountaineering expedition, but he persuaded her that this was his big opportunity, and if he did not seize it, it might not come again.

On July 3 the *John R. Bradley*, as the ship was diplomatically rechristened, sailed out of Gloucester into the north Atlantic. It had cost $30,000 to refit, but it looked magnificent, all gleaming white and gold trim. The gambler it was named after was not on board; he would join them in Nova Scotia. But Marie and Ruth came along for the first leg of the journey. Bradley joined them on July 12, and the ship crossed the Davis Strait for Greenland on July 15. Ten days later they crossed the Arctic Circle. Cook was back on familiar ground, seeing his old haunts of Godhavn and Disko Island. By late August the ship was nosing through the ice-clogged waters of Smith Sound, between northern Greenland and Ellesmere Island, toward the Eskimo settlements of Etah and Annoatok, perhaps the most northerly settlements in the world at the time.

Cook wrote: "As we entered Foulke Fjord, half a gale came from the sea. We steered for the settlement of Etah. A tiny settlement it was, for it was composed of precisely four tents, which for this season had been pitched beside a small stream, just inside the first projecting point on the north shore. Inside this point there was sheltered water for the Eskimos' kayaks, and it also made a good harbor for the schooner."

While the schooner was docked to wait out the season, the real business of the expedition got underway—at least as far as Bradley was concerned. Cook wrote: "We determined to spend as much of this time as possible in sport, since much game abounded in this region. Before we landed, we watched the Eskimos harpoon a white whale, while hares, tumbling like snowballs over wind-polished Arcaean rocks, gave another day of gun recreation."

They took the schooner's motor launch a further twenty-five miles north.

"Annoatok is the northernmost settlement of the globe, a place beyond which even the hardy Eskimos attempt nothing but brief hunting excursions, and where, curiously, money is useless because it has no value."

The settlement consisted of twelve tents and three stone igloos in a small bay. Beyond the bay Smith Sound was impassable, blocked by ice.

"Ordinarily Annoatok is a town of only a single family or perhaps two, but we found it unusually large and populous, for the best hunters had gathered here for the winter bear hunt. More than a hundred dogs, the standard by which Eskimo prosperity is measured, yelped a greeting, and twelve long-haired wild men came out to meet us as friends.

"It came to me strongly that this was the spot to make the base for a polar dash. Here were Eskimo helpers, strong, hefty natives from whom I could select the best to accompany me; here, by a fortunate chance, were the best dog teams; here were plenty of furs for clothing; and here was unlimited food."

The plan was simple. They were within seven hundred miles of the Pole. Cook would stay the winter in Annoatok, then take a small team of Eskimo and dogs the following spring to cross the polar sea. He would return a few months later, but John Bradley was not going to wait to bring him home. Instead he would travel overland to Upernavik, where he could get a boat to Copenhagen. At the last minute one of the men on the ship, Rudolph Franke, agreed to remain the winter and travel with Cook the following year.

Bradley turned south, happy with his haul of new trophies. He was back in New York by October, and telling all who would listen about his friend Cook's plans to reach the Pole. Reporters pounced on the flamboyant gambler, who was happy to supply copy. The story went on the front page of several newspapers. Typical was the *Boston Herald* of October 2: DASH TO POLE TO FORESTALL PEARY IS PLAN OF DR. F. A. COOK. More soberly, the *New York Times* carried an editorial which concluded that though Cook had a head start, Peary would be in the race. The result was by no means a foregone conclusion.

Cook, as a courtesy, had also written to the Peary Arctic Club, letting them know that he had found a new route to the Pole, farther west than Peary's, and he would be attempting it in the coming season.

That America was beginning to see the quest for the Pole as a race between two men of highly contrasting characters, showed the excitement the topic was generating. It was like the Super Bowl or World Series of exploration. No one stopped to consider that men from other nations might be interested parties in the race. It was seen as a strictly two-horse race. This was a mistake, because Roald Amundsen was beginning to form his own plans for an attack, and Nansen still had not given up on his ambitions, despite his advancing years.

Amundsen's plan required a ship, and Nansen had the ship. If Amundsen could persuade the older man to step aside and give him *Fram*, the Americans would face a very experienced, determined, and resourceful rival.

Peary did not even consider the challenge from Europe. He saw Cook as having betrayed him, and all his efforts would be to thwart his former colleague. An emergency meeting of the Peary Arctic Club was called to discuss the potential calamity. The Club had regarded Cook as a friend. In 1901 they had even sent him to rescue Peary. Now their attitude hardened. An attempt to blacken his name—which became increasingly bitter and deceitful—began with a letter to the International Bureau of Polar Research in Brussels, accusing Cook of trespassing on Peary's sphere of influence. Peary's letter asked the Bureau to refuse recognition to any claims by Cook.

Peary then wrote to the *New York Times*, saying that if Cook went to Etah and Annoatok and hired Eskimo and dogs, he would be using people and animals trained and nurtured by Peary, to which he had no right. Peary conveniently ignored the fact that these were free independent people, not his own serfs to order about. Although the commander always proclaimed a great admiration for the natives of the Arctic, he never saw them as equals, but as tools in his greater plans. He often spoke of them in a paternalistic way, as if they were wayward children who needed the steadying influence of the white man to prosper. He never bothered to learn their language, leaving that to Matthew Henson.

Peary immediately threw himself into another round of fundraising. The *Roosevelt* had to be made ready for starting in spring, 1908. There was no other option. This expedition would have to be organized very quickly, or be doomed to failure before it left port. Previous expeditions had proven difficult to organize and finance. Now he had to call in every favor owed to get this one on the water quickly. And when one of his chief backers, Morris Jessup, passed away that year, it made the job even more daunting.

But the Peary Arctic Club had achieved one thing. Through careful manipulation of the media, and through contacts with friends in high places, Peary was now seen as America's chief hope. His credentials were no better than Cook's—in many ways they were worse. But perception counts for a lot, and Peary was perceived as the country's preeminent explorer. The President, the Navy (for a change), and the entire country was behind him. He found himself pushing open doors.

Amundsen, in Norway, was pushing half-closed doors, but with equal determination. Nansen was in semi-retirement, working as part of the diplomatic corps of his country. So the chances were good that Amundsen could get his hands on *Fram*. A big part of organizing any expedition is sorting out the ship to bring you into the polar sea. The *Fram* was still the most suitable icebreaker in the world. It would give Amundsen a decided advantage.

The race was on.

23

AMUNDSEN EYES
THE POLE

The Northwest Passage was legendary in exploration circles. Following his successful navigation of it, Amundsen was now a genuine Norwegian hero, on an equal footing with Fridtjof Nansen. In terms of prestige that was certainly true, but Nansen still had an indefinable something more, a network of connections within the establishment that would always allow him to raise funds with more ease than Amundsen. He was old-school, like his backers, and Amundsen still needed to keep him on his side.

In 1906 Nansen had urged Amundsen to return home quickly from the Northwest Passage to capitalize on his growing reputation, but the younger man had rejected this advice, spending several months in America, where explorers were enjoying something of a golden period. He played the same theaters and the same lecture circuits as Peary and Cook, then crossed the Atlantic to the UK and Europe before heading home. Amundsen knew he needed to pay off his creditors if he was to get another shot at one of the few legendary targets still left to men in his unusual trade. So he accepted every speaking engagement he could get. One of his creditors was Nansen, who had paid dearly for the privilege of getting the first telegram with the news of the successful trip.

But the two men never fell out. In this they were different from Peary and Cook. Perhaps Nansen admired the chutzpah his colleague displayed. Amundsen was an intensely ambitious man, and never afraid to set high targets for himself. And Nansen consistently backed him. In fact, Nansen urged the Norwegian parliament to step in and help with the costs of the three-year trip. At his urging, on April 20, 1907, the parliament voted to award Amundsen a sum sufficient to clear all his remaining debts from the *Gjøa* expedition. His creditors were off his back, and the offers to lecture were rolling in. He had the breathing space to plan his next trip.

As he put it in his autobiography, he dreamt of new worlds to conquer.

In the autumn of 1907 he returned to America for another lecture tour, this one designed not to cover his debts, but to build up funds for the next expedition—the big one. He spoke to journalists about his lofty ambitions, telling the *New York Times* and other prestigious publications that his biggest discoveries were still ahead of him. Finally, on October 27, he announced his bold plan was to plant the Norwegian flag on the North Pole, the very tip of the world.

The timing could not have been better. John Bradley had just told the papers that Cook intended to seek the Pole in the spring of 1908. Peary had reacted by discrediting Cook, and by setting plans in motion to be on the polar sea by the winter of 1908. Now there was a third man in the race, and a very creditable contender. America was gripped with polar fever.

The three contenders had contrasting styles. Peary was using his famous Peary System of a large team of natives and dogs working in relays to leave caches of food and fuel all along his route. He was going to go from Smith Sound onto the ice. The Peary System had collapsed spectacularly on his last trip, but he had claimed a Farthest North, and he seemed to know what he was doing. Cook had a different approach— the Alpine approach of the mountaineer. He was going to travel light and fast, living off the land. It was more risky, but if everything went right, it could work. Amundsen had a completely different approach— one that had gained Nansen a farthest North a decade earlier. He would embed *Fram* in the ice and use the polar drift to carry him to the Pole. His approach was the riskiest of all; it could leave him stranded.

Amundsen told a disbelieving world that he was prepared to spend several years isolated from the world to achieve his objective.

"You cannot pick up a bag and start for the North Pole as you would go to Philadelphia," he said. "It will take all of two years to get ready. The food has to be especially carefully prepared, otherwise the men get scurvy, and it is no use to be an explorer unless you live to come back."

It would be a long and arduous undertaking, involving drifting in the frozen polar sea for perhaps two to three years before getting close enough for a dash across the ice to lay the flag.

In that interview he spoke in glowing terms of the friendliness and knowledge of the people of the Arctic, especially the Eskimo and Inuit. He had learned from them how to use the icy conditions to his advantage.

"Your Arctic explorer revels in a field of ice, as a farmer delights in a wheat field," he quipped.

Talking to another reporter, he expanded on his plans. A shy man who liked to keep things to himself, he was beginning to realize the power of the press, and to use it for his own advantage. He even began to joke with reporters, putting a human face on the Viking image. He joked about using polar bears to tow his sleds to the Pole, saying he was going to bring along a bear trainer to ensure the animals did not turn on him. People warmed to the human side of him.

He spent a lot of time in America, becoming quite an adept lecturer during his second tour. He did not enjoy the lecture circuit, but he knew that the money was essential—both for his own comfort and for his future plans. He returned to Norway, and for a while left the Pole on hold, as he concentrated on more practical matters. He began by building a house for himself outside Oslo. It was his retreat, and expressed his character; it was decorated to look like a captain's cabin, with plenty of Arctic etchings on the walls. His family had had a housekeeper, Betty, when he was growing up. He wanted to keep the woman, but he did not want to share his retreat with anyone. So he moved her into a nearby cottage, where she could be on standby; the comforts of home, along with the solitude he enjoyed.

But all was not rosy. Two of his brothers, Gustav and Jens, had business problems, and expected him to help out. Initially he was happy to, but he quickly saw that could be a bottomless pit. They felt they were entitled to a share of their brother's good fortune. His third brother, Leon, was different. The two were always close, and Leon acted as his business manager. This was important all the time, but particularly when Roald was at sea.

Sitting in his home overlooking the sea, he knew he would have to get away from family squabbles, financial worries, and the mundanity of life. The feeling of frustration and boredom was building up in him, and the only cure was a new expedition. His plan was audacious: he would sail a boat into the high Arctic and let it get frozen into the pack ice. It was known that the ice drifted across the polar sea. Whalers and sealers had often been taken hundreds of miles off their course when they were beset. The direction and speed of the drift was not known precisely, but Amundsen was fairly sure that if he entered the pack ice in the right spot, it would pull him in a circle around the pole, drifting north all the while. At some point they would be close enough to the Pole to be able to risk a dash across the frozen sea and back safely to the ship. Then it was a matter of waiting until the drift brought them south again, and the ice broke up, releasing the ship. It was Nansen's plan of 1893–1896, taken to even more extremes.

The plan had two drawbacks: it could take two or three years, and they would be on frozen water rather than land, so game would be scarce or non-existent. It would need a very tough boat, and the boat would have to be very well stocked.

The *Gjøa* was out of the question. It was too small, and it had taken a battering in the Northwest Passage. Amundsen had sold it in San Francisco, and it was eventually donated to the city. It remained a popular tourist attraction for decades, until it was returned in 1972 to Norway. Now it is in Oslo harbor, beside Nansen's *Fram* and Thor Heyerdahl's *Kon-Tiki*.

The *Kon-Tiki* was a raft made of balsa wood which Heyerdahl sailed from Peru to the Polynesian Islands in 1948, to prove that Polynesians could have populated the Americas. He sailed nearly four thousand miles across the Pacific on the raft before running aground on a deserted island. The trip made him a household name, and almost as famous as Amundsen.

The *Fram* was a more traditional craft. It had been designed by Nansen in 1892 to cope with very particular conditions. He wanted to go as far north as possible, embedded in the pack ice. The problem was that when a ship becomes iced in, the pressure on both sides can crush the vessel like a paper cup. Nansen came up with an elegant solution. He designed the hull in such a way that when the ship was crushed, it would pop up out of the ice, safely out of danger.

Fram was a three-masted schooner, thirty-nine meters long and eleven meters across. That was unusually wide, and the ship was also unusually shallow, with virtually no keel. The rudder and propeller could be pulled back into the boat, so that the ice would not destroy them. Heavy insulation meant that the crew could remain comfortable no matter how cold it got outside. There was plenty of storage room. There had to be: Nansen thought he might be trapped for up to five years. Instead of batteries, he had a windmill and a small generator.

The three ships lying beside one another in Oslo Harbor today represent three contrasting styles and periods in the history of exploration. Nansen was the elder statesman, part of the establishment. He entered public life, becoming an ambassador, and then the High Commissioner for Refugees at the League of Nations. Heyerdahl was the forceful modern man, prepared to go out on a limb for a crazy idea. His approach was completely non-traditional, and he knew how to play the media to finance his plans. Amundsen fell in between. He was modern and ambitious, feeling his way with the mass media, while still trying to maintain the traditional approaches to fundraising and planning. For instance, he liked to have a scientific aspect to his trips, as a justification. Heyerdahl didn't bother; he was exploring for the sake of exploring.

Amundsen admired Nansen, and appreciated the support of the older man. And he knew the history and qualities of the *Fram* as well as anyone. He knew why it had been designed the way it had, and he knew it was the vessel he needed for his next venture. He needed to get Nansen on board.

It helped that when Amundsen published his account of his Northwest Passage trip, he dedicated the book to Nansen. There is no reason to think that this was manipulative. His admiration was genuine, and he deeply appreciated the assistance Nansen had given him.

There was a problem. Nansen was the veteran, but in his own mind he was still a Young Turk. He felt the call of the Poles as strongly as ever and was considering one more voyage. He wanted to take *Fram* south, exploring the Antarctic. He thought he could land on the southern continent and make a quick dash to the Pole, bagging it ahead of the British, who were making valiant efforts to plant the Union Jack there. He had trekked across Greenland. How difficult could Antarctica be?

Nansen was twelve years older than Amundsen, and already moving from exploration to the life of a public figure. He was the Norwegian ambassador to Great Britain, and knew that soon his time would have passed. He had to either do it now, or pass the torch. He kept these feelings to himself. There was no public announcement. It had not got to the planning stage.

Then he got a shock. Amundsen wrote to him from America; he wanted to borrow the *Fram* for his next trip. This presented a major problem. He would have to go public with his plans and commit to a new expedition, or step aside. Technically, *Fram* was not his to give out. It belonged to the Norwegian government. But Amundsen was right to approach Nansen. One word from him could swing it either way.

Nansen did a lot of soul-searching in private. Part of him still yearned for the thrill of exploration, but his body was slowing down, and life at home had its attractions. In the end he stepped aside graciously. Perhaps deep down he knew he did not have it any more, and if his rival had the boat, he was off the hook.

Amundsen had *Fram*. He also had Nansen's blessing. He immediately began fundraising. It was a lot easier now that he had a reputation. In the fall of 1908 he presented his plans to the Norwegian Geographical Society. He emphasised the scientific value of the trip more than the dash for glory that he dreamed of. He told the audience that he would take measurements of current strength and direction, and soundings of depths in the Arctic Ocean, adding greatly to the knowledge of that region. King Haakon and Queen Maud were enthralled by the ambitious project, and immediately made a substantial donation.

It sparked a major surge in his fundraising efforts. The money was rolling in fast.

The public loved his plan. He would sail south, rounding Cape Horn at the tip of South America. He would follow the coast up to Alaska, and enter the Bering Strait—where he had exited the Northwest Passage a few years earlier. He would sail northwest until he became trapped in the pack ice. The ship would pop out of the ice and drift along with the flow while the crew took soundings to map the ocean floor, as well as monitoring air temperature, water salinity, winds, and tides. It would take four years to drift across the frozen polar sea, but eventually the drift would carry them to an exit point, somewhere between Greenland and Spitzbergen. At some point during that four-year drift they would be close enough to the Pole to make a dash on skis and with dog sleds, bagging the real prize.

Flushed with his success in Norway, Amundsen addressed the Royal Geographical Society in London on January 25, 1909. This time he emphasized the work he would do in studying the mysterious aurora borealis, the Northern Lights. Carried away on the wave of international enthusiasm, the Norwegian parliament agreed to grant Amundsen 75,000 kroner to refurbish the *Fram* to meet the challenges of the four year drift. This money allowed him to replace the bulky steam engine with a lighter and more efficient diesel one.

He was still well short of the money he needed, but more was flowing in every day, and he was not a patient man. He barged ahead, incurring debt and making deals he might not be able to honor. Another brief trip to America was called for—always good to fill the coffers. He planned on making the crossing in November.

24

COOK HEADS NORTH

Cook was oblivious to the plans of his rivals. He was settling in for a long winter at 78 degrees latitude.

"The dark veil of the long night is slowly falling over us, and these grey days, humidity and stillness serve to increase the saddening effect of the gloom of the long night," he recalled.

He and Franke constructed a simple hut from old packing boxes, and furnished it as well as they could. They had a stove for warmth, and on the very cold days they could sit on their bunks. The air was quite warm, but the ground was freezing. The air in the hut did not circulate efficiently; there was a sharp temperature gradient between floor and roof, and if either man stood too long, his head would perspire while his feet went white and numb. There the two men remained throughout the long winter, building sledges, sorting supplies, and working with the local Eskimo for their mutual survival.

Sledges were the key to the enterprise. He wanted lightweight ones that would move over the ice easily. The Eskimo were experts at building sledges, but here was one area where Cook was even more expert. He had used Eskimo sledges, European sledges in his trip to Antarctica, and Alaskan sledges. He knew the strengths and weaknesses of each design, and he worked hard that winter to create the vehicle that was perfect for his needs. What he ended up with were twelve feet long and two and a half feet wide. They weighed just fifty-five pounds each. Cook knew that the design Peary used weighed over a hundred pounds—he was eliminating all this dead weight, which he could make up in food and fuel.

He used local supplies, but had not left it to chance, bringing hickory from home as well. Instead of solid wooden runners, he used a system of light runners supported with crossbars and struts. Not only were they lighter, they were a bit flexible, making them run over the uneven ice more smoothly. He trained the Eskimo of Annoatok to work on the sledges in a workshop beside his hut. He also needed a boat for the leads they would inevitably encounter on the polar dash. He had gone for a collapsible design, a twelve-foot rowboat that he disassembled and built into the sledges. To a casual observer it did not look as if he was carrying a boat at all, but if they became trapped, he could quickly reassemble the bits into a serviceable launch and cross to safety. The beauty of incorporating bits of the boat into the sledges was that it conserved weight. Every ounce of effort would be exerted to bring food on the long journey, not needless bits of wood.

As the darkest part of winter approached, Cook tested the equipment by going on an extended hunting trip. They covered five hundred miles and the sledges performed magnificently. On another hunting trip, near Christmas, he encountered Knud Rasmussen, a Greenlander who had been educated in Denmark. He passed a letter to Rasmussen to mail when he got to civilization. The letter was to Marie, and said: "I have one hundred dogs and as many more as I desire, with fifteen of the best men of the tribe assembled here for the attack over the new route across Ellesmere Land out by way of Nansen Sound and back by Kennedy Channel, thus using to good advantage the drift and the musk oxen so abundant in Ellesmere Land. All of my equipment is ready and we hope to start for the goal late in January."

He was very happy with his progress, and confident of his ultimate success.

Christmas came and went, as Cook noted: "Christmas day in the Arctic does not dawn with the glow which children in waking early to seek their bedecked tree, view outside their windows in more southern lands. Both Christmas day and Christmas night are black. Only the stars keep their endless watch in the cold skies."

They enjoyed a native feast that day, and one of the delicacies was ice cream—but made without either cream or sugar, two key ingredients in the American version! Instead the women collected a mix of oils from seal, walrus, and narwhal. Musk ox suet was chewed until it was broken down to a fatty mass, which was mixed with the oils. This was the base for the ice cream. Flavor was provided by bits of cooked meat, moss flowers, and delicate grasses. Obviously there was no grass to be had during winter, but during the summer the natives had prepared for that; after a hunt they had cut open the stomach of a reindeer and frozen the contents, half-digested grass. This was thawed out in December for the ice cream.

"It all forms a paste the color of pistachio, with occasional spots like crushed fruit," he noted. The paste was mixed with snow until it froze.

"When completed, it looks very much like ice cream, but it has the flavor of cod liver oil, with a similar odor. Nevertheless it has nutritive qualities vastly superior to our ice cream, and stomach pains rarely follow an engorgement."

Cook sampled the delicacy, but his feast consisted of treats he had taken from the John Bradley before she sailed for home: green turtle soup, dried vegetables, caviar on toast, olives, salmon, crystallized potatoes, reindeer steak, rice, peas, apricots, raisins, biscuits, cheese, and coffee.

"I ate heartily, with more gusto than I ever partook of delicious food in the Waldorf Astoria in my faraway home city."

In January—still deep in the Arctic night—preparations began in earnest. Although Cook was going to travel light, he adopted the Peary approach for the first leg of the journey. He sent a team out, led by polar novice Rudolph Franke, to cross Smith Sound and cache supplies high on Ellesmere Island. They returned and reported that ice conditions were good. This was encouraging. In February an advance party of Eskimo, with eight sledges, pushed even farther north. Now Cook had food and supplies for the early part of the journey, but it was still too early in the season to set out. Impatience had cost Peary on some of his Greenland expeditions in the past. Cook knew he had to wait for spring. As he prepared for departure, he left a note outlining his plans for Rasmussen, whom he believed was coming north again. The note said he expected to return to Annoatok in May or June, and that Rasmussen was welcome to use the hut and whatever supplies he liked in Cook's absence.

On February 19 the sun reappeared over the horizon, signaling the end of the Arctic night. It also signaled the start of the expedition. Cook mustered 103 dogs, and divided them among eleven sledges. The sledges were loaded with supplies, spare furs, food for men and dogs, ammunition, and navigation equipment—they weighed a couple of tons. Franke was going to accompany Cook for the early stages of the trip. They were also joined by nine hand-picked Eskimo, one for each sledge. Cook found it easy to recruit the best, because he spoke their language fluently, unlike Peary. He did not look on them as childish savages, but took a real and genuine interest in their ways and traditions. Often during the long winter he had whiled away the hours sitting in their igloos, chatting with them as an equal.

All knew what they were seeking that morning—though they had different visions of the purpose of the long trek. Cook and Franke were finding the Pole, the spot on the globe where every direction was south. The Eskimo had no interest in the Pole, or the Big Nail, as they called it. They knew all about it. The spot, they believed, was marked by a big iron nail that had fallen over and been lost in the snow. Iron was very important to them, but they would stick to the nearer supplies, the giant remains of the Cape York meteorite. Peary had stolen three of the biggest fragments, but there were others he did not know about. And they could trade for iron. So they were not interested in the Big Nail. They were more concerned with finding the rich hunting grounds to the north that Cook had told them about. This was a partial truth: Cook had promised game, but this was based on belief rather than any direct knowledge. In fact, the rich hunting lands to the north never materialized.

Dog teams are difficult to control, particularly at the start of a day. The animals are very lively and relish the physical challenge of towing sledges. They leap and pull at their harnesses, and resist most efforts to quiet them down. It was a noisy camp, as over a hundred of the energetic animals yelped, skirmished, and tumbled in the snow. Finally, at 8:00 a.m., they were ready to set out. Cook snapped his whip in the air, and was almost thrown into the snow as his team lurched forward.

"The spans of dog teams leaped forward, and we were off. My polar quest had begun!"

The first day saw the eleven sledge teams make twenty miles, leaving them only thirty miles from Cape Sabine in Ellesmere Island. Temperatures hovered between minus forty and minus fifty. The second day, late in the evening, they made the Cape, the spot where Adolphus Greely, on a meteorological expedition in 1883, had lost nineteen of his twenty-five men to the cold and starvation.

On February 23 Cook met with a group of Eskimo returning to Annoatok, and their news was not good. Game was in short supply. Cook's plan necessitated living off the land. Some men, including Franke, returned with the hunting party, while there was also an exchange of dogs. Franke's instructions were to remain at the hut until summer, guarding Cook's supplies (and his valuable collection of furs and ivory, worth $10,000), and if the polar party had not returned by then, he could go home. Cook continued with stronger dog teams, each hauling eight-hundred-pound sledges. Temperatures continued to drop as they left the relative shelter of Smith Sound for the more exposed fringes of the Arctic Ocean.

"A hard wind, with a temperature of minus sixty, had almost paralyzed the dogs, and the men were kept alive only by running with the dogs." One dog died of the cold, and frostbite became a problem.

But the enthusiasm of the group was undampened, and they marched on over Ellesmere Island. Rations were reduced, but a few days later a herd of musk oxen were spotted, and three were butchered. The meat was eaten raw, by both animals and humans. The group continued up the east coast of Axel Heiberg Island, where they managed to find more oxen. On one memorable hunt, they managed to kill twenty of the animals, fueling Cook's confidence.

By the start of March they had reached the edge of the polar sea. They had not advanced any appreciable distance north, but that was deliberate. They had crossed from Annoatok in a roughly northeasterly direction, traversing Ellesmere Island rather than traveling to the top of it. Now they were ready to turn toward the Pole. Cook estimated that the polar drift would pull them to the west. If they headed out on the polar sea now and marched to the Pole and back, the drift would bring them back toward the west coast of Greenland, and the safety of Annoatok. If they had set out directly from Annoatok, they would end up coming out of the ice over deep water. If his calculations were right . . .

They were camped at Cape Svartovoeg (since renamed Cape Stallworthy), right on the tip of Axel Heiberg Island, the seventh biggest island of the Canadian archipelago, and the thirty-first biggest island in the world. The edge of the Cape was marked by high black cliffs that dropped steeply to the sea. The land around them was ice-free, fields of grass and moss with abundant game—an oasis of life in the frigid land. Beyond them the polar sea was permanently frozen.

Cook dismissed most of the Eskimo and their dog teams, taking only two men with him. From that point on he would be unsupported. They were a little over five hundred miles from the Pole, and the real journey was about to begin.

25

PEARY LEAVES FOR THE POLE

When Peary had received the letter from Cook outlining his plans to cross Ellesmere Island and travel up Nansen Strait to the top of Axel Heiberg Island, before turning north, he was livid. He could not stop a European competing in the Arctic, but he was damned if he was going to let a fellow American forestall him. Peary had not given up on the Pole. In an ideal world he would have taken a year or two out to raise funds for his next expedition, and to milk the previous one for everything it was worth. Now he was denied that luxury, and he had to act fast if he was to salvage anything.

Peary was a far more modern man than Cook, an entrepreneur who saw exploration as a business. He had incorporated the Peary Arctic Club as a fundraising tool, and he was able to generate far more funds than his rival—just as well, because his expeditions cost several times' more. The Club was made up of some very influential people, in business, politics, and the media. Peary strolled the corridors of power with ease, and he was a master of spin. His first task was to mobilize support for his own hastily organized expedition. He had one advantage: he was just back from a successful polar trip.

Whether he achieved the latitude he claimed or not, he had certainly reached the Big Lead and gone farther north than he had managed in any of his previous expeditions. It proved that his approach—the vaunted Peary System—was workable. All he needed was luck on his side. For the 1908–1909 expedition he would stick closely to the same plan. He would use the *Roosevelt* again, this time with a support ship bringing extra provisions and coal. He would base himself again at Etah, and use the same Eskimo. The only real difference was that this time he would use even more men and dogs, and he would head slightly west as well as north, to compensate for the polar drift. It was like a chess game— plan before your opening, make the right moves at the right time, and victory would come.

But even the early moves were fraught in this game. It was vital that he get funding for the trip. Even though he had his ship, he would have to refit it for the coming season, pay for provisions, buy new equipment; it all cost. One of his most important backers and the President of the Arctic Club, Morris Jessup, had passed away in January 1908. He was always a man who could be relied upon to throw in ten thousand here or there to bring the war chest up to strength. Now Peary was without one of his most important supporters. Jessup's widow did donate an unex- pected $5,000, which helped. And other funders came on board. Attorney Thomas Hubbard agreed to take over the Club, organising the fundrais- ing. He also dug into his own pocket to show his faith in Peary. Others followed suit. And money came from unexpected sources. A rich paper manufacturer arrived at Peary's office unannounced and left a check for $10,000. He was immediately offered the vice presidency of the Club.

As quick as the money came in, Peary was spending it on supplies and refurbishment. But the project was now building a momentum, and he was confident he would be leaving New York in the spring or early summer. The *Roosevelt* would winter embedded in the ice off Grant Land, the northern portion of Ellesmere Island. In the spring, Peary would set out with the best of the Eskimo he would recruit at Etah and Annoatok, on the opposite side of Smith Sound in northern Greenland.

Cook had one companion for the Arctic winter before his polar march; Peary would have many. He carefully chose a team of Americans to make the complex Peary System work. Matthew Henson would be back, of course. Not only was he Peary's personal man, he was an old Arctic hand, who knew the local language. Like Peary, Henson had a native wife, and a toddler son in Greenland. Unlike Peary, he mixed well with the natives, and was considered one of the tribe when he was in the Arctic.

The *Roosevelt*'s master, Robert Bartlett, was sailing again, as was civil engineer Ross Marvin. Marvin had been invaluable on the previous expedition, and this time would serve as Peary's assistant and secretary, handling all the correspondence. Marvin's brother was a New York advertising man, whose son, Lee, would go on to become an Oscar-winning Hollywood star. The physician this time was Dr. John Goodsell from Pennsylvania. Donald MacMillan, a professor of mathematics and physical training, and Yale athlete George Borup were on their first Arctic trip. The ship pulled out of New York on one of the hottest days the city had ever seen, sailing for one of the coldest regions the world knew. Thirteen people died of heat-related problems on July 6, which replaced the departure of Peary as the top spot on the daily news agenda.

The ship was packed. As was normal on a Peary expedition, he made the most of his departure. There were a hundred people on board, including most of the Peary Arctic Club. The *Roosevelt* passed the flotilla of supporters majestically, then pulled in for the night at Oyster Bay, Long Island. Peary and Josephine went on shore, and they dined with the President himself the following afternoon. Afterwards the President, accompanied by his wife and three youngest sons, got a tour of the ship.

As the President stepped off the ship, Peary's voice boomed over the general din.

"Mr. President," he declared, "I shall put into this effort everything there is in me—physical, mental, and moral."

The President grinned. "I believe in you, Peary. And I believe in your success—if it is within the possibility of man."

Peary was delighted to hear this. He was a patriot through and through. If you had sawn through his body and laid both sides down, you would have found the Stars and Stripes running through him like the pattern in a stick of rock candy. As he later wrote in his account of the expedition: "It is a great satisfaction to me that this whole expedition was American from start to finish. We did not purchase a Newfoundland or Norwegian sealer and fix it over for our purposes. The *Roosevelt* was built of American timber in an American shipyard, engineered by an American firm with American metal, and constructed on American designs. This expedition went north in an American-built ship, by an American route, in the command of an American, to secure, if possible, an American trophy."

With the presidential endorsement ringing in his ears, Peary turned north, facing into frigid waters few on Earth were more familiar with. They touched down in Sydney, Nova Scotia, then crossed the North Atlantic to Greenland, sailing up the coast to Cape York. A smaller supply ship, *Erik*, followed them, carrying twenty-five tons of whale meat for the dog teams, and fifty tons of extra coal for the *Roosevelt*'s engines. Now Peary was on home ground. He knew every inlet up the coast of Greenland, and knew how to avoid the dangerous ice conditions often found even in summer. It was smooth sailing, and they met none of the heavy weather they had encountered on the last expedition. They crossed the Arctic Circle shortly after midnight on July 26. It was his twentieth time to pass over the imaginary line. Those crossing for the first time felt a thrill of anticipation.

Peary also felt a thrill of anticipation, but for another reason. He was close to Etah, where he would recruit Eskimo and dogs for the following season. One question plagued him: would Cook have taken the pick of the crop, leaving Peary short? Cook was constantly on his mind. The crew learned never to mention the name, in case it triggered a tirade. He did not try to hide his bitter hatred of his rival.

They passed Cape York at the start of August. Finally they were among the Eskimo that Peary had come to rely upon. He was delighted when the fur-clad natives rowed their kayaks out to meet his boat. In his writings Peary made it abundantly clear that he had great respect for the natives of the high Arctic, who managed not only to eke out an existence in the harsh landscape, but to thrive in it. But his interest was very self-centered and paternalistic; he did not regard them as the equals of the white race.

"I have often been asked: of what use are Eskimos to the world?" he wrote. "They are too far removed to be of value for commercial enterprises, and, furthermore, they lack ambition. They have no literature nor, properly speaking, any art. They value life only as does a fox, or a bear, purely by instinct. But let us not forget that these people, trustworthy and hardy, will yet prove their value to mankind. With their help, the world shall discover the Pole."

In the end, it was all about Peary.

His attitude is in sharp contrast to Cook, who had a real respect for the Eskimo, and who learned their language and studied and reported their customs and traditions.

To Peary these people were tools, his property to further his ends.

"For eighteen years I had been training them in my methods; or, to put it another way, teaching them how to modify and concentrate their wonderful ice technique and endurance, so as to make them useful for my purposes."

This attitude led to some appalling situations over the years, such as when Peary let his charges die rather than allow Dr. Dedrick to treat them on one expedition. Peary also resented anyone else trading with the natives, as he wanted to be their only source of knives and guns. In fact, he had been known to take things from them that they had got from other white traders.

His method of recruitment was perfunctory. With Henson translating, he "selected the few men needed from that place, told them that when the sun reached a certain point in the heavens that evening the ship would sail, and that they and their families and possessions must be aboard the ship."

In a moment of megalomania, Peary wrote about the feelings of the natives toward their white benefactor: "Their feeling for me is a blending of gratitude and confidence. To understand what my gifts have meant to them, imagine a philanthropic millionaire descending upon an American country town and offering every man there a brownstone mansion and an unlimited bank account. But even this comparison falls short of the reality. My various expeditions into that region have had the effect of raising the Eskimos from the most abject destitution to a position of relative affluence."

It would be interesting to see what the Eskimo he brought to New York as a museum exhibit a decade previously would have said about that.

On August 3 the *Roosevelt* rendezvoused with the *Erik*, and two days later Peary and Henson transferred to the smaller ship, to visit a number of Eskimo settlements and recruit more men and dogs. The *Roosevelt* sailed north to Etah, where they would remain a number of weeks before setting up their winter base on Ellesmere Island, across the narrow Smith Sound in the Canadian Arctic.

Peary believed the race was truly on at last.

26

PEARY VENTS HIS RAGE ON COOK'S COMPANION

Rudolph Franke was a young man in his twenties, with no great experience of the Arctic, or of exploration in general. He had grown up in Germany, and got the wanderlust listening to old salties telling tales in the port of Hamburg. He moved to America in search of adventure, and had put an advertisement in the *New York Herald* offering himself as a volunteer for any expedition north. It was a youthful lark, but John Bradley had seen the advertisement, and taken the youngster at his word, bringing him on the Cook expedition. Now he found himself facing far more than he had signed up for. He had expected to be hunting big game for a season, not crossing unexplored regions with a madman intent on the Pole. Over-wintering in the Arctic was not part of his plans either.

So when Cook turned him back with the first party of Eskimo hunters they had encountered, he was delighted. The early days of the polar march had been marked by extremely low temperatures—more than one of the dogs had perished, frozen to death. But when Franke found himself back in Annoatok, it was hardly the relief he expected. It was still dark most of the day, and bitterly cold. When Cook had been there, he at least had companionship. Now he found himself alone in the rough wooden cabin, guarding the silver fox furs, the ivory, and the remaining supplies. The tiny village was still occupied, but unlike Cook, Franke did not speak the language. So he was fairly isolated.

Long months passed in monotony, only occasionally relieved by hunting expeditions. In March the second group turned back by Cook, at the tip of Axel Heiberg Island, returned to the settlement. They carried a letter from Cook to Franke. In the letter Cook re-emphasised the importance of guarding the furs and ivories, saying the items "must be our money on the return trip." Cook would need them for bartering with natives, and for paying for passage home to America. Even though John Bradley had covered the costs of the expedition, there are always extra expenses, and those furs might be the difference between Cook coming home comfortably or coming home to debt.

Franke remained in Annoatok as the days lengthened into spring. By late March the spring equinox had passed, and there was now more daylight than night in each twenty-four-hour cycle. By the end of May the days had lengthened so much that there was light throughout the night. The sun dipped below the horizon briefly around midnight, but the land was bathed in twenty-four-hour light. Within another few weeks they would enter the days of the midnight sun, when the golden orb never set. And still there was no sign of Cook. He was due home in May, and by the end of that month there was no news of him. The longer he was away, the more likely it was that something had gone wrong. He could have perished on the ice, in which case he would never be seen again. Or he might have been carried farther than he planned by the drift, and could end up missing Annoatok altogether. There was a cut-off point; if Franke waited too long, he would be trapped for another winter. He would have to head south at some point, to catch a ship home. Complicating the situation, he was weakening by the day. Cook was a great advocate of eating raw meat. With Cook gone, Franke had reverted to the preserved supplies. His condition had deteriorated. It could be seen in the gray tone of his complexion, and in the way his skin seemed to hang limply. His teeth yellowed and his gums began to bleed. He was in the early stages of scurvy. He could have reversed the condition with a few hearty doses of seal liver, but he did not even realize how ill he was becoming.

July 5 was the date Cook had nominated as the cut-off point. When that day dawned with no sign of the explorer, Franke reluctantly packed a sledge and got a team of Eskimo and dogs to pull him south, taking the precious furs and ivories with him. The work of waiting was done; it was time to go home. But it was not easy. Though it was summer, a ferocious storm swept down, pinning the travelers for a few days. When they got moving again, the ground was rough and difficult to travel. But they got to Etah eventually, in early August. They had been hoping to meet a passing whaler, but they had already gone south for the season. Instead they found just two ships there. *Roosevelt*, Peary's icebreaker, was in harbor, and beside her was the *Erik*, a steamer hired by the Peary Arctic Club to bring extra supplies of coal for the expedition. The *Erik* also contained several paying customers, eager to explore the Arctic from the safety of a well-provisioned ship. It was all part of the fundraising efforts of the Peary Arctic Club.

Franke must have been a sight when he rowed out to the *Roosevelt*. He was weak and emaciated, and had not bathed in months. His hair was long and matted and he had a straggly beard. His eyes were bloodshot, and he was hunched and weak. He called up to the deck, asking to speak to Peary. Matthew Henson described him thus: "We were met by the most hopelessly dirty, unkempt, filth-littered human being any of us had ever seen, or could ever have imagined: a white man with long matted hair and beard, who could speak very little English and that only between cries, whimperings, and whines, and whose legs were swollen out of all shape from the scurvy."

A head appeared over the bulwarks and told him that Peary was away for a few days. He was allowed on board for a few minutes, but the steward who met him refused to give him anything to eat or drink— not even a coffee. Everyone knew Peary's irrational dislike of Cook, and anyone associated with Cook was bad news. Franke had to get back on his little launch and row back to the tents of the village.

When Captain Robert Bartlett heard the next morning how Franke was treated, he was furious. This was not the way one white man should treat another in such an isolated place. He was not scared of Peary, and immediately went ashore to find the young man. He brought him back to the ship and fed him, apologizing profusely for the way he had been treated on the previous day. When he told Franke that *Erik* was returning to America soon, the young man pleaded to be allowed travel with her. This was beyond the authority of Bartlett; he was just the captain of the *Roosevelt*. He explained that it was Peary who could grant that request, and Peary alone.

Franke did not have long to wait. That very afternoon Peary returned to Etah, along with the expedition physician Dr. John Goodsell and a group of Eskimo. Franke grabbed the explorer by the sleeve, and pleaded his case: "Please, dear God, take me away. I can't stand it."

He thrust a letter into Peary's hand, the letter from Cook, giving him permission to leave his post at Annoatok on July 5. Peary's face blackened when Cook was mentioned. Franke could not have known it, but it was the one word that was almost guaranteed to leave him stranded. But he needed to know the whereabouts of his great rival, so he controlled his anger, asking as casually as he could what news there was. Franke explained that the doctor had not been seen since he departed Axel Heiberg Island five months previously. As he said this, his voice trembled, and he held shaking hands over his face. He was a pitiful sight. As Dr. Goodsell led him away for a medical examination, Peary turned to the crew.

"That, gentlemen, is an example of what can happen to a white man in the Arctic," he said.

He agreed to let Franke travel south with the *Erik*, departing for Newfoundland on August 21. But he exacted a high price for the privilege. He insisted on Franke handing over the supplies of furs and ivory he had with him. He took every last item, insisting on a signed release from Franke.

As the young man later recalled: "In a critical condition, and under duress, I was obliged to hand over all the property belonging to Dr. Cook. Peary put the alternative to me: the furs, etc., or you stay here. That meant, in my invalid condition, to perish."

Not only did Peary steal the items Cook had earmarked for trade, he insisted that the release also cover any other items Cook had left in that part of Greenland, including the contents of the hut in Annoatok.

To ensure the piracy was complete, he sent a crewman, John Murphy, north to Annoatok to take possession of the hut, giving him a letter of instructions which said: "Franke has now turned over all these supplies and equipment to me so that Dr. Cook has no longer any claim upon them."

The fact that these items belonged to Cook and not to Franke—so the young man had no right to hand them over—did not bother Peary in the slightest. He instructed Murphy that if Cook reappeared, Murphy was to still remain absolutely in charge of the hut, and to continue to use the items inside for trade or any other purpose he saw fit. The doctor was not to be given access to his own possessions. If Cook needed supplies, Murphy was allowed sell them to him—in effect, Cook would be charged for receiving his own food, or taking possession of his own books and supplies.

One of the men on the expedition was a big game hunter, Harry Whitney. He had been due to sail home, but was not happy with what he had shot so far, so he decided to stay a winter in Greenland and try his luck next season. Peary gave him permission to use the hut in Annoatok. And Whitney could use the supplies in the hut as he saw fit to survive the winter. Unlike Cook, he would not be charged for them.

27

COOK REACHES FOR THE POLE

In the shadow of the lofty black cliffs that marked the end of Axel Heiberg Island, and the start of the Arctic Ocean, Cook camped for a brief period. Though he had announced jubilantly on February 2 that they were off, this marked the start of the challenging part of the journey. Once they left the island and headed out onto the broken ice, they were truly underway. And the real danger would begin.

There were a number of concerns. The first was that game would now become scarce. They would still find the occasional seal and walrus, and they might encounter a polar bear. But hares, musk oxen, and reindeer did not venture onto the ice, no matter how solid. There was no vegetation to support them. So the party would have to rely on what they could pull on their sledges. And they were 520 miles from the Pole. That meant a return journey of over a thousand miles, with limited opportunities of living off the "land."

Their other concerns related to the conditions. The ice was not smooth, like a frozen pond. Sea ice is rough and serrated, broken by pressure ridges, refrozen cracks, and mini bergs. These would all slow progress in the days ahead. Another danger was the leads of open water that could open up at any moment in the ice, necessitating long delays and posing a real danger. A plunge into the water would probably prove fatal. Salt water freezes below the freezing point of distilled water, and the temperature in the sea would be below freezing. Hypothermia would set in immediately. In the unlikely event of surviving a plunge into the sea, frostbite would follow swiftly. Cook was under no illusions; he knew that this was one of the most dangerous journeys he had ever undertaken.

Still, he was confident. Reviewing the progress to date, he felt they had traveled fast enough to make the polar dash realistic: "Starting from our camp at Annoatok late in February, when the curtain of night was just beginning to lift, when the chill of the long winter was felt at its worst, we had forced progress through deep snows, over land and frozen seas, braving the most furious storms of the season, and traveling despite baffling darkness, and had covered in less than a month about four hundred miles—nearly half the distance between our winter camp and the Pole."

Cook's first task was to decide who would travel with him. He wanted a small party, and the qualities he was looking for were strength and character. He wanted fearless companions who would brave the risks without mutiny.

He considered his options. He knew that the Peary System called for sending out advance parties to cache supplies, then relaying more supplies farther along the route. Although he had over a hundred dogs, he did not favor this approach. More men on the ice meant more supplies had to be hauled, becoming a vicious cycle of increasing loads. It was time to show the courage of his convictions, and travel light.

Two young Eskimo hunters had stood out in the trip so far. Both were about twenty, eager to work, and uncomplaining. He also found their company easy. So he chose Etukishook and Ahwelah. He felt they could be trusted to follow to the limits of his own endurance—a march to the bitter end, if necessary. The wages he promised them may seem small by modern standards, but to an Eskimo they were the wealth of years. Each young man would receive a rifle and a good knife on their return to Greenland. In a primitive society a rifle would make you a man of wealth, able to provide for a family in great comfort. Both men jumped at the chance.

Cook decided on two rather than three sledges. One of the sledges was the one with the collapsible canvas boat built into it. On the polar sea that could prove its worth. As supplies were eaten, Cook planned on reducing the load by ditching one of the sledges for the return. He also picked twenty-six of the strongest dogs, thirteen for each sledge. The dogs were as expendable as the second sledge; he planned on butchering the animals regularly, using their carcasses to feed their companions. On the return, the remaining sledge would grow lighter by the day, and Cook hoped to reach safety with just one sledge and six dogs. This was an approach used a few years later with great success by Amundsen in the Antarctic.

Loading the sledges took all day, and was supervised closely by Cook. The three travelers would bring food for eighty days. Pemmican would be the backbone of their diet, with occasional delicacies to relieve the monotony. They carried over eight hundred pounds of beef pemmican and 130 pounds of walrus pemmican, with fifty pounds of prime musk oxen tenderloin and twenty-five pounds of oxen fat. They also packed tea and coffee, twenty-five pounds of sugar, forty pounds of condensed milk, sixty pounds of biscuits, and a supply of pea soup for variety. The dogs would get a pound of pemmican a day. The men would get a pound of pemmican every day too, supplemented with biscuits and other provisions.

The sledges also carried wood alcohol and petroleum, as well as a plentiful supply of candles and matches. In addition to these they had to leave room for the non-perishable supplies, which included a tent, two canvas sledge covers, fur groundsheets, reindeer-skin sleeping bags, and carpentry essentials such as wood and screws, for running repairs.

They had plates and cutlery, but reduced to the minimum, as well as a selection of knives. They brought two guns and 110 rounds of ammunition. They would not see much game, but if they encountered a polar bear the guns would save their lives. Polar bears are vicious predators, and would think nothing of making a meal of the polar party.

For clothing, Cook had decided everyone should bring at least double of everything, so that if one set of clothes got wet—either from the weather, from the sea beneath them, or through perspiration—they had a change of clothes ready. So each man had four pairs of boots with fur stockings, a woolen shirt, three pairs of sealskin mittens, two pairs of fur mittens, and a sealskin coat. Their daily walking apparel consisted of fox fur coats over bird-skin shirts, bearskin pants, sealskin boots, and stockings made from hare skin. Every animal played its part. Each man also had a blanket for extra warmth, and a sewing kit. Everyone was responsible for his own equipment.

To top it all, Cook issued each man a pair of snow goggles. Sunlight glinting off the ice has the power to burn the inside of the eyeball, damaging the retina. Snow blindness is a painful condition, and makes travel in polar and mountainous regions even more difficult. Although the Eskimo were not used to the snow goggles, everyone wore them. It was a simple way of avoiding a very major problem.

Finally, there was Cook's personal equipment. He took binoculars, a pocket compass, a liquid compass as backup, an aluminium surveying compass with azimuth attachment, a surveyor's sextant with attached terrestrial and astronomical telescope, and sundry bits such as thermometers, an artificial horizon, four watches, a pedometer, barometer, and a camera. He also brought a supply of notebooks and pencils to keep an accurate record of his achievements.

When everything was ready, the polar party turned their backs on the black cliffs and bade farewell to their companions.

"Taking their hands in my manner of parting, I thanked them as well as I could for their faithful service to me. '*Tigishi ah yaung-uluk*!' (The Big Nail!) they replied, wishing me luck," he recalled.

Those who were going no farther turned back south and began their trudge down Nansen Sound toward Ellesmere Island. A strong wind was whipping up the snow, and they soon disappeared in the whiteness. But for a long time their voices could be heard, carried on the wind. Then they too faded, and the three men were left with their thoughts.

Instead of immediately setting out, the men retreated into an igloo to escape the gale. At noon the following day the dogs were harnessed, and the journey recommenced. The going was rough but exhilarating. Cook led on foot, and the dog teams followed, each in the charge of one of the Eskimo youths. Two other Eskimo, Koolootingwah and Inugito, came along for the first few days, carrying extra supplies. They would turn back after three days, leaving only three for the final dash.

"Dashing about transparent ultramarine gorges, and about the base of miniature mountains of ice, we soon came into a region of undulating icy hills. The hard irregularity of the ice at times endangered our sleds. We climbed over ridges like walls. We jumped dangerous crevasses, keeping slightly west by north; the land soon sank in the rear of us."

When the two extra men turned back, it was a poignant departure.

"About us was a cheerless waste of crushed wind and water-driven ice. On the horizon Svartevoeg, toward which the returning Eskimo were bound, was but a black speck. To the north, where our goal lay, our way was untrodden, unknown. The thought came to me that perhaps we should never see our departing friends. With it came a pang of tenderness for the loved ones I had left behind me."

Now they were truly alone, and for the first time a primeval fear began to creep into the minds of the two Eskimo men left with Cook. They were a tribe who thrived on the edges of the polar sea, exploiting the game that roamed the vast lands of the northern latitudes. They never ventured onto the ice cap of the interior of Greenland, and they never ventured far onto the frozen polar sea. It went against all their instincts to be so far from land. Cook understood this fear, and he did his best to alleviate it. He had told the two men that they would encounter new and unknown lands on their journey toward the Big Nail, and those lands would teem with game. Now he took advantage of a phenomenon of the icy region. Low cloud cover in the distance led to a mirage on the far horizon. Although there was nothing there except the shadow of the low lying clouds, it could easily be mistaken for land.

"*Noona* (Land)," Cook shouted, pointing and reassuring his men that they were not as far out from safety as they feared. This was a trick he pulled continuously on the journey, managing to convince his companions that they were never more than a few days from land. This harmless deceit kept them marching, but it was to have a nasty side effect after the expedition. When questioned by people skeptical of Cook's claims, the two men said that they had wandered the Arctic always within a few days of land. The truth was that only Cook could navigate, and the accounts of the two men as to where they were could not be relied upon. Whether or not Cook reached the Pole, they were many days from land for much of their march.

Progress was steady if unspectacular. The team managed roughly two and a half miles an hour, and averaged fifteen miles a day. On March 22, with the temperature close to minus sixty, Cook spotted a dark line in the pearly white of the clouds in the distance. This was bad news, often an indicator of thin ice or worse, a lead. By six o'clock that evening they had reached a line of high-pressure ridges in the ice, beyond which they could see a jumble of floes. It was not looking good as they slowly picked their way between the obstacles. After a few hours they climbed over a raised block of ice, and Cook's heart sank.

"Twisting snake-like between the white field, and separating the packs, was a tremendous cut several miles wide, which seemed at the time to bar all further progress. It was the Big Lead, that great river separating the land-adhering ice from the vast grinding fields of the central pack beyond, at which many heroic men before me had stopped. I felt the dismay and heartsickness of all of them within me now."

This was the Big Lead that had put an end to Peary's hopes in his last expedition. The fact that Cook had reached it and described it in detail proves that he reached quite a high latitude. It does not prove that he attained the Pole, but it does show that he was on the journey, and not loitering about near land, as Peary and others were later to claim. He had only four hundred miles to go—if he could cross the Big Lead. But it stretched for miles in either direction. The only thing to do was to make camp and sit it out, in the hope that the intervening water would freeze, or the wind would drive both shores together.

"We retired. Ice was our pillow. Ice was our bed. A dome of snow above us held off the descending liquid air of frost. I could not sleep."

The following day there was a stretch across the two-mile wide lead of new ice, thin and uncertain. Cook knew it would not bear the marching party, but if they spread themselves thin, they might edge across it without plunging through. The dogs were put on very long leads, to keep them well ahead of the sledges. Slowly they began to inch their way across.

"I knew, as I gently placed my foot upon the thin yellowish surface, that at any moment I might sink into an icy grave. Yet a spirit of bravado thrilled my heart. I felt the grip of danger, and also that thrill of exultation which accompanies its terror."

The ice moved beneath him like a sheet of rubber, and there were regular loud cracks. But the new ice held. They took a few hours to make the crossing, but to Cook it felt like years. Finally they made it, and they surged forward exultantly. This was the great barrier; now they were on the permanent ice of the polar sea, free from the continental shelf. The road to the Pole was smooth before them.

Of course, it would not be an easy path. A few days after crossing the Big Lead, the party were forced to camp during a vicious storm. That night there was a terrifying loud crack which woke the three men up. Finding nothing wrong, they went back to sleep. A few minutes later the crack was repeated, louder than before. And suddenly a crevasse opened beneath them, running right through their igloo. Cook was plunged into the freezing water. Luckily his two companions were spared a ducking, and pulled him to safety. Because he had been in his sleeping bag, he had not got wet. That probably saved Cook's life.

"Gratitude filled my heart. I fully realized how narrow had been the escape of all of us. The experience, while momentarily terrifying, was instructive, for it taught us the danger of spreading ice, especially in calms following storms."

They broke camp and marched on. At that latitude, as Cook noted, life was devoid of pleasure. It was just a case of putting one foot in front of the other, and carrying on until you were ready to drop.

By the end of March, according to his own sextant readings, Cook had passed Peary's Farthest North. He was now officially the explorer who had come closest to the Pole.

Here we are in unknown territory. Most historians accept that Cook crossed the Big Lead. His account of the open water tallied with what Peary found at a similar latitude, and his Eskimo companions confirmed what he saw, and how many days' march from Axel Heiberg it was to the lead, even though they could not confirm his sextant readings or other observations, being untrained in such matters. Accepting that he got to the other side of it, we can accept that he beat Peary's fictional Farthest North of the 1906. He may even have beaten the earlier Italian mark of Umberto Cagni. He noted things such as the fact that shadows do not lengthen and shorten through the day, as they do every place else on earth. Instead, the shadow of a man maintains the same length, just rotating around his body as the sun rotates around the sky at an even height. This is true only of the Polar Regions, and Cook did note it. His companions also noticed the odd behavior of shadows. It is on such anecdotal evidence that Cook's claim needs to be evaluated. As he had no one to confirm his navigational observations, we can only take him at his word, or not.

You cannot leave a flag at the Pole for the next man along to find, because the polar drift means that within hours that flag will be a number of miles from the Pole already.

Cook said that in early April he was less than three hundred miles from his destination, and traveling fast. They were still averaging less than fifteen miles a day. This is quick going, a lot faster than Peary made the following season. But it is not extraordinarily quick; other explorers had made similar distances in the past. If the weather conditions were not too bad and the ice relatively smooth, such distances were possible, especially to a light team intent on speed.

Cook continued his gentle deception that they were close to land.

"Discoveries of new land seemed often made. But with a clearing horizon the deception was detected. The boys believed most of these signs to be indications of real land—a belief I persistently encouraged, because it relieved them of the panic of the terror of the unknown."

Observations were not possible every day. In the days before GPS, fixing one's position was a difficult task, involving precise measurements and many calculations. The observations had to be taken at noon exactly—which is why Cook had brought along so many watches. He had to align the sextant to the horizon precisely, using the artificial horizon he had packed. Then he took the angle and direction of the sun, and worked out position. If the weather was cloudy or stormy, as it often was, they had to rely on instinct and dead reckoning. He managed to get readings on a number of occasions, but by no means every day.

He took the first reading on March 25, showing latitude of 83 degrees 31 minutes north. Five days later they had reached 84 degrees 50 minutes. He would take about half a dozen observations over the coming few weeks, and only managed three on the return journey.

For a number of days the travelers had been moving past low-lying land to the west, which Cook named Bradley Land. He described it thus: "The lower coast resembled Heiberg Island, with mountains and high valleys. The upper coast I estimated as being about one thousand feet high, flat, and covered with a thin sheet ice."

He even took a photograph of his two companions in harness with the land in the distance. It is a grainy photograph and impossible to make out details. Subsequent exploration has revealed that there was no land to the west at all. It is possible Cook mistook massive bergs for distant hills. Sometimes huge chunks of the continental ice sheet off Greenland—several miles across—can break off and become trapped in the polar sea, drifting for years. But these generally are only a hundred to two hundred feet high, rather than the thousand feet Cook described. Cook's companions maintained afterwards that the photograph was not taken halfway to the Pole as Cook claimed, but was shot far closer to Axel Heiberg. Although an exact match for the blurry features on the image has not been found, some experts believe that the picture was taken off Ren Bay, Ellesmere Island. Previously Cook had taken a picture of a peak in the McKinley range and tried to pass it off as the summit. Was he doing the same again?

By Cook's own account, once the group passed Bradley Land the Eskimo boys became more concerned, as they were now too far from land for their own comfort. He had to cajole, threaten, and promise to keep them marching. They were beginning to suffer from exhaustion, and from the monotonous diet, lacking in fresh meat. Each night now they were too tired to build igloos, instead sheltering behind hummocks in the ice. Sleep eluded them. The landscape was barren, and no life was spotted— no game, no seal holes, no birds. They were alone in a lifeless world.

They began to slow down. On April 8 Cook recorded a latitude of 86 degrees 86 minutes, meaning they were now covering less than ten miles a day. By April 11 they had reached 87 degrees 20 minutes. Half their food was gone, and they were down a number of dogs, having sacrificed some to feed the others. They had 160 miles to go, which Cook estimated would take thirteen days at their current average. The ice was getting thicker, and the going was easier, so they could improve on the nine miles a day, bringing it closer to the fifteen they had been making earlier in the trip. But his companions were getting increasingly concerned.

Finally, on April 13, Ahwelah refused to move. He was hunched over his sledge, crying silently, his tears dropping into the snow. "It is well to die. Beyond is impossible," he whispered.

It was a moment that pushed Cook's leadership skills to the limit. He knew how close they were to the goal of a lifetime. If he had taken the Peary approach he would have just ordered them to stand up and get to work. One crew member of the *Roosevelt* put it like this: "Rule by the iron hand, without the velvet glove." But Cook was a gentler soul. He admitted that he had his moments of despair too, but explained how close they were. He asked for five more days, certain he could cover the one hundred miles in that time. Reluctantly the two Eskimo agreed. Within two moons they would be back among their people, and it would all be over. The whips cracked, and the dogs were off again.

According to Cook's account, they made rapid progress over those five days, on one of them doing a double day's march to cover the ground as swiftly as possible. By April 19 they had reached a latitude of 89 degrees 31 minutes. They were within thirty miles of the North Pole!

"I suppose I created quite a commotion about the little camp," he noted with characteristic understatement. His companions were equally excited, not so much about the Pole, but about the prospect of turning back and going home. They prepared a good meal, then set out for a double march, to bring them to their destination.

In the early hours of April 22, they knew they were as close as it was humanly possible to determine at that period to the top of the world.

"We are at the top of the world. The flag is flung to the frigid breezes of the North Pole!" Cook later wrote in his account of the expedition, *My Attainment of the Pole*. "I knew that I was at a spot which was as near as possible, by usual methods of determination, a spot toward which men had striven for more than three centuries—a spot known as the North Pole, and where I stood first of white men. We had reached our destination. My relief was indescribable."

They built an igloo, and Cook spent that day and the following walking around what he had assured the Eskimo was the Pole, taking observations. The ice beneath them was fourteen feet thick, and beneath that the sea fell another four thousand feet. Cook hung Old Glory from a flag pole. His companions hung their wet clothing nearby, taking advantage of a day's break from marching to dry out their skins. Cook found the juxtaposition of flag and trousers incongruous.

So had they really reached the Pole? We have only Cook's word for it. Up to 1906, he was a man who could be taken at his word. But after making a dubious claim to McKinley, all his subsequent claims must come in for scrutiny.

Almost certainly he crossed the Big Lead that had stopped Peary the previous season. Whether he got much further is open to doubt. His Eskimo companions believed they were never more than a few days' march from land. It is possible he convinced them—and perhaps himself—that Bradley Land was a real place. Equally possible is that he traveled a bit north, battled with the storms and the fears of his companions, and greatly exaggerated his claimed distances. He could have spent several weeks on the ice and not have come closer than a few hundred miles to the Pole.

This makes sense when the polar drift is taken into account. The top of the globe, unlike the Antarctic, is sea rather than land. The sea is permanently frozen, and the ice slowly drifts in a giant circle around the Pole. Nearer the Pole, you are closer to the axle of the drift, and so you move less. Farther away the drift is faster, and takes you farther. Cook had traveled to Axel Heiberg before turning north deliberately, so that the drift as he traveled to the Pole would bring him home over northern Greenland. He hoped to make land in Smith Sound and get to his base at Annoatok. But if he did not get near the Pole, the drift would have affected his party far more than he anticipated. The fact that their return from the pole was beset with so many difficulties bears out this interpretation.

It is highly probable that Frederick Cook struggled through reasonably high latitudes, but never came close to the Pole. His polar camp on April 22 was a sham, staged to convince his two companions that they had achieved success. They were his only witnesses, and they had no way of checking his navigational observations. If he told them they had found the Big Nail, they were happy to agree. Cook may have fooled them, but he would not have fooled himself. He was too experienced a navigator to be in any doubt about his true location.

Whatever the truth, on April 23 it was time to break camp and turn south. They were coming home, to claim the spoils.

28

PEARY HEADS NORTH

As Peary's winter came to an end he still had no idea where Cook was. Could he be holed up somewhere, waiting out the winter, ready to return with the devastating news that he had attained the Pole? It seemed unlikely. Judging by the time he set out, and Peary's own experience at those latitudes, Cook should have returned to civilization long before the winter set in. He might have returned too late to get a ship home, but he could have sent messages south with word of his whereabouts.

Peary decided that his rival must have died on the ice, and would never be heard from again. It was the perfect scenario, from his point of view. He would get to the Pole, and no one could claim priority.

Having reached this conclusion, Peary made it public, by nailing a sign to the door of Cook's cabin in Annoatok, where he had left John Murphy in charge, with Harry Whitney as a guest. The sign read: "This house belongs to Dr. F. A. Cook, but Dr. Cook is long ago dead, and there is no use to search for him. Therefore I, Commander Robert E. Peary, install my boatswain in the deserted home."

It was a callous note, and not everyone on the expedition was comfortable with the level of animosity Peary displayed. His assistant

Marvin wrote home to say that he could not reveal the full extent of the situation, but he made it clear he was not happy. "The Dr. Cook affair is a tangle and a hard nut to crack," he admitted. However, they had a job to do, and everyone was behind the forceful leader.

A year later, Peary was writing his account of the expedition and by then he knew that Cook had survived his year on the ice. So he tried to sanitize the story, writing: "Boatswain Murphy was a thoroughly trust-worthy man, and I gave him instructions to prevent the Eskimo from looting the supplies and equipment left there by Dr. Cook, and to be prepared to render Dr. Cook any assistance he might require when he returned, as I had no doubt he would as soon as the ice froze over Smith Sound (presumably in January) so as to enable him to cross to Annoatok from Ellesmere Land, where I had no doubt he then was."

This version seriously contradicts the cold note left on the hut door, and the recollection of members of the expedition, such as Henson and Marvin. It is reminiscent of the way Peary tried to justify himself after leaving Verhoeff in Greenland on his second expedition, and after his falling out with Dr. Dedrick several years later. Those two incidents had been sideshows, but his treatment of Cook was to become a crucial part of the two men's story in the years to come.

Peary did not winter at Etah. He recruited there, but he crossed Smith Sound to Ellesmere Island, and set up his winter quarters at Cape Sheri-dan, on the northeast coast. He was a little over five hundred miles from the Pole, around the same distance as Cook was when he turned north at Axel Heiberg, two hundred miles further west. During the winter a large supply of food and fuel was ferried across the island to the northernmost tip, Cape Columbia. Aside from the very tip of Greenland—inaccessi-ble because of the ice sheet over the interior of that country—it was the most northerly land mass in the world. The distance to the Pole was just 478 miles. Peary could not have found a more perfect starting point.

His fears that Cook might have left him short of men and dogs was unfounded. He had 246 dogs and twenty-two experienced Eskimo sledge handlers (along with their families) in igloos around the *Roosevelt* at Cape Sheridan. It was the largest Arctic assault party ever gathered.

In February 1909 the final leg began—the push from winter quarters to the Pole. More supplies and people were sent to Cape Columbia from the *Roosevelt*, and on February 22 Peary himself set out. He did not take all the dogs, but it was still a massive party on the trail. He had six American or Canadian companions with him, nineteen Eskimo, and 140 dogs. He divided his force into six groups. The plan was an elaborate military siege of the high Arctic. Teams would march ahead to break trail or lay depots. Then the next group would take over and push further north, while earlier groups went back down the line to pick up more supplies from Cape Columbia or the other caches, and bring them forward. With the forward and backward marches the teams would cover far more than the 480 miles there and back. But one team was not involved in the hectic activity.

The entire train was designed to pull Peary to the Pole, and in order to conserve his resources for the final push, he just traveled in the one direction. This meant that his team would be the strongest and best rested when it came to the later stages of the march. In his accounts of the expedition, Peary said that he was the only one not to have a dog team. He walked alongside, always heading north. This was not quite true. Because of the damage done to his feet a decade earlier, when he had lost all his toes to frostbite, Peary was not capable of long marches day after day. In addition, his broken leg from the second Greenland expedition (the one with Cook) was acting up for the first time in years. This might have been due to nutrition; old wounds tend to flare up again when the body runs low on vitamin C, and Peary was still no fan of raw meat. His assistant Matthew Henson gave the true picture. Peary tried to walk at the start of the trip, but quite soon gave up, and spent a lot of the expedition on a fur-lined seat on a sledge, being pulled. He walked at times, but in general he led from the rear, and traveled in more comfort than his companions. At fifty-three he was the oldest of the party by a decade, and the years had taken a hard toll on his body.

According to Henson, when they came to the final portion of the march Peary did lead from the front, and "he kept in the lead and did his work in such a way as to convince me that he was still as good a man as he had ever been."

Just as in his previous expedition, the Peary System began well. There were occasional hitches, such as when one team crashed and destroyed a sledge on the first day, and had to unload on the snow and return to Cape Columbia for a spare sledge. But there was strength in numbers, and they coped well with such setbacks. The lead team was alternated every five marches, so that each team would share in the burden, and get its fair share of rest. The plan called for the lead team to break trail, advance between ten and fifteen miles, and then establish camp. When the main party arrived at this camp, the lead team would take off again. This meant that the main party was spared some of the work in building camp each night, and also meant that orders could be passed up and down the line, as the groups came together briefly every day.

Robert Bartlett, the captain of the *Roosevelt*, was in charge of the first lead group. He made twelve miles, into a gale, on the first day. On the second day the lead party made roughly the same distance, but the followers were stopped by a lead of open water roughly a quarter of a mile across. The weary travelers had to make camp themselves that night, and wait for the lead to close. The following morning, before the lead had fully frozen over, they made a perilous crossing, and continued. Of course the moving ice and drifting snow had obscured Bartlett's trail, so they had to waste another hour finding the tracks again. But these setbacks aside, the first few days on the ice went smoothly enough. Their progress was encouraging.

But a few days later progress was halted once again—and this time the lead was far bigger than the one they had to wait out overnight. Peary's heart sank. This was the Big Lead that had scuppered his chances last time. Would it do the same now? Peary knew there were two problems. The immediate one was how to cross over the lead and onto the permanent iced sea. The second problem was potentially more serious—they would encounter the same lead on the way home, and if they could not cross it then, they were condemned to a slow death and an icy grave. That problem could wait, though. He pushed it from his head. He looked out and did not like what he saw.

"I found the familiar unwelcome sight which I had so often before me on the expedition of 1905–1906—the white expanse of ice cut by a river of inky black water, throwing off dense clouds of vapor which gathered in a sullen canopy overhead, at times swinging lower with the wind and obscuring the opposite shore of this malevolent Styx."

Climbing a nearby pinnacle in the ice, he could see that the lead was a quarter of a mile across, and extended as far as the horizon on both sides. Peary did not record the height of the pinnacle, but if it was one hundred feet, then the horizon would have been a little over twelve miles in each direction. The lead was a huge obstacle.

Cook had prepared for leads by packing a collapsible boat on one sledge. Although Peary had been stopped by a lead on his previous expedition, he had not learned the lesson, and had no boat with him. They had no option but to wait until the weather conditions forced both sides of the lead together, or until the intervening water froze. It was a frustrating number of days. They were only forty-five miles out from Cape Columbia, and they were no longer moving.

"Five days passed in intolerable inaction, and still the broad line of black water spread before us."

The long delay made Peary and his American companions taciturn and tetchy, but it had a worse effect on the Eskimo. Those who had been on the last expedition remembered how the conditions had almost trapped them permanently on the polar ice, and they were terrified. It was not long before fear turned to dissent in the camp.

"Finally two of the older men, who had been with me for years and whom I had trusted, came to me pretending to be sick. I have had sufficient experience to know a sick Eskimo when I see one, and the excuses of Poodloonah and Panikpah did not convince me," said Peary.

This was a test of his leadership, and he failed miserably. Instead of quelling the incipient mutiny, he fired the two men, among his most experienced dog handlers. One of the men was the father of Etukishook, one of Cook's companions from the previous season. Both men turned around and headed back for Cape Columbia, carrying "a note to the mate of the ship, giving instructions in regard to these two men and their families."

The dismissal of the two fanned the flames of mutiny, and the long days of idleness did not help. The situation was only resolved when Professor MacMillan began to organize football games, wrestling, and races on the ice, to keep everyone occupied. Once they had something to do, everyone began to calm down. By the sixth day the lead was beginning to close, and the group gingerly made their way across to the other side. No one was happy on the crossing—least of all the Eskimo—but once they were across Peary was confident it was their last substantial obstacle before the Pole. They made twelve miles that day, camping well north of the Big Lead. The march brought them over the eighty-fourth parallel. The next two days they kept that average up. The lead rotated, and Matthew Henson took over, breaking trail to the north.

But the Arctic began to take its toll. After a few more days MacMillan began to limp. When he removed his boot that evening he found that his heel was badly frostbitten. There was no alternative; he would have to return to base. It was a blow to Peary, as the professor had proven himself a useful companion. Still, it showed the value of his approach. The loss of one man, even a good one, would not slow their forward progress. In fact, the Peary System called for people to be sent back at regular intervals. Peary had decided that Dr. Goodsell would be the first to turn south, as he felt that it was important to have a physician back at base. Now the physician would have a patient on the march back to base.

Peary had kept everyone in the dark as to how far they would go. Everyone knew that the plan called for parties to return to base when their usefulness to the expedition as a whole had ended. All knew that Peary and perhaps one or two companions would make the final dash, with a team of the strongest Eskimo. But none of them knew who he would select. Captain Bartlett had been promised that he could come past Umberto Cagni's Farthest North mark of 1900, but no promises had been made to anyone else, and no further promises to the captain. Despite knowing they might be sent back at any moment, the men worked selflessly on behalf of Peary.

Now the polar party consisted of sixteen men, twelve sledges, and one hundred dogs. Peary had chosen the best of the dogs from Goodsell and MacMillan's teams and taken them for himself, giving them the weaker animals and Eskimo for their return journey. This was a very sensible approach, as the strongest were needed for the longest period on the ice. Peary divided the remaining marchers into four groups: three support parties, and his own group. "Forward, march!" he boomed, and they were off again.

They hadn't got far before they hit another lead—but this one was a lot smaller than the Big Lead, and they were able to skirt it. They came close to disaster when one group of dogs slipped into a crack in the thin ice they were crossing, and plunged into the freezing sea. Borup, the Yale athlete, leapt forward and halted the sledge, preventing it from following the dogs. Had they lost the sledge, with its five hundred pounds of food and supplies, it would have dealt them a crippling blow. They also managed to rescue the dogs.

Camp that day brought them to a latitude of a little over 85 degrees. Three years earlier it had taken Peary twenty-three days longer to get that far north.

Despite his great heroism that day, the following day Borup was turned south with three Eskimo. Peary chose him because, despite his strength, he was the least experienced on the ice. The young man was disappointed, but hardly surprised. Peary wrote: "It was a serious disappointment to Borup that he was obliged to turn back; but he had reason to feel proud of his work. He had carried the Yale colors close up to eighty-five and a half degrees, and had borne them over as many miles of polar ice as Nansen had covered in his entire journey from his ship to his farthest north."

Now there were twelve men, ten sledges, and eighty dogs still traveling into the unknown. Now they traveled as three groups. One party was led by Henson, one by Bartlett, and Marvin's party merged with Peary's own. Bartlett took the lead.

Surprisingly, they rarely stopped to take observations. In fact, they took the first observation on March 22, after a month on the ice. Up to that point they had relied on dead reckoning. There were three people on the trip who were able to use a sextant and do the complex calculations to determine their position: Peary himself, Marvin, and Bartlett. Peary asked Marvin to take the observation. The reason for this was that it would provide an independent determination of their latitude. No one could accuse Peary of exaggerating if he had not taken the observations. It was a wise precaution.

The process of taking the observation was long and involved, but in the end Marvin determined their position as 85 degrees 48 minutes north. This corresponded to within a few miles of their dead reckoning estimate, confirming they were still on target. A quick calculation showed that they had averaged ten miles north a day, on the days that they had marched. Worryingly, they had only managed to march on three days out of four, because of delays caused by leads and other factors.

But they were only 252 miles from the Pole. A third of their journey was behind them.

Three days later Marvin took another reading, showing they had reached 86 degrees 37 minutes. They were less than three days' march from Peary's previous Farthest North, and well ahead of schedule. It was the last reading Marvin took. The following morning he was ordered to take two Eskimo and turn back to Cape Columbia. As the three set out, with one sledge and seventeen dogs, Peary watched them go, then turned north once more.

"Forward, march!" his voice boomed, and they were off. He little dreamed that he would never see Marvin again.

Marvin's journey back to Cape Columbia remained for many years one of the enduring mysteries of the Arctic. The two Eskimo boys, Kudlooktoo and Inukitsoq, arrived safely at the base, and told the stunned crew of the *Roosevelt* that Marvin had slipped through thin ice near the Big Lead. They had been spread out at the time for safety, and neither Eskimo could reach him before he slipped under the water and was lost forever. The explanation was accepted initially, but there were always doubts over it. Some people thought Marvin had taken his own life. Others suspected there was more that the two Eskimo were not telling.

Finally, in 1906, Kudlooktoo gave a different account of the incident to explorer and missionary Knud Rasmussen, after he had been baptized by him. He said that Marvin had become unstable on the return journey, and that when they reached the Big Lead he had become involved in a violent row with Inukitsoq. He had tried to abandon the young Eskimo on one side of the lead, which would have condemned him to a slow and painful death through exposure and starvation. Seeing no other way to save his companion, Kudlooktoo had taken a rifle and shot Marvin. This new version raised as many questions as it answered. Kudlooktoo had been close to Marvin, but did not get on with the other Eskimo, making it unlikely that he would side with him against the American. And if he had a gun, he could have resolved the issue without having to shoot Marvin. To this day no one really knows what happened on the ice. Cook always maintained that there was "something unnatural" about the disappearance of Marvin.

Oblivious to the drama unfolding farther south, Peary continued his slow advance toward the Pole, now with Bartlett or Henson leading, and he following. The speed of the party had increased to around fifteen miles a day. Surprisingly, they came across the tracks of two Arctic foxes, several hundred miles from land. They crossed the eighty-seventh parallel, not far from where Peary claimed he had turned back three years previously. As he put it: "Now, three years older, with three more years of the inevitable wear and tear of this inexorable game behind me, I stood again beyond the eighty-seventh parallel still reaching forward to that goal which had beckoned to me for so many years."

But there were two hundred miles to go, and nothing was guaranteed. The following night the ice snapped underneath their camp, separating Peary and Henson from the others, and almost plunging a dog team into the sea. Nothing could be taken for granted.

"That night we slept with our mittens on, ready at a moment's notice for anything that might happen," Peary noted.

The following day they reached a huge lead, and in dense cloud could not see to the far side of it. The lead looked big enough to be the fabled open polar sea, Peary said. It was frustrating, but they lost another day of marching while they waited for the lead to close. They raced forward again, eager to make up for lost time.

Two days later, April 1, was the final separation. Bartlett was turned back. The sailor was bitterly disappointed. He knew that Peary would take one companion with him to the Pole, and he really believed that his chances were better than Henson's. He was performing strongly. He was a master dog sledge driver, and he had navigational skills that Henson simply didn't possess. This alone should have ensured his place on the final polar party. He could take the sextant observations that would corroborate Peary's observations, removing all possibility of doubt.

Yet Peary chose Henson.

The morning Bartlett was to turn south he took one final observation, placing them at 87 degrees 46 minutes 49 seconds north. He had been up earlier than Peary and had walked five miles north of the camp, hoping that walk would push him over the eighty-eighth parallel. The sextant reading showed that he had fallen several miles short of this. He had traveled farther north than any man apart from Peary, but for him, the race was over. Bitterly disappointed, he turned south, and began the long trek home.

"I felt a keen regret as I saw the captain's broad shoulders grow smaller in the distance and finally disappear behind the ice hummocks of the white and glittering expanse toward the south. But it was no time for reverie, and I turned abruptly away and gave my attention to the work which was before me," he recalled.

Henson noted in *A Negro Explorer at the North Pole*: "Captain Bartlett bade us all farewell. He turned back from the Farthest North that had ever been reached by anyone, to ensure the safe return of him who was to go to a still farther north, the very top of the world, the Pole itself."

That left six in the polar party. There was Peary and Henson, and four Eskimo: Ootah, Egingwah, Seegloo, and Ooqueah. They were still 130 miles from their final destination, and at the rate they were traveling, that should take ten days. Bartlett had been the strongest of the party, and had broken trail for the past five days. Now they would have no one ahead of them, and that could slow their progress. But they were finally traveling light; at the end they were using Cook's approach.

Peary went to bed that night knowing his chances were good but not certain. However, he knew he had chosen his traveling companion wisely. Bartlett had enormous strengths, but there were two things in Henson's favor that no amount of ability, loyalty, or endurance could trump. Henson was not white, and he could not read a sextant. Peary wanted to be the undisputed first white man at the Pole. He could discount the natives, as the world would. And Henson, being a Negro, would not spoil his party.

And, if he fell short of his mark, as he had on several occasions before, Henson would not be able to take the observations that could expose this.

29

A CURIOUS NEWSPAPER HEADLINE

One of Peary's strongest supporters was Harold Bridgman of the Brooklyn *Standard Union* newspaper. Bridgman had interviewed Cook after his first trip to Greenland with Peary, and the article had irked Peary, being printed without his permission. But the two had become firm friends, and Bridgman was an important cog in the Peary Arctic Club. As the years progressed, Bridgman had moved from neutral observer to firm camp follower of the commander—and, by extension, a critic of Cook.

He had used his extensive media skills to build up Peary during the vital fundraising phase of the polar expedition. But with Peary on the ice, and no prospect of news for months, Bridgman took matters into his own hands.

In the edition of the paper published on Wednesday, April 14, 1909, Bridgman carried an intriguing headline: Peary Due North Pole Twelve Midnight, Thursday.

This was incredibly prophetic—and inaccurate. Peary had been ahead of this schedule when Captain Bartlett had turned south. Bartlett was the only one who could carry news of the final stages of the expedition, until Peary himself returned. And to get news back to America, he would have had to race across the ice to Cape Columbia, travel south to Cape Sheridan, cross Smith Sound, and travel south to Upernavik or one of the other inhabited spots of Greenland to use a telegraph. That would have taken several weeks or months.

Only two explanations are possible; either Bridgman took a wild guess, or he and Peary had arranged the article before the commander set sail. This was the explanation Cook favored. He wrote: "Is Mr. Bridgman a psychic medium? How, with Peary thousands of miles away, hundreds of miles from the most northerly wireless station, did he sense the amazing feat? Were he and Peary in telepathic communication? Or, rather, does this not seem to point to an agreement entered into before the departure of Peary, about a year before the attempt was made, to announce on a certain day the 'discovery' of the Pole?"

The most likely explanation is that Peary took an audacious gamble. He knew that Cook had a year head start on him. But he also knew that polar exploration is often not a straightforward task. He had frequently been trapped in the far north over the winter, and he knew the same could happen to Cook. He might reach the Pole a year after Cook, but he was determined that his story would get out first.

No other papers took up the *Standard Union* story, but it illustrated the lengths Peary was willing to go to, to ensure he would be credited with the discovery of the North Pole.

30

COOK RETURNS

When you get to the top of Everest, it is all downhill home. Climbing downhill has its dangers, but you are swiftly moving toward safety, warmth, thicker air, better weather. Not so when you turn from the Pole. You face the exact same journey that brought you to that bleak spot. Every one of the dangers is just the same. Only difference is, you are weaker, and you have fewer supplies.

Whether Cook turned away from the North Pole on April 24, 1908, or whether he turned away from a spot a few days' march north and west of the Big Lead (more likely), he still faced a big challenge to get to safety. Not only was he navigating in a featureless landscape, the polar drift meant that he was navigating on a moving landscape.

The North Pole and the South Pole are completely different. The southern end of the globe is covered in a large continent, which is buried beneath two miles of ice. The North Pole is situated in the open Arctic Ocean, which is almost fourteen thousand feet deep at that point. Because of the extreme cold of the region, it is covered permanently in ice. There is a layer of ice roughly ten to fifteen feet thick covering the entire Arctic Ocean. This is a thin skin, and can crack and buckle, causing the troublesome leads. It can also melt—it is estimated that by

2016 the actual Pole itself will be in open water for a few weeks every summer, due to global warming.

All the world's oceans are dominated by huge ocean currents, such as the warm water Gulf Stream, which flows from the Gulf of Mexico to Europe, and the cold water Labrador Current that flows across the north Atlantic. These currents ensure that the world's oceans are never stationary. As a consequence, the skin of ice over the polar sea is never stationary. The polar drift can carry an explorer several miles off course during the course of a single day. A vicious storm can magnify the effect, leaving the explorer hopelessly lost. This was a huge problem a century ago, as position could only be determined by sextant observations, which could only be taken once a day, and only during clear weather.

So when Cook turned south he was facing enormous obstacles. He had hoped that the drift would carry him east, so that if he headed directly south he would make land in northern Greenland. He was not as familiar with the area as Peary, but he knew it well enough to work his way to safety from there. It had taken them two months to reach the Pole—or wherever they had really turned back from—so it should have taken roughly the same time to reach land.

Before leaving their Farthest North, Cook buried a bottle in a crevasse describing his accomplishment. It was a pointless gesture: with the polar drift it could be back in civilization before him. He knew this, but felt if it was ever discovered, its location might give information on the polar drift. After depositing the message, he and his two companions turned south and began racing toward land.

They did not try to follow their outward trail, for two reasons. One was that drifting snow obscured much of it, and Cook did not expect they could follow it far. The second was the drift. Cook also decided that the return trip could lead to possibilities of exploration.

He had "an eager desire to ascertain what might be discovered on a new trail farther west. It was this eagerness which led to us being carried adrift and held prisoners for a year."

On April 25 the party crossed five crevasses, which slowed them down, but they still managed sixteen miles, according to Cook. As the enthusiasm for home conquered their fatigue, they maintained these speeds for the next few days. By April 30 they were 120 miles from the Pole, but had drifted east. Their sextant reading showed them off course, so they turned their course southwest, and marched on. But on May 6 a vicious storm broke over them, pinning them in a makeshift camp for a number of days. With snow and crystallized ice being driven into their faces by gale, and a wind chill dropping the temperatures to an inhuman level, they had no choice but to wait it out. Food supplies were dwindling, and the prospect of starvation loomed.

There was another worry.

"For many days no observations had been possible. Our location could only be guessed at."

It was May 24 before the sky cleared enough for another observation. They were down to 84 degrees north, but had drifted west. They could not see Bradley Land, which should have been close to them, had it existed. The ice was crossed with pressure ridges, and they could see open water and leads in the near distance. Conditions were nasty. Worryingly, they had only averaged twelve miles a day since leaving the Pole, and now they were slowing down rather than speeding up. They had two options: make for Nansen Sound, between Axel Heiberg and Ellesmere Islands, or go west and try for game on Bradley Land.

"The new land westward was invisible, and offered no food prospects," Cook judged. It was a wise call. To have gone west and found nothing would have been a fatal detour. Cook knew that the polar drift was eastward, and using that knowledge he plotted a course to the west of Cape Svartevoeg. The drift would bring them to land safely. The drift is normally determined by ocean currents, but can also be influenced by nearby land masses, and by local weather. It was a gamble to try and read it, but it would have been a gamble to ignore the drift too. Cook thought he had made the right decision.

The temperature was rising now every day, approaching zero. The ice was changing, breaking up as summer approached. The three men were no longer shivering. Crossing the eighty-third parallel, they found their way barred by a large lead to the east. The shores of the lead were characterized by broken and ragged sheets of ice and small bergs.

Launching the boat was impossible, and trying to land on the other side looked equally impossible. The lead was not going to close or freeze, so Cook had to travel south on the west of the lead. The wind shifted to the east, pushing them farther west. For twenty days they traveled south and west, with no idea of their position. Fog reduced visibility to a short distance, and they were damp and miserable as food was reduced to half rations.

When they eventually managed to take a reading, Cook was shocked.

"Since leaving the eighty-fourth parallel, without noticeable movement, we had been carried astray by the ocean drift. I took observations. They gave latitude 79 degrees 82 minutes, and longitude 101 degrees 22 minutes. At last I had discovered our whereabouts, and found that we were far from where we ought to be. Our situation was indeed nearly hopeless."

They were in Crown Prince Gustav Sea, far west and south of where they needed to be. Axel Heiberg was to the east, with the low mountains barely visible on the horizon. Their planned line of retreat was on the opposite side of that landmass. That was where their supplies had been cached, and where the game roamed. That way lay salvation. Instead, they found themselves on a rapidly melting ice sheet a full fifty miles off shore. They had half rations enough for ten days, and they faced crushed ice and open leads. The task was impossible. Perhaps they could make it south instead, to the uninhabited wastelands of Ellef Ringnes Land and Amund Ringnes Land. With no option, they moved into Hassel Sound and tried to reach the more eastern of the islands.

On June 15 the men were woken from their camp by a sound in the air, and a flutter of wings. It was a snow bunting, and the first animal they had seen since they had noted the fox tracks on the ice about four months previously. The following day they made land, on a small, low-lying island, completely devoid of life. But a few days later they spotted the tracks of a small rat, then they saw old bear tracks. They began to track these, hoping to bring down the massive beast. One bear would be the difference between life and death. They eventually located the bear, and tried to move to the windward side of it, so as to give its sensitive nose no indication of the hunters on its trail. But soon the bear looked up, and then began moving purposefully across the ice.

"He was as hungry as we were, for he made an airline for our changed position. We were hunting the bear—the bear was also hunting us."

It was an uneven contest. Polar bears are among the most ferocious predators in the world, and weigh close to three quarters of a ton. But the humans had a gun. They spent a day gorging themselves and their remaining dogs, then continued on their journey, with a sledge full of food. More bears appeared, and other game. The threat of starvation was past. The party continued south, trying to reach Lancaster Sound, where they could hitch a ride on a Scottish whaler. It was a risky undertaking, and in the end they failed. By September they were in Cape Sparbo, on the northern shore of Devon Island. Situated in Baffin Bay, it is the largest uninhabited island in the world. Although the island was not inhabited, it was occasionally visited by explorers, sealers, and native hunters. Cook decided the party had no option but to spend the winter in this isolated spot, and try for home the following spring. They made a cave habitable, and spent the autumn hunting musk oxen and other game to stock their larder for the long dark months to come. Hunting was difficult, as they were out of ammunition. They had to fashion spears and axes from bits of their sledges, but they stockpiled enough to eat well for the winter.

November to February was spent in the cave. In February, like bears emerging from hibernation, the three men were ready to march once more. The sea ice was still frozen, so they knew they could make it east to Axel Heiberg Island, then cross it to their caches. It took two brutal months, which reduced them to walking skeletons. But at last they were across Smith Sound and heading for Annoatok, where Cook knew he had supplies for trade, as well as food. Late on the evening of April 15 they arrived at their destination.

"So weak that we had to climb on hands and knees, we reached the top of an iceberg, and from there saw Annoatok. Natives, who had thought us long dead, rushed out to greet us. There I met Mr. Harry Whitney . . ."

Cook's year in the wilderness was over. But his troubles were just beginning.

31

COOK REACHES EUROPE

Cook was shocked when he discovered that his hut had been commandeered by Peary. He had expected to return to civilization and have the use of a house full of provisions. Instead he found himself at the mercy of his rival, having to undergo the indignity of paying for supplies that he owned. He was also furious that his supply of valuable furs had been confiscated.

"Now if Mr. Peary required my supplies for legitimate exploration, I should have been glad to give him my last bread; but to use my things to satisfy his greed for commercial gain was bitter medicine," he complained to anyone who would listen. The problem was, the men in charge were Peary's men, and they didn't care.

The only one who did care was the independent sportsman Henry Whitney, who was just along for some game hunting. He found Cook an engaging companion, and the two men often whiled the hours away in conversation as Cook regained his strength at Annoatuk. Eventually Cook opened up to his new companion, telling Whitney that he had reached the Pole. But he swore the other man to secrecy, knowing that he needed to control the release of the story.

Cook was eager to return to southern Europe, both to get his story out, and to begin his journey home to his family. He decided that his best option was a sledge trip through Greenland. He would travel seven hundred miles south, reaching the Danish trading post of Upernavik, where he could easily get a ship to Denmark. It would not be an easy trip; he would face mountains and glaciers, open leads of water, and endless hardship. Whitney suggested waiting until the end of the summer, when a boat would be sent to pick him up. He said that Cook was welcome to share the ride home. But Cook decided he could get back more quickly by taking the sledge route.

Cook hired two Eskimo for the trip, as his companions on the polar journey had already returned to their people. But on the day before he set out, one of his new Eskimo got sick. That meant they could take one sledge less. He would have to leave some provisions behind. He discussed the matter with Whitney, who suggested that he leave stuff that he would not need immediately on the sledge journey. He could bring only what he needed to survive, and Whitney would bring the rest of the stuff back to America at the end of the summer.

Cook agreed. He immediately boxed much of his paperwork, his meteorological data, ethnological collections, geological specimens, and some furs and spare clothing. He also boxed much of his navigational equipment, which he would not need for the trip to Upernavik. These included his sextant, compass, artificial horizon, barometer, and thermometer. He kept his manuscript, diary, and some original field papers with astronomical calculations and sextant readings. The remainder of his papers went into the three boxes he was leaving with Whitney.

He was taking a risk. These papers and the instruments would have to be assessed by academics and experts to verify his claim to the Pole. But he trusted Whitney. The hunter knew the vital importance of the boxes left in his care.

Before leaving, Cook instructed Whitney to hand the cabin back, not to Peary, but to Etukishook and Ahwelah, the two Eskimo who had accompanied him to the Pole. It was a "thank you" for their loyal service.

In a dig at Peary, he also left a letter allowing Peary's men Murphy and Pritchard (who had been left in charge of Cook's cabin) to stay there until the end of the season. He said that instead of charging them rent, he would consider their free tenancy to be balanced against the cost to Peary of letting Franke return to America with Peary's support ship some months previously.

He turned south in the third week of April, making good progress despite violent storms. On May 21 he reached Upernavik. He sought out the Danish governor, who put him up in guest quarters while he waited for the next ship south. It was a long wait; he was stuck in Upernavik until August, when a ship docked three hundred miles south. He hopped on a coastal trawler and joined the *Hans Egede*, which departed for Copenhagen on August 9. The night before they departed, the captain and crew threw a dinner for Cook, attended by many of the locals, including explorer Knud Rasmussen. Although he had not gone public with his claims yet, he could not conceal his success from the happy revelers. Rasmussen revealed that the discovery of the Big Nail was the talk of the Eskimo tribes in the region. Word was getting out.

Rasmussen, half Danish and half Inuit, was a bit of a visionary, almost a shamanistic character. He congratulated Cook on the greatest victory in Arctic history, but struck a warning note: Peary, a man with a bad name among the natives for his greed and domineering ways, would not be happy. It was a sobering warning, which Cook did not take as seriously as he should have.

The *Hans Egede* took three weeks to complete its voyage south. Cook, who didn't have the money to pay for his passage, composed a long article about the Pole, which he hoped to sell to finance his return to the world. On September 1 the captain landed Cook at Lerwick, on the Shetland Islands, where he sent a lengthy telegram to the *New York Herald*. He asked for a fee of $3,000, which the newspaper was happy to pay. Now he could afford his passage, and a good suit of clothes when he landed in Copenhagen.

By the time the ship pulled into the Danish capital, he was the sensation of the year. There was a telegram from the Prime Minister congratulating him, hundreds of people on the pier, and dozens of reporters. One of them, Philip Gibbs from the London *Daily Chronicle*, knew nothing at all about polar exploration, and decided to hide his ignorance by going on the attack in his interview. He demanded to see Cook's diary and papers. When Cook gently explained that most of his papers were still in Greenland, the reporter was incredulous.

"What evidence can you bring to show that you actually reached the North Pole?" he asked.

Cook knew he was in for a tough ride. He didn't know just how tough.

But he pushed the thought aside, and threw himself into the celebrations. Among the many people clambering to meet him was one familiar face. Old friend Roald Amundsen had traveled from Norway, and was there to offer his congratulations—and share a bottle of wine. It was a great homecoming.

And when news broke a week later that Peary was also claiming to have reached the Pole—but a year later than Cook—the doctor was magnanimous: "I am proud that a fellow American has reached the Pole. As Rear Admiral Schley said at Santiago: 'There is glory enough for us all.'"

32

AMUNDSEN SETS OUT FOR THE NORTH POLE

The most difficult and dangerous mountain to climb is not Mount Everest. The tenth highest peak, Annapurna, is a far bigger challenge, and has only been climbed a small number of times. For every one person who has made the summit of Annapurna, twenty have reached the top of the world. And you are five times more likely to die on the smaller mountain.

These are facts every explorer knows and the public remains largely ignorant of. Some geographical targets are glamorous, and some are obscure. Perception can be more important than reality when it comes to planning expeditions. Amundsen knew that the Northwest Passage had gained him respect, but true fame and financial independence would only come if he achieved a really crowd-pleasing first. That was why he had persuaded Nansen to give him *Fram*, and why he was determined to set the Norwegian flag on the North Pole.

His plans were progressing well, with funds flowing in, but not fast enough. This was a common problem for explorers. His first lecture tour of America had been a success, so he hoped to repeat that success with a second tour, in November 1909. He was a hero in Oslo, and enjoyed the new opportunities this gave him. Up to this time he had been too busy—or away too long—for relationships. But with a few years at home, with money in his pocket and every door open to him, this had changed. For the first time in his life, Amundsen found himself in love.

Of course, it could not be simple. The woman he fell for, Sigrid Castberg, was already married to a well-known Oslo lawyer. A passionate man, Amundsen tried to persuade her to leave her husband, obtain a divorce, and marry him. She knew he was planning a trip that would take several years, so she declined, telling him that she would consider such drastic moves when he returned. Nevertheless, the two remained inseparable companions as he planned his expedition, setting many tongues wagging in the close-knit community.

Success is never certain, but the last Viking was confident of his plan. It had a good chance, particularly if the expedition was properly staffed and equipped. He began looking for suitable companions for the long voyage, as he oversaw the production of his book about the Northwest Passage. He needed a special breed of explorer to accompany him, as the plan involved being frozen into the polar sea for up to seven years. That was a huge commitment for something that was not guaranteed to succeed.

Amundsen hoped to enter the Arctic Basin through the Bering Strait, the fifty-mile gap separating Alaska from Russia. He would then sail northwest until the *Fram* was completely immobilized in the pack ice. The ship would then drift at the mercy of the ice for between four and six years, crossing the high Arctic before emerging somewhere between Greenland and Spitzbergen, the large island far north of Norway. The slow pace of the drift would give the crew plenty of time to take ocean depth soundings, and to map the ocean floor. They would also take daily readings of air temperature, humidity, water salinity, and wind and tide observations. The result would be the most comprehensive survey of the Arctic Ocean ever. This was window dressing; Amundsen couldn't care less about the science, but he knew it would get him backers, and funding.

He also began modifying *Fram* for the task. *Gjøa* had performed well in the search for the Northwest Passage, but was battered beyond use by the end. *Fram* was on loan, so he would have to make sure it came back in good condition. More importantly, his life and the lives of his crew depended upon the reliability of their vessel. One of the first things he did was install a diesel engine to the boat. This was a major innovation, as marine diesel engines were cutting-edge technology. *Fram* was the very first polar vessel to be fitted with one, and one of the first oceangoing vessels. It would perform far more efficiently than the gas engine the *Gjøa* had struggled with. For one thing, its output was fifteen times the horsepower of *Gjøa*'s engine, meaning it could ram effectively through broken pack ice and thin sheets.

No expedition is organized easily, but Amundsen was enjoying the challenge. Based largely in Oslo, with a woman he loved at his side, and with a new home overlooking the bay, this was as good and as stable as his life had ever been.

The summer of 1909 passed in a swirl of social engagements, meetings, and planning sessions. He had only raised a quarter of what he would need, but he knew the American trip was coming up in a few months. He was optimistic.

Then, in September, his world came crashing down. On September 1 the *New York Herald* carried the front page headline which rendered his plans meaningless. THE NORTH POLE IS DISCOVERED BY DR. FREDERICK A. COOK. The story was taken up by all the major European papers. Then, only a week later, the papers began to carry another report just as distressing for the Norwegian. Now Peary was claiming to have reached the Pole as well.

At best, he was racing for third place.

33

PEARY REACHES THE POLE?

One hundred thirty-four miles to go, and not enough strength or provisions for the ten days, at a minimum, that it would take them to reach their goal. Yet Peary seemed optimistic. His life, after all, was based on overcoming insurmountable obstacles. The fact that hc had often failed did not bother him.

"We had five sledges and forty dogs, the pick of one hundred and forty with which we had left the ship. With these we were ready now for the final lap of the journey."

His plan was simple; he would make five forced marches of at least twenty-five miles each. If the final march did not bring them to the Pole, they would make that last day a double march, and keep going until they arrived at 90 degrees north. The plan ignored a number of factors. Weather or open leads could delay them. They were weak after two months on the ice. And they were averaging well under thirteen miles a day. Now he wanted his small team to double their speed. It was a hopelessly optimistic schedule.

In fairness to Peary, he tried his best. The next week was characterized by long days of wearisome toil, which left everyone exhausted at the end of a march. The days began the same way. The camp would wake, and breakfast would be prepared. Then, as Henson and the Eskimo got the sledges loaded and the dogs ready, Peary would put on a pair of snow shoes and shuffle out onto the ice ahead of them, moving slowly with his familiar half-lame gait. He would break trail so that they would have something to follow at the start of the day. After an hour or so they always caught up with him. Peary then kicked off the snow shoes and sat in the fur-lined seat in the sledge under Egingwah's control. The other four sledges were loaded with supplies. Even Peary, who was doing less physical work than the others, felt the strain. He had cut a third hole in his belt to keep pace with his shrinking waistline.

"Every man and dog of us was as lean and flat-bellied as a board, and as hard," he noted.

Matthew Henson acknowledged the toughness of those final days, writing: "The memory of those last five marches is a memory of toil, fatigue, and exhaustion."

They tried to travel in as straight a line as possible. The temperature had risen to minus twenty-five, and the wind had died down. Conditions could not have been better. The first day they marched for ten hours. Peary estimated they had covered thirty miles, but decided twenty-five was more realistic. He noted that the northerly wind had died down, and was no longer driving the ice south. He speculated that there might be a "rebound," and that the drift might temporarily switch direction and help them out.

Henson noted: "We marched and marched, falling down in our tracks repeatedly, until it was impossible to go on. We were forced to camp, in spite of the impatience of the Commander."

The next day Peary estimated that delays had slowed the group down, and they had probably covered twenty miles. He put a fourth new notch in his belt. He believed the next day they covered twenty-five miles, and the following day something similar, noting: "I had not dared to hope for such progress as we were making."

Henson's recollection is a bit different: On April 3 he slipped and fell into an open lead, only being rescued from certain death by the swift intervention of Ootah. By the time he had dried off and caught up with the others, he found that Peary too had taken a ducking. To peel off the sodden furs after a plunge into the water, dry off, and dress again in new furs was not as simple a matter as shrugging out of one coat and into another. Every setback cost the group valuable time.

On the evening of April 5, Peary allowed everyone an hour of extra sleep. He had taken a latitude reading that showed their position to be 89 degrees 25 minutes, or thirty-five miles from the Pole. This should have been cause for jubilation, but Henson noted that the Commander seemed disappointed. No one could confirm the observation, and they all took Peary at his word. But it is possible that his observation that evening showed the group much farther south. The reality is that they were unlikely to be traveling as fast as Peary's optimistic estimates. Instead of being within a march of the top of the world, they were still a week short of their destination. Time was running out. Peary, as the sole navigator, knew this. But he gave the false reading, and told his companions they were nearly ready to turn for home.

That day's observation had not been taken at noon, so could not be relied upon, whether it showed what Peary claimed it showed or a completely different latitude. In either case, he had to take another observation the following day, at the right time. By midnight they were on the march again. The twenty-four-hour light meant it mattered little whether they traveled by day or by night, and the early start meant that they could get in a long day on the trail before his next observation, at noon on April 6.

"When we had covered a good fifteen miles we halted, made tea, ate lunch, and rested the dogs. Then we went on for another estimated fifteen miles. In twelve hours actual traveling time we made thirty miles."

He put their speed down to having a small party on the ice: a large party moved slower. They ended their double march at ten o'clock on April 6, and Peary told everyone that they were within the vicinity of the Pole. After setting up camp, he took his observation at noon, and discovered he was only three minutes of a degree short of his target. That was just a handful of miles—for all practical purposes, he had arrived. But he was too exhausted to make the last few steps.

Actually, he was incapable of walking that distance himself, and his companions had unhitched the sledges for a well-earned rest. So, exhaustion or not, he had no way of crossing the remaining distance. Peary was a forceful man; he could have ordered everyone to harness up for a few more hours. This was the culmination of twenty years' hard work, the dream of his lifetime. Yet he didn't issue that order. Was there significance in that? At this remove, we can only speculate.

"I was too weary to take the last few steps," he simply said in his later account of the trip.

So they ate and slept. After a few hours Peary was awake again, and he noted in his diary: "The Pole at last. The prize of three centuries. My dream and goal for twenty years. Mine at last! I cannot bring myself to realize it."

A sledge was prepared for a quick dash the final few miles north. It was a light sledge, carrying only a tin of pemmican, the navigational instruments, and a few skins for warmth. Drawn by a double team of dogs, it swiftly raced over the frozen ground, covering an estimated ten miles in a few hours. At midnight, they stopped and Peary took advantage of the twenty-four-hour day and a break in the fog to take some new observations. They had overshot their target! According to Peary, their dash had brought them over the Pole and now they were heading south. He had passed from the western to the eastern hemisphere in a few miles. Although they had not deviated from their course, they had begun by marching north, and now they were going south. They had to retrace their steps.

Fixing the exact spot of the Pole is difficult, because the instruments Peary had at his disposal were accurate to within a few miles. He would never be able to say conclusively that he had stepped on the actual spot of the Pole, but if he could walk in a tight circle around the Pole, and criss-cross that circle, he could legitimately claim to have discovered the North Pole. This he proceeded to do. A measurement at 6:00 a.m. on April 7 showed them four or five miles south of the Pole in the direction of the Bering Strait. So he headed into the sun for eight miles, crossing the polar vicinity once more, then turned toward the camp, arriving in time to take a reading at noon.

According to Peary, the numerous observations he had taken proved he had indeed been in the immediate vicinity of the North Pole, to within the limits of accuracy allowed by the scientific instruments of the time. This was success, by any standards Peary would be called upon to satisfy.

Happy, he planted five flags at what he claimed was the Pole. One of these was an American flag that his wife had made for him a number of years previously and which he carried on all his expeditions. A strip had been removed and left at each Farthest North. Now he had no more need to tear off the strips; there was no farther north.

He also raised the flag of his old fraternity, Delta Kappa Epsilon, the Navy League flag, the World Ensign of Liberty and Peace flag, and the Red Cross flag. As the flags were raised, Henson and the Eskimo gave three lusty cheers, then everyone shook hands in a semi-formal gesture a bit out of keeping with their ragged appearances and the wilderness of their surroundings.

Henson remembered the discovery of the Pole a bit differently from his commander. He did not recall Peary taking any measurement at the camp on April 6. He said that when they stopped to set up camp, Peary unfurled a flag and placed it over the igloo his Eskimo had built for him. He then told Henson: "This, my boy, is to be Camp Morris K. Jessup, the last and most northerly camp on the earth." Henson and the Eskimo then gave three cheers for the end of their journey.

He said that it was on the next day that Peary took his observations.

The chief difference in both accounts is that in Peary's version, he took an observation on April 6 which showed he was very close to the Pole, and the following day he fixed the spot with as much exactness as he could. In Henson's version, he declared on April 6 that they had reached the Pole, then took observations the following day to confirm that. It seems a small discrepancy, but if Henson is correct, then Peary committed a serious blunder by declaring their success without bothering to check his actual position. If he knew that they were up to a hundred miles short of the Pole, he would not have needed to take any observations. He would be faking them, in any case. If he had made the decision to pretend that they had got farther north than they had, then Henson's version makes perfect sense.

Peary had turned back the only other man who could take a sextant reading (Captain Bartlett), and was accompanied by four uneducated

Eskimo, and a servant who was not a navigator. If he could convince the five that he had gone far enough, it would be easy to convince the rest of the world.

So did Peary reach the Pole on April 7? It seems highly unlikely. In the weeks leading up to the final dash he was averaging around thirteen miles a day. The five days since Bartlett had turned back were not trouble-free marches. Peary acknowledged that the second day had been difficult, and they had not traveled as far as he would have liked. Then, on April 3, both he and Henson had taken plunges into the sea. It is scarcely credible that they could have almost doubled their speed under the circumstances. Far more likely is that they continued at their same pace, or perhaps a little faster. If we assume that they traveled fifteen miles a day, and on one long day achieved twenty miles (rather than the thirty Peary claimed), then they would have fallen fifty or sixty miles short of the Pole. Of course, they could also have slowed down slightly, and been a lot further away than that. Four to six more marches might have got them to their true destination, but that would have meant four to six more marches back—prolonging their time on the ice by well over a week, with dwindling supplies, and their support teams far south. Peary almost certainly judged the reward not worth the risk. He had gone far enough to be able to make a credible and uncontested claim on the North Pole. In his First Greenland Expedition he had exaggerated his penetration of the ice sheet. In his Second Greenland Expedition he had made claims to have discovered the northern extent of the island, which were later found to be exaggerated. The final camp, on April 6–8, 1909, was just one more exaggeration.

Sometime later, when the claims of both Peary and Cook were being considered by panels of experts, a subcommittee of the Committee of Naval Affairs examined Peary's journal, which he had brought with him on the expedition. The subcommittee were concerned that the page for April 6 contained the ordinary observations of the day, with no mention of the discovery of the Pole. Instead, a note on a separate sheet of paper had been inserted at that page proclaiming the discovery. And the pages for April 7 and 8, when Peary was supposedly taking observations to confirm his discovery, were embarrassingly blank. The journal was clean and not smudged, which the subcommittee thought odd, as conditions on the ice had been brutal. Although they did not say that the journal was a fabrication, clearly they had concerns. They accepted Peary's word that he had been to the Pole, but they were not happy with his proof of the fact.

Modern explorers and experts are even less happy with his proofs. Irish adventurer Pat Falvey, who has been on fourteen Arctic expeditions, said: "Most modern polar explorers think that the timings and the logistics put forward by Peary would suggest that he did not achieve what he said he had achieved, and his record is very much in doubt, according to those who know what we can achieve now."

On his sudden surge of speed at the end of the expedition, Falvey said: "If he was going for five hours a day prior to turning back the last people before his final dash, he could have decided to lengthen his marches. You can do that for a while. You can go day and night to achieve a goal; endorphins will keep you going. But the experts I have spoken to doubt that Peary kept it up and got to the pole."

On the ice, Peary was not troubled by such future concerns. Happy he had gone far enough, it was time to turn around and race toward Cape Columbia. As every mountaineer will tell you, the mountain isn't climbed until you return safely to base.

34

PEARY RETURNS

On April 27 Captain Bartlett, safely back on the *Roosevelt* at Cape Sheridan, spotted a dark figure moving on the ice several miles out from the ship. He squinted into the distance, and was sure it was Peary and his team, returning from the Pole. Excited, he rushed off the ship and onto the ice, trekking north to meet them. When he reached the weary travellers, he walked up to Peary and said: "I congratulate you, sir, on the discovery of the Pole."

Peary looked at him with tired eyes.

"How did you guess it?" he muttered. Then he continued trudging toward the ship.

He said nothing more. For a man with a reputation for blowing his own trumpet, it seemed strange. But Bartlett thought nothing more of it.

An hour later Peary was back on board. He said nothing to his fellow expedition members about the trip, and made no claim to have reached the Pole. He retired to his cabin without giving any account of his trip. Borup and the others must have found it strange. But they all put it down to exhaustion.

Henson had also noticed Peary's reluctance to talk about his great achievement. At the Pole itself he had attempted to shake Peary's hand at one stage, only for the commander to turn away from him. Henson put it down to a gust of wind blowing ice crystals into Peary's eye, making him turn. But he found it strange that there had been no talk at all of the Pole on the return trip. In fact, Peary rarely spoke to Henson, and this silent treatment continued for several days. And when Peary finally resumed talking to Henson, it was always about matter-of-fact matters, never about the Pole.

We now know why Peary reacted so strangely. On the ice it had been an easy decision to reach: if he had pressed north for another five or six days, he risked the Eskimo rebelling, or worse, running out of food and being trapped in the far north, cut off from potential rescue. So giving a false reading to his companions had seemed an easy option. But now he was back among his equals, white men who understood navigation and who knew the conditions of the ice. Would they believe his account of the five-day "sprint" for the Pole? Or would they realize that he was incapable of the speed he claimed? If they suspected that, his whole claim would collapse. Captain Bartlett had taken the last independent latitude reading, showing the party 134 miles short of the Pole. Yet Peary expected everyone to believe that five days later he had reached the top of the world. They knew the condition of his feet. They knew the weakness of his men. Would they take him at his word? Peary knew that his word, on this matter, was as good as a three-dollar bill.

The simple solution was to say nothing, and put off the discussion.

The *Roosevelt* spent a while more in Cape Sheridan before Peary ordered the expedition to set sail for Greenland, the first leg of the journey home. He did not seem to be in any great rush to share his big news with the world. Instead of hurrying, they took a leisurely cruise across Smith Sound, and actually stopped along the way for a walrus hunt. Peary spent long hours alone in his cabin, brooding. His hand had been forced by circumstances. Several expeditions had seen him always fall short of his goal. This time he had come agonizingly close. And he knew that his age and physical condition—not to mention the finances—meant there would be no more chances. He had given it his best shot, and fallen short of the mark by roughly ninety miles. But he was a forceful man, and he knew that he had a better than even chance of bluffing it out. He had got close enough for that to work.

Then they reached northern Greenland, and everywhere they heard the whispers: Cook had reached the Pole a year ahead of Peary. This was the jolt he needed. Suddenly his mood of depression turned to fury. Was another man going to claim his prize? He went into war mode.

The first thing he did was to locate Ahwelah and Etukishook, and bring them on board the *Roosevelt*, where they were interrogated about their trip with Cook. After several years in the Arctic, Peary still had not learned the native tongue. But he prepared a list of questions, and hoped that Henson's pigdin Eskimo would be sufficient for the job. Dr. Goodsell, the expedition physician, did speak the language fluently. He volunteered to help, but was brusquely turned down by Peary.

Both natives were questioned separately. They were shown maps and charts, and asked where they had been on their epic trip. Neither man could read, and neither had ever used a map. They might as well have been shown Egyptian hieroglyphics. But Peary was happy. It was ammunition against his rival. He prepared to sail south, and get his own story out.

Henry Whitney was still waiting for the ship he had arranged to pick him up after his summer of game hunting. But there was no sign of it. Peary had a word with the younger man, warning him that if he did not leave Greenland soon, he ran the risk of being iced in for the winter. He offered the hunter a berth on the *Roosevelt*, which Whitney was glad to accept.

A few hours later a line of natives arrived at the ship with all of Whitney's luggage. There were boxes and crates and trunks, even a sledge. As Peary stood on the deck the items were brought up the gangplank. Then his voice rang out with chilly decisiveness: "Have you anything belonging to Dr. Cook?"

Whitney paused, then pointed to three boxes and the battered sledge.

"Well, I don't want any of them aboard this ship," Peary said.

Whitney was now caught in the same dilemma as Rudolph Franke had been the previous summer. Accept the lift home and abandon

Cook's possessions, or remain faithful to the doctor and spend a winter on the ice. Peary's attitude made it clear there would be no compromise.

Whitney sought advice from a senior member of the crew, who suggested that he quietly repack and sneak Cook's items on board. This is what he did. But just before they sailed, Peary summoned Whitney to his cabin.

"When I said I did not want anything belonging to Dr. Cook aboard this ship, I meant I did not want a single thing he had," he said, looking steadily at Whitney. "I am going to place you on your word of honor as a gentleman not to take a thing belonging to Dr. Cook aboard this ship."

Reluctantly, Whitney gathered up Cook's items and placed them in a big gun chest, nailing it shut. He took the chest out and hid it behind some rocks on the shore, in the hopes that it would not be spotted by looters. He was determined to return for the box the following season. On August 20 the *Roosevelt* turned south, and headed for home. Three days later they passed the *Jeanie*, the ship that was coming for Whitney. Whitney left the *Roosevelt* and joined the *Jeanie*. Now he had a choice; go back north and pick up the chest, or continue south to the good hunting grounds for one final shoot before he returned home. A silly factor shaped his decision. He had promised guns to Ahwelah and Etukishook, and he felt he could not go back without the guns. So he ordered the *Jeanie* to turn south. He could always buy Cook new instruments. And how important were the papers in any case?

It was a decision that changed the course of Cook's subsequent life.

On the evening of September 5, the *Roosevelt* reached Indian Harbour in Labrador, and Peary went ashore the following morning. The morose leader had now morphed into a man of action. He spent several hours in the wireless station, getting his news to the world.

"Have made good at last. I have the old Pole," he wired his wife, Josephine. He followed this up with sixteen more telegrams, including one to Herbert Bridgman with the news that the expedition had been a success. He told the Associated Press and the *New York Times* that he had nailed the Stars and Stripes to the North Pole. He left an element of intrigue, promising an explosive story to come. Now the world had two men claiming the greatest prize in exploration.

35

AMUNDSEN CHANGES HIS MIND

When the European press began to carry reports on Cook's claims in September 1909, Amundsen was horrified. But he tried to remain gracious in defeat. Not only was he an admirer of Cook, they were genuine friends. Part of him must have exulted in the glory of his former companion, while the rest of him lamented his lost opportunity. Then, on September 7, there came the second bombshell. A headline in the *New York Times* proclaimed: PEARY DISCOVERS THE NORTH POLE AFTER EIGHT TRIALS IN TWENTY-THREE YEARS.

Cook claimed to have attained the top of the world in the spring of 1908, while Peary reached the spot a full year later. Controversy immediately arose. Had both men reached the spot, or was one a fraud? Some backed Cook; more backed Peary. It was of little consequence to Amundsen. Someone had got there before him. It scarcely mattered who.

Cook was in Copenhagen at the time, and Amundsen immediately traveled south to meet him. They stayed in the same hotel for a weekend, and were seen in each other's company all the time. Reports suggest that both men had a very enjoyable reunion. Amundsen had no doubts about the veracity of his friend's claim. He seemed genuinely happy for Cook.

At one point during the weekend, perhaps after a few beers too many, Cook jokingly suggested that Amundsen should travel south instead of north, and bag the South Pole. Amundsen just laughed. The idea was preposterous. Even getting to the right region was a monumental task, and conditions in the Antarctic were far tougher than those in the Arctic.

After Cook left Copenhagen, Amundsen returned to Oslo, where he still had a lot of work to do before his trip to America. He finally arrived in New York in November, and by that stage he knew that Cook's claim was controversial. What he did not know was just how controversial it had become. It was polarizing people. Cook was being widely discredited, and Peary and his supporters were doing their best to undermine the New York doctor. Both men had sailed together in the past, and been friends. That was forgotten now. Peary was on the war path, and using all his extensive contacts to crush the claims of his rival.

Amundsen was warned by the Norwegian consul in Chicago, Fredrik Herman Gade, to keep his mouth shut and not involve himself in the controversy. But as soon as his ship docked in New York, the reporters began hounding him.

Although he would have preferred to have promoted his own trip, he could not stand by and see his friend being vilified. He announced his support for Cook, adding, "Peary's behavior fills me with the deepest anger and I want to proclaim publicly that Dr. Cook is the most reliable Arctic traveler I know, and it is simply unreasonable to doubt him and believe Peary."

Not the answer the American establishment wanted, but it was widely reported nonetheless. So were his views on more mundane subjects, such as American football, and the feasibility of driving a racing car on ice.

Amundsen stayed in Chicago with Gade, who had been at school with him. Gade had a business brain, and he put a number of sponsorship deals in place which would help supply the upcoming Norwegian North Pole expedition. But interest was waning; the objective had been achieved. Who wanted their products associated with the third man to the Pole?

He knew the trip was now in trouble. But deep in the recesses of his mind, a plan had been forming to salvage the situation. It was a bold and audacious plan. It might even see him accused of duplicity. But if he succeeded, he would be crowned in glory, pushing the squabble between Peary and Cook onto the back pages. He said nothing, not even to his closest associates. Nansen was not taken into his confidence. Nor were the crew he recruited for the *Fram*. He did confide in his brother Leon, his business manager, and in Gade, who was helping him in America.

As he put it himself: "Just as everything was about ready, the world was electrified by the news that Admiral Peary, in April 1909, had reached the North Pole. This was a blow indeed! If I was to maintain my prestige as an explorer, I must quickly achieve a sensational success of some sort. I resolved upon a coup."

When he returned from America, funds still not fully in place, he threw himself into final preparations for his polar trip. He knew that he could get credit on promises. He would be out of touch with civilization for a few years—the creditors could hardly chase him. And on his return, he would settle bills with the proceeds of lectures and a book. So he never lost faith, working furiously to the end. During the long winter and hard spring of 1909–1910 he continued to train in the snow, hardening his body for the ordeal ahead. He got to know his men, training with them as they went about their final preparations.

Aside from that, he shunned society. He refused to answer the phone, did not encourage visitors, and spent hours studying the accounts of previous polar explorers.

In America the war of words raged between Cook and Peary. Amundsen turned his mind away from all that, concentrating on his own project. Third to the Pole, but his would be the most interesting route, and the one that would bring the greatest scientific benefits. If he could not be the first, he could be the best. That was the plan, as far as the public were concerned. The Norwegian government and Nansen also believed this. So did the crew of the *Fram*, and the polar party itself. But secretly, some were beginning to doubt what they were being told. For one thing, money began to appear from American sponsors.

Why were they backing the man who was starting after the race had been won?

Then there was the prefabricated shed that appeared in Amundsen's garden at Uranienborg. It was large, with a kitchen and sleeping accommodation for nine. It would be useless on the frozen Arctic Ocean, where the plan was to stick with the ship until it was time to leave for the Pole. Once on the ice, a massive structure like the hut would be useless—the team would use tents and igloos.

Helmet Hansen, an old hand from the *Gjøa* expedition, and traveling again, was told the hut was an observatory.

"I told Captain Nielsen that no power on earth would get me to sleep in that house, built on drift ice," he said. But the captain changed the subject, and would not talk about the house. Captain Nilsen was probably one of the few in on the new plan. And he said nothing.

In April, Britain's top explorer, Robert Falcon Scott, visited Oslo. Scott, even by that stage, was a world-famous figure. A dashing hero, the British idolized him. His life was about to become entwined with Amundsen's.

Scott was born in 1868, the son of a Plymouth brewer. But there was a strong naval tradition in the family, and he went to sea as a cadet at the age of thirteen. Had he remained in school, Scott would have probably gone to university and studied science or engineering. He had a brilliant mind, and an instinctive grasp of those subjects.

After two years as a cadet, Scott passed out of HMS *Britannia*, the training ship, as a midshipman, seventh out of a class of twenty-six. A few months later he was on the *Boadicea*, on active duty in the seas around South Africa. During his years as a midshipman, posted to various outposts of the British Empire, he encountered Sir Clements Markham, the Secretary of the Royal Geographical Society. Markham, a former naval officer himself, and an explorer, was a closet homosexual with an obsession for the Antarctic. Scott impressed the older man, who kept an eye on him as his career progressed.

Scott came from a comfortable family, but in 1894 his father made a bad investment and lost the family brewery. He died three years later, a broken man. Financial security was a thing of the past; the young officer would have to make his own mark on the world, and support his mother and sisters. Promotion now became vital. Chance threw the opportunity his way; on a London street, he bumped into Clements Markham. The older man was still fascinated by Scott.

The Royal Geographical Society, with the help of the Royal Society and the Navy, was planning an Antarctic expedition. Scott volunteered to lead, and Markham backed him to the hilt. Scott was given command of the *Discovery* Expedition. The appointment was controversial. Markham wanted a Navy man in command, but the RS and the RGS wanted a scientist to lead. In the end Markham prevailed. Scott was actually the perfect choice. As the scientists who served under him would attest, he spoke their language and facilitated them in every way he could. The command also gave Scott promotion to the rank of commander, and a pay increase.

Discovery left England in August 1901, with fifty men on board. They also brought dogs and skis, but did not know how to use them. Amundsen relied on dogs and skis for his expedition, but he had grown up in the Arctic and understood the tools of his trade. Cook and Peary had learned from the Eskimo. Scott would not have this chance; Antarctica is uninhabited, and there would be no one to learn from. He would have to make it up as he went along.

The region around the South Pole is completely different from that surrounding the North Pole. The North Pole is located under a thin sea of frozen ice. The South Pole is in the center of the Antarctic continent, a vast island at the bottom of the world. The interior is covered in a layer of ice about two miles thick, which dwarfs the Greenland Ice Sheet. Penetrating the interior involves finding a route from the sea ice surrounding the continent, onto the polar plateau itself. Mountains more than ten thousand feet high ring the interior. Aside from penguins and marine mammals around the coast, there is no game or any other source of food inland, and temperatures can drop to extremes undreamed of in the north.

The expedition was not an unqualified success; the group found the conditions brutal beyond imagining, and one member, George Vince, slipped over a precipice to his death in March 1902. But there were highlights. There was one long march south, in which Scott, Ernest Shackleton, and Edward Wilson established a farthest south of 82 degrees 17 seconds, about 530 miles from the Pole. That trip nearly killed them. The following season, Scott opened up the Polar Plateau on another long march. They also made important geographical and biological discoveries before returning to England in 1904.

Scott was a national hero to the English, and spent a number of years enjoying the notoriety, moving in the highest social circles, and rubbing shoulders with the King and the royal family, no less. He married a slightly scandalous American sculptress, which only added to his allure, became Assistant Director of Intelligence for the Navy, and was promoted to captain. His companion on the Farthest South, Ernest Shackleton, returned to Antarctica and got to within a hundred miles of the Pole. So by 1909 Scott was actively organizing a return to the mysterious southern continent. He was determined to claim the last great geographic mark for the Crown and the Navy—and to get there before Shackleton.

Scott visited Norway in April 1910 to test out a new innovation in polar transport, a motorized sledge. It was the forerunner of today's snowmobiles and skidoos. It was a large and cumbersome machine, but performed well enough on the plateau between Oslo and Bergen. But when it eventually got to the Antarctic it proved a complete disaster. One machine fell through the sea ice and was lost; and their second was abandoned after a few useless miles. Scott was accompanied by his glamorous wife Kathleen. They met with Nansen and discussed the upcoming British Antarctic Expedition. Scott also tried to meet with Amundsen, but without success. Amundsen was busy, and could not find the time.

This surprised Scott. He understood the hard work of finalizing an expedition, but surely the man could have found a few hours for him? The truth is, Amundsen knew that if he met Scott face to face and discussed their respective expeditions, he could not conceal from the English man his daring new plan to match Cook and Peary.

Scott returned to England with his snowmobile, and eventually set sail for Antarctica on June 15. His ship, the *Terra Nova*, had sixty-five on board. They stopped in South Africa and Australia before docking in New Zealand, their stopping-off point before the Antarctic. Scott left the ship in Melbourne for some last minute fundraising.

Two months after Scott departed England, Amundsen left Oslo in the *Fram*, bound for the Bering Strait. There were nineteen men on board, and five times that number of dogs. Their trip took them into the mid-Atlantic, where they would stop at Madeira, taking on extra provisions, before rounding South America and heading for San Francisco.

On September 9 they made ready to cast off from Madeira. Amundsen called all the crew together. As he surveyed them on the deck, he must have been apprehensive. This was his coup: a change of plan as dramatic as any imaginable. If the crew did not agree, he was lost. He drew a breath, then began to speak.

"It is my intention to sail southwards, land a party on the southern continent, and try to reach the South Pole."

The crew looked at him, mouths open. They were stunned. Aside from the commander of the ship, Thorvald Nilsen, none had any idea of the change in plans. But then the smiles broke out, and the cheering began. The race was on.

When Scott arrived in Melbourne in October, he found a telegram waiting for him, which explained Amundsen's reluctance to meet with him in the spring. The telegram outlined the Norwegian's changed plan to sail south and try to reach the South Pole. Scott was stunned. He had believed he had the continent to himself. Now he faced the challenge of a well-prepared and worthy adversary.

It was a race that would grip the whole world.

36

PEARY REACTS TO COOK CLAIM

Three days after leaving Indian Harbour, the *Roosevelt* arrived at the Strait of Belle Isle, separating Newfoundland from Labrador. Here Peary got some replies to his telegrams—including a message of congratulations from his rival, Frederick Cook, passed on by the *New York Herald*. He was furious. He replied immediately, telling the paper that they should not take anything the doctor claimed too seriously, and adding that Cook's story was not supported by the Eskimo who supposedly accompanied him. This was a bold claim, and the first real shot in the media war that was to come. Peary also wired the *New York Times*, saying: "Don't let Cook story worry you. I have him nailed."

This was a bit late. Several papers had already carried extensive accounts of Cook's claim. The *New York Herald* had carried an extensive article by Cook himself. Peary was furious, and fired off a wire, saying: "Do not imagine *Herald* likely to be imposed upon by Cook story, but for your information Cook has simply handed the public a gold brick. He's not been at the Pole April 21, 1908, or at any other time."

Those were fighting words. In a way Peary had no choice but to go on the attack. Cook could be gracious; he had won the race. But unless Peary completely destroyed Cook's claim, he would always be remembered as the second man to the Pole. And by "always be remembered," he understood the truth—no one remembers who came second. It is also possible that he genuinely believed that Cook had not achieved the goal. After all, if his own claim was fraudulent, why not that of his rival?

After disparaging Cook so publicly, Peary then went silent for a number of days. He refused to tell any of the reporters that constantly flocked around about his experiences at the Pole. There was a practical reason for this. He wanted to see what Cook said first. What if there was land at the Pole? Or islands nearby? He told reporters that he would not give Cook information; but the truth was that he wanted to know what Cook had seen before risking going public himself. He threw out the challenge to Cook—produce an account of his journey, and then he would do the same. He justified the fact that he had brought no one to the Pole who could take an independent navigational reading and confirm his position.

"After a lifetime of effort I dearly wanted the honor for myself. I am the only white man who has ever reached the North Pole," he told the Associated Press's John Regan.

Cook arrived back in New York on September 21, 1909. After the adulation in Copenhagen, he was somewhat prepared, but even so the massive turnout moved him. Thirty thousand well-wishers lined the streets and the press were out in force. There were the inevitable questions about Peary. One reporter asked whether he looked on Peary as a friend or an enemy. Cook looked momentarily confused, replying: "I must say I do not know. I have treated Mr. Peary as a friend, and until I know more about the situation, I shall continue to do the same."

He had bigger worries than the bitterness of an old foe. In his absence there had been an economic crash. The failure of the Knickerbocker Trust had wiped out his wealth and the more substantial wealth of his wife, and when he returned to America it was to the news that he was now homeless, and his family were staying with various friends after losing their house to foreclosure. He was confident that once his claims to the Pole were ratified, he could begin the lucrative lecture circuit, and the inevitable book deal would also help. All he had to do was wait for Whitney to return to civilization with his logs and instruments.

Less than a week after his arrival in New York, while he was staying at the Waldorf Astoria, Cook received a telegram from Whitney. It read, in part: "Peary would allow nothing belonging to you on board. Said to leave everything in cache, Etah."

The telegram ended with a breezy "Good shooting."

Cook went pale. This, he knew instantly, was a devastating blow. Any panel of scientific experts would want to examine his instruments to see they were calibrated correctly. They would also want to see the original log of the journey, not the rough notes Cook had brought home. Without the materials he had entrusted to Whitney, the only proof he had was his word. And against an implacable opponent like Peary, that would not be enough.

It was tempting to return to Greenland immediately to retrieve the chest, but the lateness of the season made that impossible. Etah would be unreachable until the early summer. And by that stage, unless the Eskimo had been very sternly warned, there would be nothing left. It was a harsh environment, and a trunk left unattended would not survive the winter. Though outwardly he professed confidence that his records would eventually make their way home, privately Cook knew that all was lost on that front.

Admitting that he did not know to how great an extent this setback would complicate things, he told a reporter from the *Philadelphia North American*: "I had counted on him bringing the instruments and everything with him. Naturally, I am disappointed."

In this latest setback, at least Cook had public support. Many saw Peary's hand clearly in the calamity, with the *Philadelphia Inquirer* saying: "Mr. Peary insists that Dr. Cook prove his story, but it would seem as if Peary has been doing everything possible to hinder Cook."

The *New York Evening Journal* accused Peary of trying to sabotage Cook, because he clearly believed the claims of the doctor. Within days public support for Cook was growing at an alarming rate. A *Pittsburgh Press* poll showed that 96 percent of their readership believed Cook got to the Pole—and a massive 70 percent believed Peary had fallen short.

Only the *New York Times*, which was paying him large advances for articles, sided with Peary.

The Peary Arctic Club rowed in behind their leader, criticizing Cook's claim to have averaged fifteen miles a day on the ice. They pointed out, rightly, that more experienced polar travelers had not been able to achieve speeds as impressive as this. But when Peary finally gave his account, and claimed speeds in excess of thirty miles a day, they wisely dropped this line of criticism. But there were other promising lines of attack. One proved very damaging for Cook.

In October the club released an affidavit signed by Edward Barrill, the blacksmith who had accompanied Cook to the top of Mount McKinley in 1906. The affidavit was a sworn legal statement which alleged that the pair got nowhere near the top of the mountain. Barrill swore that they had gone no higher than eight thousand feet—less than halfway up the formidable slope. It was first published, in full, in the *New York Globe*, and was reprinted by papers across the country in the following weeks.

Cook responded instantly, declaring in the *New York Evening Mail*: "The Barrill affidavit was paid for, I am sure. It is a lie, made from whole cloth."

In 1989, when the Peary papers were finally made available to researchers, a copy of a bank draft for $5,000 (over $200,000 in today's terms) was found that backs up Cook's immediate gut feeling. The attorney who organized the affidavit, J. M. Ashton, drew up the bank draft, payable to himself from the account of General Hubbard. It was dated three days before the Barrill affidavit was sworn. Barrill was bribed, and bribed handsomely. He bought a five-bedroom home and an orchard with the proceeds, and was the first resident of Darby, Montana, to own a car. His betrayal of Cook guaranteed his financial security for the rest of his life.

Of course, Cook knew none of this at the time. He only knew that Barrill was lying. They had gone far higher than eight thousand feet. The problem was that many in the mountaineering world had found Cook's claim unbelievable from the start. They were quick to seize on this new evidence of his duplicity. It was a staggering blow to the doctor. As far as the public were concerned, if you could lie about one geographical First, you could lie about another. Suddenly the polar question became a different question; if Cook could not prove he climbed Mount McKinley, then his claim to the Pole fell.

Peary, pulling the strings in this media manipulation, took less than a week to follow home his new advantage. He released a fourteen-point, twenty-five-hundred-word rebuttal of Cook's claim. In the document he recounted how he had questioned Cook's Eskimo companions, and they had said they were never far from land. He didn't bother to mention that they were questioned without a proper interprcter, and that they did not understand maps, so could not have told Peary where they were during their year in the wilderness of the far north.

Cook was in the middle of a lecture tour and media blitz, making seventy appearances in less than a month. But increasingly he was finding hostile audiences, firing unanswerable questions at him. His health began to suffer. In late October he canceled the remainder of his tour and went into seclusion. He still had hopes; the University of Copenhagen was going to analyze his papers, and their verdict could prove critical. Unfortunately he did not have the original papers he had hoped Whitney would bring home, so he did his best to reconstruct the log from what he had. In late November he sent what he had to Copenhagen, with a letter urging the panel to consider a neutral judgement until the following season, when he might be able to retrieve his original notes.

Two weeks later, the report of the Copenhagen commission was published. They found Cook's proofs inadequate, and returned a verdict of "Not Proven" on his polar claim. "Not Proven" is a very neutral verdict, but in America the media took it at its most negative. They quickly reported that Frederick Cook had not reached the Pole, and the city which had initially honored him as a hero had now withdrawn its backing for him. This was not strictly true, but perception is often more important than reality. To the American media and the American public, Cook had been exposed as a fraud. The verdict of the Copenhagen commission, coming only months after the Barrill affidavit, had destroyed the last vestiges of his reputation.

Financially in ruins, with the lecture circuit now closed to him, Cook crossed the Atlantic to Europe, and went into hiding.

As Cook retreated to Europe, his tail between his legs, Peary discovered a harsh truth. He had convinced the world that his rival had not reached the Pole. Now he had to convince the world that he himself had.

He did get a boost when the National Geographic Society asked both him and Cook to present their proofs for review. Peary had history with the Society. They had backed some of his earlier expeditions. He gave them copious notes about the early stages of his trip, but held back the notes from the crucial five days at the end. When they asked for these notes, he met the three-man committee and handed over a box of instruments and papers. The three men peered inside, didn't read a single paper, then proposed going off for dinner with Peary. Two days later they produced their report. Unlike the Copenhagen commission's verdict on Cook, the National Geographic verdict was unequivocal: Peary had reached the Pole on April 6, 1909.

A bill was brought to Congress by Peary's supporters, recognizing him as the discoverer of the North Pole. This was not quite a formality; a Congress subcommittee described the National Geographic Society's examination of Peary's data as "perfunctory and hasty," and asked to see the data for themselves. Peary declined, and they adjourned the matter.

Peary spent some time in Europe, accepting honors on the basis of the endorsement of the National Geographic Society. They were the only public body so far to come out in full support of his claim, but gradually public opinion was turning. By the end of 1910, most people accepted that the North Pole had been reached by Peary, not by Cook. At the end of the year his book, *The North Pole*, came out, furthering his position.

In January 1911 he appeared before the Congressional committee for three days of questioning. Many aspects of his trip troubled them. There was no note in his diary for the thirty hours he purportedly spent at the Pole, and no mention in the diary itself of the historic feat. Instead a loose leaf had been inserted at the relevant page, saying: "The Pole at last, the prize of three centuries, my dream and ambition for twenty years. Mine at last." That note could have been written at any time, and inserted in the diary.

Peary had no answers to some of the questions, prompting Representative Ernest Roberts to label his testimony "vague and uncertain." Committee Chair Thomas Butler concluded that they had only Peary's word and his proofs to judge. He accepted Peary's word, but found his proofs inadequate. In the end it came down to a character judgement: did they believe Peary?

By a four to three vote, they did.

The Bill was placed into law by President Taft on March 4, 1911, acknowledging Peary for his work in the Arctic, and crediting him with reaching the North Pole. Perhaps in deference to Cook, who was not completely discredited yet, they amended the bill to say "reached" the North Pole, rather than discovered the North Pole.

A second Bill was passed by Congress promoting Peary to the rank of Rear Admiral in the Navy, on his retirement. It provided a useful boost to his pension.

Peary, aware that his records did not bear close scrutiny, never made them available for examination again. The Congressional sub-committee were the last people to see those records until the 1980s, when Peary's descendants finally opened the papers up to researchers, several decades after his death.

As the years passed several explorers tried to verify many of Peary's discoveries, including Crocker Land, an island in the high Arctic. Disappointingly, many of his discoveries proved nonexistent. Cook had reported that Crocker Land did not exist; later explorers proved the truth of this, verifying that Cook had at least got to the polar region, even if he had not got near the Pole itself. But Peary ignored all this activity. He enjoyed a quiet retirement on Eagle Island, off the coast of Maine. He rarely spoke of the Pole, and pursued other interests. He even learned to fly.

Perhaps he thought it wise to let sleeping dogs lie. After all, his claim to the Pole was every bit as bogus as Cook's. And he was determined it would never come under the same scrutiny that Cook's had.

37

RACE FOR THE SOUTH POLE

Captain Scott was horrified when he got the telegram from Amundsen in Melbourne. The Englishman had that nation's deep-rooted sense of fair play, and he felt he was being grievously wronged once more. In 1907 his former shipmate, and the man who had accompanied him on his farthest south in 1902, Ernest Shackleton, had led his own expedition and almost reached the South Pole.

There are two traditional routes to the pole. Antarctica is a large island situated slightly east of the Pole, with a huge peninsula located to the west. If you were to draw a line across the narrowest point of that peninsula, the line would be over six miles long, but would pass close to the Pole. The continent has two huge bays, the Weddell Sea and the Ross Sea. Both seas are permanently frozen, so the only way to get to the narrowest point of Antarctica, and thus to the Pole, is to set up base at the edge of the frozen sea (or ice barrier), then trek several hundred miles across the barrier until you reach the land. Then you have to climb up to the polar plateau, roughly nine thousand feet. From there you have a few hundred miles more before reaching your destination.

In a nutshell, the distance from base to Pole is twice as far down south, in far rougher conditions.

Scott pioneered the approach from the Ross Sea. He had expected Shackleton in 1907 to do the decent thing, and pioneer his own route. Shackleton opted also for the Ross Sea, and tried to get onto the Ross Ice Shelf at the Bay of Whales. But when he failed, he sailed on to McMurdo Sound, where Scott had made camp in 1901–1903, and used his old commander's hut. Scott felt this was a major betrayal, and it drove a wedge between the old friends.

Scott was nowhere near as possessive as Peary, who saw the route from northern Greenland to the Pole as his exclusive front yard, but he was offended by Shackleton slavishly following his footsteps. How would Amundsen treat the quest? Would he have the effrontery to show up at McMurdo Sound and also exploit Scott's work?

Reporters were naturally eager to hear Scott's thoughts about the situation, but he was cautious in his reply. He said that he would not change his plans and indulge in a race. He was not prepared to sacrifice the scientific goals of the expedition just to beat Amundsen to the pole. However, he wrote in his diary that Amundsen had a fair chance of success. He knew he was facing a serious and well-equipped challenger.

Scott's expedition was an impressive one. Between the ship and the shore party there were sixty-five men, chosen from the cream of eight thousand applicants. The team included seven men who had been on Scott's earlier *Discovery* expedition, as well as five veterans of Shackleton's trip. Scott's friend and companion on his previous Farthest South, Edward Wilson, was the chief scientist. The team also included a meteorologist, a physicist, a geologist, a botanist, and a zoologist. They also brought a Norwegian skiing expert.

To cope with whatever the environment threw at them, they used a mixed strategy when it came to transport. They brought dogs, which Amundsen would rely upon, and which had proved so useful to both Cook and Peary. But they also brought hardy ponies, which could pull far heavier loads, if they could cope with the environment. Ponies were never a traditional form of transport in Arctic conditions, so Scott was taking a gamble with them. They also brought giant snow tractors, which proved to be a complete waste of space. But at the end it boiled down to one thing: the British were prepared to adopt the energy-sapping process of man-hauling. Man is a species capable of huge endurance, and on British expeditions to Greenland and the Arctic in the previous century, teams of men had hauled their own sledges. They were slower than dogs, but the system did work.

Amundsen would never dream of man-hauling, and neither would Peary or Cook. It was very popular among British expeditions, but it never spread beyond that because it wore down the men rapidly and was slower than using dogs. Scott's problem was that he was not a trained dog handler, and did not realize how useful the small animals could be when properly handled. He genuinely believed that man-hauling was a more efficient alternative. So his plan was to use all his different forms of transport to bring men to the top of the polar plateau, but the final few hundred miles would be powered by men in harness.

Scott listed the main objective of the expedition—which was financed to the tune of $5 million in today's money—as the discovery of the South Pole. But he insisted the scientific work was every bit as important. This was in sharp contrast to Amundsen, who saw science as a side show.

Scott left Australia with a heavy heart, rejoining the *Terra Nova* in New Zealand where he told his men they were now in a race. But he downplayed this. The ship left for Antarctica at the end of November, overloaded and sailing low. A heavy storm a week later nearly sunk them, and they lost two ponies, a dog, ten tons of coal, and sixty-five gallons of petrol to the crashing waves. On December 10 they entered the pack ice around Antarctica, and spent twenty days negotiating this barrier before reaching the open seas surrounding the continent.

But by early January they had arrived in the vicinity of McMurdo Sound. Scott chose not to use his old hut, but instead set up base fifteen miles north, on Cape Evans. He hoped that area would remain ice-free during the southern summer, allowing the *Terra Nova* to come and go. In winter those seas would freeze over, allowing easy access to the old hut at Hut Point. This gave the team a double base.

By January 18 everything had been unloaded, and a prefabricated hut, fifty feet by twenty-five feet, was in place for the men. Now all they had to do was sit out the harsh winter, and the following season they would be ready for the polar dash. The time would not be spent in idleness, however. There was scientific work to be done, and they would also lay out caches of food and fuel for the following season, at least across the Ross Ice Shield.

The Ross Ice Shield does not move like the polar ice in the north, because it is anchored to the land. So it was quite safe to lay out the depots. They would slowly drift toward the sea as glaciation from the land pushed the ice out, but they would not drift east or west, and the push out to the sea was a small one, a matter of a few miles each season. So any depots laid out that season would be safely there for the following season.

On September 9 Amundsen turned south from Madeira rather than north, and made no other stops before reaching the Ross Sea in January 1910. He was completely unaware of the storm of controversy his telegram to Scott had unleashed. Even Norway turned against him, and fundraising for the expedition, which had continued while he was sailing for Madeira, dried up completely. Oblivious, the crew spotted icebergs for the first time on New Year's Day, and by January 14 they had anchored in the Bay of Whales.

His was a smaller affair than Scott's—there were only nineteen men on board, and only seven were to land. None were scientists. Instead they were all hardy outdoor men, used to skis and dog sledges. If this was a race, Amundsen was only picking men with a proven record of traveling fast over ice and snow. He had also studied the writings of both Scott and Shackleton. Shackleton had abandoned his attempt to set up a base at the Bay of Whales, because he felt the ice was unstable. But Amundsen felt the Irishman had misread the conditions, and he took a gamble that the ice was stable enough for a base to survive. Setting up the base at the Bay of Whales meant that he was already more than seventy miles closer to the Pole than Scott. Balanced against this was the fact that Scott knew a route up the Beardmore Glacier to the polar plateau; Amundsen would have to pioneer a route. If he was unlucky it could cost him weeks. So the race was fairly even from the start.

Amundsen set up his quarters for the winter. It was less cramped than Scott's, as there were only seven men sharing the hut. But there was constant noise from one hundred energetic dogs. Dogs were all he brought; no ponies and no tractors. He was sticking with what he knew worked. Each man was issued with specially commissioned skis, designed by Amundsen, and a mix of Eskimo and European clothing to ward off the cold. The skis were unusually long, to prevent the men slipping into crevasses.

To prevent boredom during the long winter, the hut, called Framheim, was stocked with a library of three thousand books and a large collection of records. Everything was in place by the end of January.

In early February the group had unexpected visitors. Back at McMurdo Sound, Scott had dispatched a group of men to explore King Edward VII Land, and they had set out on the *Terra Nova*, sailing west under Victor Campbell, seeking a possible landing point. They were stunned when they spotted a ship at anchor in the Bay of Whales. Although the British party had not obsessed on the Norwegian challenge, Scott had convinced himself, and the team, that Amundsen would do the honorable thing and make his base in the Weddell Sea. Now they had proof that he was actually only a few days' march from their own base—and seventy miles nearer the Pole.

The meeting on February 3 was an awkward affair. Both groups behaved in a very civilized manner, but it was impossible to completely conceal their animosity. Officers from the *Terra Nova* boarded the *Fram*, where they were given breakfast. Later some of the *Fram* crew boarded the *Terra Nova* for lunch. Amundsen had been relieved to find out that *Terra Nova* did not have a wireless telegraph. He had seen from Cook and Peary how vital it was to be not only first to the Pole, but first with the news. There had been a certain amount of gamesmanship in the meeting; Campbell had boasted about the efficiency of the snowmobiles, which worried the Norwegians. Amundsen urged Campbell to camp nearby, but Campbell left the Bay of Whales that day to bring news back to Scott.

He got back on February 22 and Scott was furious. His first instinct was to load up a sledge, cross to Franheim, and have it out with Amundsen. But he soon realized the futility of this, and calmed down, recording in his diary: "One thing only fixes itself in my mind.

The proper, as well as the wiser, course is for us to proceed exactly as though this had not happened. To go forward and do our best for the honor of our country without fear or panic."

Before winter set in, Scott continued his depot laying, leaving caches of food and fuel at points along the great ice barrier (as the Ross Ice Shield was then known). His final cache was One Ton Depot a little short of 80 degrees south, before the Beardmore Glacier and the route to the polar plateau. It was a major undertaking, and the snowmobiles had already been abandoned as not up to the job. Six of the eight ponies involved in the process died. On April 23 the sun set, and the long Antarctic Night began. Men busied themselves with scientific work, and tended to the remaining ponies and dogs. Scott also insisted on a series of lectures, on a variety of subjects, as the only practical form of entertainment, and regular football games in the dark to maintain fitness.

Amundsen also laid depots, and had more success than Scott, managing to push his final cache to well beyond 82 degrees south. In all he laid three caches, containing a ton and a half of seal meat, as well as fuel. The sun set at Franheim on April 21 and the four-month night began. Amundsen was sure of his men and dogs, but spent the months of darkness in torment, wondering about the snowmobiles. Would they prove his undoing? He was determined to get off early the following season, to forestall this possibility. By late August he was ready— but temperatures as low as minus 72°F prevented the eight men (one remained at Franheim) and seven sledges from leaving. They finally set out on September 8.

Their initial progress was good, but after four days they were all suffering from the cold, and the dogs were beginning to suffer frostbite. Amundsen had to admit that his plan was a panic reaction to the nearness of the British, and he turned back to Franheim. It was a brutal retreat. Several dogs died, and others had to be put on the sledges to get them home. It was a disastrous start to the season. Part of the fallout was a violent dispute between Amundsen and Hjalmar Johansen, a polar veteran who had been on Nansen's Farthest north. The result of this dispute was that Amundsen decided only five men would travel to the Pole when they set out again.

They waited until October 19, then tried again. This time there were five men and four sledges, towed by fifty-two dogs. Fog hampered their initial progress, and they wandered into a field of crevasses, which nearly cost them the life of Amundsen. But they managed to reach their final depot on November 5. Twelve days later they reached the end of the Ross Ice Shelf. In the shadow of the Transantarctic Mountains they faced their first real difficulty. Scott had a way through the mountains onto the plateau beyond—the Beardmore Glacier used by Shackleton a few years earlier. Amundsen would have to find a similar route, or his race would end right there.

It took them several days of exploration, with plenty of climbing to gain ground and survey the surroundings. Finally they could see what looked to be a clear route, a steep glacier thirty-five miles long, leading up to the plateau. Amundsen named it the Axel Heiberg Glacier. It was a far tougher challenge than the team were expecting. But at the end of three long days they were on the top, and the road to the Pole lay open before them.

Scott laid his plans with military efficiency. Like the Peary System, it involved teams laying depots and turning back at various points along the way, but it did not involve Peary's relay work. Sixteen men would set out, using the two surviving motor sledges (one had plunged through the ice), ponies, and dogs. They would cross the barrier to the Beardmore Glacier, where the dogs would return to base, and the ponies would be shot for food. From there to the Pole, it was man-hauling: three teams of four, with just one group carrying on the whole way. They were doing it the hard way.

The motor party left base on October 24 for the two-hundred-mile journey to latitude 80 degrees 30 minutes south, to lay a depot. After fifty miles the motor sledges were abandoned in the snow, and the four man team man-hauled the remaining 150 miles to lay the depot. The remaining three teams set out on November 1, catching up with the earlier team on November 21. It was now time to turn the dogs back, but progress had been slower than anticipated, and Scott changed the plan. Now the dogs would continue south, at least for a while. On December

4 the expedition reached the Gateway, the entrance to the Beardmore Glacier. A blizzard prevented them mounting the glacier for nearly a week. At the end of the week, the remaining ponies were shot, and their carcasses cached for the return journey.

Two men returned to base, carrying the message: "Things were not as rosy as they might be, but we keep our spirits up and say the luck must turn."

On December 22, the team had reached the top of the glacier and were on the polar plateau. They laid down another depot, then eight men—hauling two sledges—continued south. Initial going was good, and they were confident they could make up the time they had lost on the barrier and the Beardmore. They were already a month behind Amundsen, who had reached the top of the Axel Heiberg Glacier on November 21.

Amundsen pushed toward the Pole with only eighteen dogs. The camp at the top of the glacier had been a difficult one; twenty-seven dogs were sacrificed. Each sledge driver had to cull most of his team, killing the dogs and skinning them. The meat was divided between the surviving dogs and the men.

"We called the place the Butcher's Shop. There was depression and sadness in the air; we had grown so fond of our dogs," Amundsen wrote in his account of the journey, *The South Pole: An Account of the Norwegian Expedition in the* Fram*, 1912.*

Three sledges were loaded with supplies for sixty days, and on November 25 the party set out across the plateau in persistent heavy fog. The ground was lined with crevasses, and some of these were covered in snow, making the going very difficult and dangerous. But by December 4 they were out of the danger zone, and on surer ground. On December 8 they passed Shackleton's Farthest South record, and were into the unknown. They began scanning the ground ahead, looking for telltale tracks in the snow, or any other sign that Scott was ahead of them on the trail. But each day brought virgin snow. On the evening of December 13 they made camp and took their evening observations. They were delighted to discover they were less than twenty miles from the Pole.

Olav Bjaaland wrote in his diary that night: "The excitement is great. Shall we see the English flag?"

The following day Amundsen took the lead, marching ahead of the dogs. At 3:00 p.m., as near as their instruments could determine, they reached the South Pole. There was nothing to distinguish it from any other point on the plateau; howling winds, freezing cold, thin atmosphere, and blinding white show under a vivid blue sky. There was no Union Jack. They were the first. Amundsen had won the race.

The moment was a bit anticlimactic—five cold men and seventeen starving dogs, standing in the middle of a vast plain of emptiness. They shook hands and raised the Norwegian flag. As a way of showing his gratitude to the men, Amundsen insisted that all five hold the flag pole as it was raised.

Three days later, after making all the observations to prove their discovery, the five men turned back on their tracks and began the retreat to Franheim.

As Amundsen turned toward home, Scott was still struggling with the early stages of the Beardmore Glacier. By the time he got to the top, on December 21, the race was already over. But he did not know that. Full of confidence, the eight men made good progress. Their yardstick for measuring their progress was Shackleton's account of his trip in 1908–1909. Within a week or so they had caught up with their imaginary rival, and on January 3 they made camp at 87 degrees 32 minutes south, less than two hundred miles from the Pole.

Here Scott made his most serious error since deciding man-hauling was more practical than using dogs. Instead of turning back four men, he turned back only three, proceeding to the Pole with a party of five. This was a major error, because he had only food and provisions—and equipment, and tent space—for four men. They had only four sets of skis; one man would have to struggle along on snow shoes. Changing the plan at the last minute jeopardized everyone. The five in the final party were Scott, Edward Wilson, Lawrence Oates, Edgar Evans, and Henry Bowers. Unknown to Scott, Evans was nursing a serious hand injury, while Oates was in the early stages of scurvy. One of the symptoms of scurvy is that old wounds tend to reopen, and Oates had been badly injured in the Boer War. That injury was slowing him down terribly in the daily marches, but he stoically said nothing.

On January 9 the five men passed Shackleton's Farthest South, still a month behind Amundsen. Scott was not losing time to his rival, despite the fact that he was man-hauling instead of using dogs. The cause of his ultimate failure would not be his choice of transport. As the five men continued their long forced marches, they saw no indications of Amundsen's presence, and they began to hope that they had won the race. But on January 16, when they were only fifteen miles from their destination, they saw a black speck on the horizon. Their hearts sank. They camped for the night in deep despair.

The following day they completed their march, arriving at the tent Amundsen had left to mark the spot. Their mood was bleak; morale was at an all-time low. Scott, a skilled writer, summed up his thoughts memorably in his diary: "The Pole. Yes, but under very different circumstances from those expected. Great God! This is an awful place and terrible enough for us to have labored to it without the reward of priority. Well, it is something to have got here."

On January 18 the group turned north to begin retracing their steps. It was a march that would lift them from the pages of history and onto the pages of mythology.

Amundsen was cautious on the return from the Pole, limiting marches to fifteen miles so as not to exhaust the men and remaining dogs. By January 7 they were down from the plateau and on the Ice Shelf, breaking into their depot for much needed supplies. On January 25 at 4:00 a.m., they arrived at Franheim. Of the fifty-two dogs that started, only eleven survived. The entire journey had taken ninety-nine days—and they arrived home in base ten days ahead of schedule, surprising the three men they had left behind. They had covered 2,150 miles.

They didn't hang around. There was a final celebratory dinner at the hut, and on January 30 they were off, racing for Hobart in Tasmania. Amundsen knew he had beaten Scott to the Pole, but he had no idea by how many days. For all he knew Scott could be back at McMurdo Sound already, and preparing to bring the news to the world. Amundsen was determined to beat him again. They arrived in Hobart on March 7, and Amundsen was not greatly surprised to learn that there had been no news from Scott. Gleefully he sent his telegrams. His instincts proved correct; winning the race was all it took for him to be forgiven for entering the race. He never got full credit; it is Scott who is still remembered from that epic clash. But the achievement of the South Pole cemented Amundsen's claim to be one of the greatest polar explorers of the golden age, and of all time. He telegrammed the *New York Times* and the *Daily Chronicle* in London, and both papers carried the news, along with a photograph of Amundsen, on Friday, March 8.

THE SOUTH POLE DISCOVERED: NORWEGIAN EXPLORER REACHES COVETED GOAL.

Both papers paid £2,000 (approximately $330,000 in today's money) for the privilege of being first to carry the news, which was quickly taken up by papers throughout Europe and America. It was a massive sum, and more was to follow, as Amundsen sold more detailed accounts of his journey, and prepared the book of the expedition. His days of financial troubles were over. He might have been beaten to the North Pole, but he had placed his mark on the globe. It would be another year before any word emerged about Scott.

While Amundsen was racing to tell his news, the Englishman was racing for his life. His men were depressed when they left the Pole; they had lost the race. But they were still full of fight, and determined to get home as quickly as possible. For three weeks, they made good progress. But they were slowly starving, and were suffering the effects of vitamin C deprivation. In addition, autumn was coming, and the weather was getting colder. Scott began to worry about the condition of his men, particularly Oates and Evans. On February 7 the group reached the edge of the plateau, and prepared to descend the Beardmore Glacier. They now realized that they were in real danger of not making it back safely. Compounding their problem, they had not marked their depots well, and they nearly failed to find the one on the glacier. The trip down was not straightforward, with Evans falling behind regularly, and on one fall he hit his head and was severely concussed. It changed his personality, making him negative and depressed. On February 16, near the bottom of the glacier, he collapsed. The following day he did not get up. The other four left him behind, expecting him to follow them. When it became obvious he would not, they had to go back for him.

Scott wrote in his diary: "He was on his knees, clothing disarranged, hands uncovered and frostbitten and with a wild look in his eyes." He was placed on a sledge. At the end of that day's march he was comatose, and he died during the night.

The four survivors continued, but the weather had deteriorated badly. Even then it was known what the average temperatures in Antarctica were. Scott was encountering temperatures fifteen degrees colder than the average. Not only did this further weaken the men, the snow was too cold for the runners of the sledges to slide over it easily. As much as anything else, this was a major factor in slowing them down. And Oates was also a problem. His Boer War wound limited his speed, and he was weakening by the day. Everyone knew that they risked not getting to the next depot in time at the pace he was limiting them to.

His feet became badly frostbitten, and the others were unwilling to abandon him. So they slowed down even more. They needed to make nine miles a day, to reach each depot before starvation. But sometimes they were making just three miles, pathetic progress compared to what they were doing on the polar plateau, and what Amundsen had managed on his return from the Pole. On March 15 Oates told the others that he could not continue, and urged them to abandon him. But they refused. The next day they only managed a few miles once more. The situation was becoming desperate. Perhaps there was talk in the tent that night about doing the decent thing—talk that Oates, as an honorable soldier, would have been influenced by.

On the morning of March 16, Oates got up earlier than the others. He did not bother putting on his boots, a process that could take half an hour in the frozen conditions. He simply said: "I am just going outside and I may be some time."

No one was under any illusions about what was happening, and no one tried to stop him. Scott noted: "We knew that Oates was walking to his death. It was the act of a brave man and an English gentleman."

The temperature outside was minus forty. He would not have survived more than half an hour. Hypothermia can be a peaceful death. It is likely he only got a few hundred yards, sat down in exhaustion, and fell asleep. In the end it was a pointless sacrifice. Too much time had been lost. Scott and his remaining companions struggled another twenty miles toward One Ton Depot, but a blizzard stopped them on March 20, forcing them to remain in their tent for a number of days. They were only eleven miles short of the depot, and the food and fuel that might have kept them alive and on the march. But they had run out of food, and the weather was desperate.

Little is known about those final days. Blizzards rarely last more than a few days, and it is likely that they could have struggled on again by March 22. But Wilson and Scott were at the end of their endurance. Bowers might have made a dash to the depot and returned with food, but he was unwilling to abandon his companions—or to face the journey alone. They remained in the tent, slowly starving as a week passed. Wilson was the first to die. They arranged his body neatly in his sleeping bag, and zipped him in. Scott died next, and Bowers—one of the toughest men ever to journey to the polar regions—lovingly posed his leader, arranging the body so that Scott was sitting up in his sleeping bag, diary and pen in hand.

A day or so later, Bowers himself succumbed.

Their bodies were not discovered until the following season, when a search party from McMurdo Sound found the tent. The diaries were recovered, so that their story could be shared with the world. Then the tent was collapsed onto the silent men, becoming their tomb.

Scott's final diary entry was moving and eloquent: "Every day we have been ready to start for our depot eleven miles away, but outside the door of the tent it remains a scene of whirling drift. I do not think we can hope for any better things now. We shall stick it out to the end, but we are getting weaker, of course, and the end cannot be far off. It seems a pity but I do not think I can write any more. R Scott.

"For God's sake, look after our people."

That last entry, in which Scott was thinking of the other expedition members even as he was dying, sealed his fate. He was the heroic martyr, the man who in defeat was the moral victor. Another entry read: "Had we lived I should have had a tale to tell of the hardihood, endurance, and courage of my companions which would have stirred the heart of every Englishman. These rough notes and our dead bodies must tell the tale."

And tell the tale they did. Britain and Europe were in need of heroes, as the continent faced the First World War. Millions of young men, the pride of a generation, would be sacrificed to the guns of the trenches. What better inspiration could they have than the story of Scott of the Antarctic? To this day when people think of the South Pole they think of Robert Falcon Scott and that lonely tent, rather than of Roald Amundsen, the man who beat him to the "awful place."

38

COOK AND PEARY AT WAR

Peary continued to press his advantage after Cook's reputation began to crumble. Bribing Barrill had been a master-stroke. It was difficult to come back from such a devastating revelation. All Cook's protestations meant nothing unless he could prove that Barrill had taken a bribe, and Peary's agents had been very careful to conceal their trail.

For one thing, Peary was not involved. The affidavit had been sought by General Thomas Hubbard of the Peary Arctic Club, not by the commander himself. Reporters did go after the General, but he was brusque in his denial of any wrongdoing. Asked directly if the sum of $5,000 ($120,000 today) had been given to the Montana blacksmith, he replied: "No money was given to him for his signature."

There was a problem with the affidavit. Barrill's account differed completely from his previous accounts of the climb. Which meant that he was either lying now, or had been lying earlier. Either way, he was a liar. That dented his credibility. But shortly after the publication of the affidavit, two other members of the expedition also expressed their doubts about Cook's claims. Belmore Browne and Herschel Parker raised their concerns, which were widely reported. They also mentioned the summit picture Cook had presented to the world, pointing out that it was taken at a secondary peak some miles from the actual summit of Mount McKinley. It was their testimony, following so swiftly on the flawed testimony of Edward Barrill, which finally destroyed Cook.

Suddenly newspapers that had been backing Cook began to cool off. He began to face hostile crowds at lectures. The massive support he had built up faded away as quickly. The stress began to affect his health. He began to pull out of lectures and public appearances.

Typical of the press he faced was this, from *The Globe*: "The similarities between the Mount McKinley hoax and the North Pole hoax are readily discernible. In one case, as in the other, there was a dissipation of the party and a reduction of the number of witnesses. In both there was a careful preparation of a fabricated record. Measurably successful in fooling the world concerning one mental journey, one can understand why the other was projected, and why an objective was selected whose pretended attainment would fructify into a fortune from lecture receipts.

"The Mount McKinley revelation means the exit of Cook, the intrepid explorer, and the entry of Cook as one who has chosen a queer road to immortality."

The few reporters who actually took the trouble to seek out Cook were impressed by his sincerity and seeming integrity, but the general view was that he was a fraud who had been caught out. To this day that is the view that prevails. Many believe that Peary genuinely thought he had achieved the pole; few believe that of Cook.

Explorer Pat Falvey said, in 2014: "I think that Cook's descriptions and his timings prove that he did not get there. Most people in the adventure world believe that Cook's claim was fraudulent. I hate to call either Cook or Peary a liar, but sometimes people can get caught up in their own belief. Does it really matter to me whether they were the first to the Pole or not? The simple fact is that theirs were amazing achievements, however far they got.

"Sometimes honorable people make mistakes, and are criticized afterwards. But they added a huge amount to the annals of history. I do not think that Peary went out of his way deceitfully to dishonor. Cook may have. But let's give them their credit. If they did get close to the

Pole, but didn't reach it, we are right to challenge their stories. But don't take everything away from them. Don't throw the ducks out with the water, and say that they did not achieve anything or were complete crooks. I honestly believe that they were basically honorable people."

Cook might not have agreed with that, as he watched the Peary machine slowly destroy his life and reputation.

Following the Barrill affidavit Peary's supporters had another trick to pull. They got Congressman Simeon Fess to read a speech in Congress which was subsequently published as a pamphlet. Fess did not write the speech; it was prepared by Peary supporter Lucien Alexander and given to the Congressman, who merely read it and put his name to it. The speech went into detail on how Cook had fooled the world, both on McKinley and the Pole. Afterwards 100,000 copies of the pamphlet containing the speech, entitled THE NORTH POLE AFTERMATH, were printed and distributed. Copies were sent to members of the American Medical Association, all the school districts in the midwest (a Cook stronghold), and to every YMCA, Elks, Rotary, and other civic clubs. Copies were also sent to newspapers, and to organizations in towns where Cook was scheduled to lecture.

Under the relentless onslaught, Cook realized that he was finished unless he could pull off a spectacular coup. If the North Pole and South Pole were gone, that left only one suitable target: Mount Everest. As the years passed after his return from the polar expedition, the new plan began to take shape.

"Mount Everest is the last challenge to the explorer. For four hundred years men with veins bursting for physical action who did not care to sacrifice themselves on the altar of war, turned to the farthest north or the farthest south. But now the slogan must be—highest up— nearest Heaven," Cook wrote.

But his new expedition was dogged by trouble from the start. He hoped to travel around the world making a film documentary, and climb in the Himalayas to take in Everest en route. But everywhere he went, the Fess pamphlet had been posted ahead of him by Peary. So Cook's reputation was tarnished before he even set foot on foreign soils. Coupled with this, war had broken out in Europe, and the world was plunged into madness. A strange American wandering the world with a camera was a figure of suspicion.

Cook set out in May 1915, intending to sail from San Francisco to Calcutta, taking in stops in Hawaii, Hong Kong, and Singapore. From Calcutta he would travel to Kathmandu in Nepal, then go up Everest. But the journey was beset by difficulties. In Penang, Malaysia, the British authorities seized their camera equipment, suspecting them of espionage. A few days later they were arrested, and it took the intervention of the American Consul to get them back on their journey again. But once they reached Calcutta they found themselves whiling away interminable weeks, before being refused permission to travel north to the mountains. The British authorities still took them as spies.

Defeated, they headed to Borneo, where they made a documentary about the local tribes. It was a commercial failure. Then they began to wend their way home. The only highlight was a successful winter ascent of Mount Fuji in Japan. They arrived back in the United States in January 1916, with nothing to show for their troubles.

As Cook was trying and failing to rehabilitate himself, Peary had retired to a palatial home on a small island just off shore in Casco Bay, Maine. He took no further interest in exploration, but did become involved in the war effort, by advocating aviation. He even took the time to learn to fly, and his advocacy was crucial in the establishment of the Naval Reserve aerial coastal patrol units. These units were set up to detect enemy shipping and submarine activity from the air. A young naval officer with ambitions to make his mark, Richard Byrd, benefited from the new interest in aviation to give his own career a good boost.

Peary's reputation grew as Cook's dwindled, and he enjoyed his retirement, gladly accepting what honors came his way. But it was not all basking in past glories. He was also involved in the planning of a system of air mail routes. He drew up eight possible routes across the USA, which became the basis for the US Postal Service air mail system.

Peary, the oldest of the four men whose destinies became entwined in the search for the North Pole, made his last public appearance at the National Geographic Society's headquarters in the spring of 1919, when he presented the annual Hubbard Gold Medal to Canadian polar explorer Vilhjalmur Stefansson. He appeared weak, his once robust frame ravaged by disease. He was receiving regular blood transfusions, which were having limited effects on his health.

By the end of the year he was in a very weak condition. In February 1920 he slipped into a coma in his home, and passed away on February 20. His burial at Arlington Cemetery showed the esteem he was held in by the time of his death. The Vice President, Thomas R. Marshall, and the Chief Justice Edwin White were there, along with Gilbert Grosvenor of the National Geographic, and inventor Alexander Graham Bell.

His nemesis dead, Cook might have expected his fortunes to improve. It was not to be. In a desperate attempt to improve his finances, Cook moved to Texas and became involved in the oil business. He set up the Texas Eagle oil company with finance of $300,000. But the cost of sinking a single well was $100,000, so he was seriously underfunded. To compensate, he set up Texas Eagle Producing and Refining Company, and sought investors.

The brochure promised investors that profits of 100 percent were not uncommon in the oil business. They hoped to transform a field near Fort Worth into one with a capacity of ten thousand barrels a day, and profits of $9 million a year. They were bold claims, but no bolder than other companies were offering. Some companies were set up honestly, and really expected those profits. Many achieved them. But other companies were set up to dupe investors into giving money to men who were little better than con artists.

Cook was trying to be honest. His mail campaign drew in $800,000 in investors, but the money was swallowed up with no oil finds to show for it. Cook became one of the victims of a precarious business. At the end of a year, a notice was issued to the investors. Instead of the $9 million profit promised, the company had made no money but was in no danger of going under. They were going to leave the original field undeveloped and concentrate on acquiring new wells and marketing crude oil instead. In 1921 the company dissolved, and was taken over by Revere Oil.

In March 1922 Cook launched a new venture, the Petroleum Producers Association (PPA). In a massive mail-order campaign he sent out a quarter of a million letters to potential investors. They would take cash investments, or would allow other companies to merge with the PPA by exchanging their old stock for face value plus 25 percent. By the end of the year the PPA had merged with 313 companies, and the exchange of old stock for PPA shares had netted it nearly $90 million. But the costs of Cook's aggressive promotional methods were astronomical, and little was left over for actual oil exploration. It was a house of cards, ready to collapse.

Cook's reputation as a fraud, and the huge potential losses that his company could incur, brought him under increasing scrutiny. Post Office inspectors began a limited investigation of oil companies in 1922, and the PPA quickly became the focus of their interest. Others also began to focus their attention on the company, which had failed to find any profitable oil wells.

To compound his woes, Cook was surprised by a policeman while in a state of undress in a hotel room, with a woman and a pint of gin. In the early days of Prohibition, this was a serious charge and a major embarrassment—especially since the woman was not his wife. Marie filed for divorce. Though she had stood by him through all his troubles, and remained loyal to him up to his death, the couple's marriage now came to an end.

In March 1923 a Grand Jury was convened to investigate PPA, and on April 20 the Grand Jury handed down eighteen separate indictments against Cook for mail fraud. He was arrested, and the fate of his company sealed. Other companies were also targeted. The directors of General Lee Oil Company got ten year sentences—but fled to Mexico while on bail. Cook was advised not to seek a plea bargain, as it was felt he would get a far lesser sentence. But due to a shortage of judges, Judge John Killits from Toledo was brought in to preside over the trial. Not only was he a tough and uncompromising jurist, he was also a friend of the late Robert Peary.

The trial opened on October 15, and Cook himself took the stand on November 9. The trial lasted until the end of November, and the jury, after several weeks of evidence, took twenty hours to arrive at a verdict. Cook was convicted of eight of the twelve charges against him.

The judge's summary was vicious. Addressing Cook, he said: "Cook, what have you got to say? This is one of the times when your peculiar and persuasive hypnotic personality fails you, isn't it? You have at last got to the point where you can't Bunco anybody. You have come to a mountain and reached latitude which are beyond you. . . . I cannot express the abhorrence I have for such a crook as you are."

The sentence was very harsh—fourteen years and nine months in prison, and a fine of $12,000, the maximum allowable. Cook was also liable for the cost of the trial, a further $12,000. Even the prosecuting District Attorney thought it unduly harsh. Cook's legal team lodged an immediate appeal, while Cook was removed to the county jail, where one of his first visitors was his ex-wife Marie. Eventually the appeals procedure ran its course, without success, and Cook was transferred to Leavenworth Prison, Kansas, to begin his sentence. That large penitentiary was to be his home until 1930, when he qualified for early release.

It was the good doctor's final disgrace. His claims of reaching the North Pole were never taken seriously again—though when Peary's claim came under increasing scrutiny the doctor did find some champions. Though he had not reached the Pole either, Peary had won the race decisively.

39

AMUNDSEN AFTER THE SOUTH POLE

A mundsen had also entered a bleak period following his return from the South Pole. A brief lecture tour of Australia filled the almost empty coffers, while Amundsen's men continued from there to South America, en route home. Amundsen took a commercial liner, and joined them in Argentina. But he reassured his backers that his stay in Norway would be brief. He had promised that the South Pole was just a diversion in his original plan to use the polar drift to get to the North Pole. Now he intended to honor that commitment by sailing north for a number of years. Some of his crew agreed to stay with him for the Arctic adventure.

In April, while Amundsen was lecturing in Australia, and his men were traveling to South America, word had come about Scott. It was vague and lacking in detail. At that stage his relief ship only knew that he was not on board. He was late back from the Pole, and had missed the ship. To the world it was reported that he had lost the race to the Pole but was still in Antarctica doing his scientific and exploration work, and would return to civilization in 1913. The great tragedy remained an untold story, and the crew of the relief ship had no idea of Scott's true fate.

Amundsen took advantage of his rival's failure to return during 1912. He used his time in South America to write a book about his experiences, returning to Oslo on July 31. He was honored wherever he went. The Norwegian parliament voted him a huge grant for the next leg of his *Fram* expedition, an annual pension, and wanted to establish a professorship for him. The French made him a Grand Officer of the Legion of Honor, while he was presented with a medal by the King of Sweden. He spent the remainder of the year on a whirlwind circuit of lectures, personal appearances, and grand social events. He was lionized everywhere he went. Winning had been everything; he was completely forgiven for how he had entered the race.

In November he arrived in London to address the Royal Geographical Society. This was the big test—Scott was a hero to the British. Amundsen had never been well received in that country. But the night proved a success. There was a good crowd, and they received him enthusiastically. Some of the officials, including Lord Curzon, were less enthusiastic, and to his death Amundsen felt that they had tried to insult and belittle him at the event. After Britain, he went to America, where he was more comfortable, and was very well received.

In February 1913 the truth of Scott's fate was finally revealed to the world, when the *Terra Nova* returned to New Zealand. Amundsen was shocked, saying: "I would gladly forego any honor or money if thereby I could have saved Scott his terrible death."

He seemed deeply moved and troubled by the news, saying to one reporter: "While those brave men were dying out there in the waste of ice, I was lecturing in warmth and comfort in Australia."

Privately Amundsen felt that part of Scott's problem was that he had not used dogs, and that much of his planning was amateurish. He had set himself up for failure. While there is an element of truth in this, Scott was a good leader who inspired loyalty in his men, and man-hauling had worked in the past. Scott was doomed by two things; his decision to take five to the Pole rather than four, and the uncharacteristically cold autumn. In a normal year, he might have staggered back to Hut Point with most of his men alive. Amundsen was careful to keep his views to himself, though. In his lectures and his press interviews he was always full of praise and sympathy for his rival.

Life returned to some semblance of normality. Amundsen knew he was committed to the polar drift, but he was unenthusiastic. He was only going over old ground broken by Nansen, then walking to a spot already reached by Cook and Peary. But he continued to maintain the fiction that this was what he was working on. In personal terms his life was unsettled; his lover Sigrid Castberg had not waited for him, moving on to a paramour more near at hand. It left him free to move on, and he began a secretive affair with the Norwegian wife of an English businessman. But as she would not leave her husband, the affair was unsatisfactory and led nowhere.

Getting *Fram* home and refitted proved a headache. The new Panama Canal was to be used to get to the Atlantic, but there were delays of several months. It was soon obvious that the polar drift would not begin until the 1915 season. While he waited impatiently, Amundsen took up a new hobby. He learned how to fly, getting the first civilian license from the Norwegian authorities in the summer of 1914. He planned on taking a plane on the *Fram*, which would be the first time an aircraft was used in Arctic exploration. But the world marches on, ignoring the dreams and ambitions of dreamers and explorers.

In August, the First World War broke out. The second leg of the *Fram* expedition was postponed indefinitely. Amundsen was off the hook. Finding himself unemployed, but with plenty of money to invest, Amundsen became the businessman his father had been. Over the following few years he invested wisely, played the markets well, and ended up a wealthy man. But his affair with the married woman was going nowhere, as she would not leave her husband, and he was getting itchy feet. It was time for another expedition.

In 1916 he announced that he was going back north, taking the *Fram* into the pack ice once more. However, when he examined the *Fram*, he discovered that the years spent in the waters around South America, waiting for the polar drift expedition to get underway, had taken their toll. The ship was in terrible condition, with much of the wood rotting. It would be cheaper to scrap it and start afresh. Amundsen commissioned a 120-foot oaken ship with a 240 horsepower diesel engine, designed for crushing through the ice. The *Maud*, named for the Norwegian Queen, was ready in the summer of 1916, and was fitted out for a trip through the Northeast Passage. Amundsen had already navigated the Northwest Passage; this trip would complete the circumnavigation of the top of the world.

To add a bit of spice to the trip, Amundsen returned to his plan of bringing along a plane, to perhaps "fly to the North Pole from the nearest point that we pass on the ship." The reporters loved that bit. But there was a war on. Planes were valuable commodities, and it soon became clear one would not be made available for such frivolous purposes as a polar jaunt. Amundsen was disappointed but realistic: it would be a sledge ride to the Pole.

At the start of the war Amundsen had been neutral, with a slight lean toward Germany. He had enjoyed his time there, and liked the country. He could not say the same of Britain. But he kept his views to himself. In 1917 it all changed. Suddenly the German U-boats began targeting civilian shipping. In October a U-boat torpedoed a Norwegian merchant ship, then sank the lifeboats as they were launched. Norway, a neutral country, was horrified. Amundsen was furious. He put all the awards and medals that he had been given by Germany and its institutions since the South Pole into an envelope, and marched into the German legation in Oslo. He confronted the ambassador—a man he knew socially—and handed over the envelope, asking it to be returned to the Emperor.

He even considered joining the British Navy. But now in his late forties, and unused to the rigid structure of a military organization, he was more useful staying where he was and galvanizing public opinion. Addressing Scandinavian Americans he said: "No man can be a slacker and at the same time a patriot. Every idle man who takes a day a week off just to suit his own whim may be the cause of death to many more men, some of whom may be dear and close to you."

He also had an expedition to organize—and the war was not making it easy. Most of his supplies had been ordered from America, but once the USA entered the war in 1917, it became difficult to get the supplies. The *Maud* Expedition was postponed until 1918.

On June 24, 1918, the *Maud* sailed north. The day was chosen because his contacts in America told him that the U-boats were no longer targeting the Arctic waters, and had moved south. Tension was high until the Maud passed across the top of Norway and turned into the Northeast Passage. This was the sea above Russia, which had once been considered a possible route from Europe to the Orient. Like the Northwest Passage, it was difficult to navigate because of the ice, which persisted most of the year. Amundsen hoped to cross the passage to the Bering Strait in one season, and from there enter the ice and begin the drift. But the weather was against him, and the team were frozen in at Cape Chelyuskin, Siberia, in mid-September. It was an uneventful winter—aside from Amundsen being mauled by a polar bear and having his shoulder mangled so badly it took months before he could use it again. To the end of his days the shoulder troubled him. On another occasion he became so absorbed in his work that he failed to notice a smouldering kerosene lamp was slowly poisoning the room with carbon monoxide. He staggered out into the snow before collapsing, but damage had been done. It would be months before his strength returned. He had always been a fit and meticulous explorer, carefully planning every move. Was he losing his touch?

The ice cleared the following September, and *Maud* got underway again. But it was a brief respite. It was very late in the season, and after eleven days they were beset again, between the New Siberian Islands and Wrangel Island. They were two-thirds of the way across Siberia, but it was going to take a third year to make the trip. Finally, in the summer of 1920, they broke free and got to the Bering Strait, two years behind schedule. Ironically, Amundsen had rejected the idea of sailing across the Atlantic, through the Panama Canal, and up the west coast of America to the Strait as being too time-consuming.

Once in the Strait, Amundsen decided they needed to visit Nome in Alaska for some repairs, and to stack up on provisions. Then they headed north again, becoming embedded in the ice in the western Bering Strait. After the third season frozen in, they retreated south to

Seattle for repairs, in the summer of 1921. The expedition was proving to be a nightmare; three seasons and nothing to show for it. Amundsen took the opportunity to return to Norway, to look after some business affairs. He rejoined the *Maud* in Nome in June 1922. They were four years into the expedition, and for all they had achieved they could have been four weeks into it.

It was time to change their approach. Amundsen divided his forces in two. One team would remain on *Maud* and resume the original plan to drift over the Pole. The second team would attempt to charter a plane and fly over the Pole. It descended into a farcical shambles and the *Maud* team fared worse. They drifted for three years at the mercy of the ice, before the ship finally made Alaska, where it was seized by Amundsen's creditors because of his mounting debts.

The second team, which he led himself, was equally unsuccessful. Amundsen was joined by Oskar Omdal of the Royal Norwegian Navy. They traveled to Wainwright, Alaska, in the autumn of 1922 and set up a base at a place they called Maudheim. They cleared the ground for a runway. Then Amundsen took a team of dogs and a sledge and went to Nome, returning in May 1923 for the flight. The attempt would be made on June 20. It needed to be a success; funds had run out, and Amundsen had run out of places to hide from his creditors.

While Amundsen had been away, Omdal had been busy, assembling the Junkers plane from the contents of three huge crates that had been delivered to the remote spot. It had both skis and landing wheels. They made the first test flight on May 11, but one of the skis collapsed on landing, crumpling like a piece of cardboard. The plane was badly damaged in the botched landing. On June 10 they were ready for a second test flight, after many hours of improvised repairs. The ski crumpled again. They could not use the plane. The attempt was over before they even took off for real. It was a devastating blow.

All the lecture tours in the world could not lift him out of this morass. He needed a dramatic comeback. It came in the form of an American investor. Haakon H. Hammer was a Danish American shipbroker and businessman who quickly gained the explorer's confidence. Hammer was a dreamer, whose dreams were as big as the Norwegian's. And he had the money to back those dreams.

Their plan for 1925 was audacious. They would buy three very expensive Dornier-Wal flying boats, with big pontoons that could withstand the force of a landing on ice or snow. The planes did not have quite the range required for a flight to the Pole and back, but they would take off fully laden from Spitzbergen, then land near the Pole. The fuel from the third plane would be pumped into the two other planes, which would then take off with everyone on board and fly to Alaska. The third plane, despite the huge cost of purchasing it, would be abandoned on the ice.

Amundsen did not rate himself as a businessman. His brother Leon had helped through most of his career. Now he signed over a power of attorney to Hammer, and let him manage the affairs. It was a costly mistake. It took Amundsen a while to realize it, but the businessman was not just a dreamer, but a fantasist. He did not have the money, and did not have the ability or contacts to raise the money for the three planes. Oblivious, Amundsen continued the preparations through the autumn of 1923 and spring of 1924, but a huge hole was forming in his finances which he had no way of filling.

The house of cards came tumbling down in April 1924. Amundsen fired Hammer, who fled immediately to Japan. Then the Norwegian tried to untangle the mess he was left with. His affairs were in complete disarray, and he had debts he could never hope to repay—many incurred without his knowledge under Hammer. To compound matters, his brother Leon became anxious, and tension between the two mounted. Leon had managed Amundsen's affairs for decades, often running up debts that would be settled after a successful expedition. Now he could see that he would be left equally bereft by Hammer's activities. The feud between the two brothers is not known in full detail, but there was a cooling off followed by a major fall-out.

Amundsen had one way of saving himself: sell his home and sell the *Maud*. But Leon was worried that this would leave Roald with no resources, so Leon's chance of recovering anything would be lost.

So he sought a legal injunction to prevent the sale of the house. The ship was seized in Alaska, and was sold off to pay some of the creditors. The whole affair became a mess, and deeply tarnished Amundsen's reputation. He had been a hero to the Norwegian people. Now even they abandoned him. He was seen as a figure of fun, a pathetic relic of the past living off former glories and slowly becoming a liability to himself and others.

In September 1924 he declared bankruptcy, and a few months later, when it got free of the ice, *Maud* was seized. His ruin was complete.

"This was the most painful, the most humiliating, and the most tragic episode in my life. After thirty years of determined work, and after a life lived to the highest of honor, that my name should then be drawn down in the dirt was an intolerable humiliation."

The adventure, at least for the moment, was over.

40

BYRD SPREADS HIS WINGS

While Amundsen was trying to follow up his South Pole success, the third claimant to the North Pole was still not ready to take his first tentative steps in the Arctic. When Richard Byrd finished high school he moved on to the Virginia Military Institute, already sure a career in the armed forces was for him. The Military Institute in Lexington is the oldest military college in the USA, and prepares students for entry to the officers' corps in the army, navy, air force, and marines. Students graduate with a BA, and are fast-tracked into the officer ranks. Byrd spent two very happy years in the grueling and macho atmosphere of the institute, which had and still has many traditions which seem arcane to modern eyes.

One of the traditions is that cadets take it in turn to stand sentry guarding the college twenty-four hours a day. Byrd would have taken his place alongside the other cadets, in full college uniform, but armed with a live gun. Another tradition was the Honor Code, a very strict code of conduct codified in the early years of the century, before Byrd enrolled. The code was brutally stark: "A cadet does not lie, cheat, steal, or tolerate those who do."

It would prove a difficult code for anyone involved in the polar exploration trade.

After two years Byrd transferred to the University of Virginia in Charlottesville to complete his primary degree. One of the most magnificent campuses in the States, it was conceived and designed by Thomas Jefferson, and retains many of the architectural gems from that period. It also had an honor code as strict as that of the Military Academy; lie, cheat, or steal, and you are expelled. One strike and you are out.

Byrd was out after a year, but not because of a violation of the honor code. His wealthy family experienced a financial crisis, and the funds were no longer there to keep him in the college. So he transferred to the United States Naval Academy in Annapolis, Maryland. It was a comedown; this was the more mainstream route into the armed forces, and he was mixing in less exalted company. But classes were small, and he settled in well, thriving in the environment. Undergraduates were called midshipmen, and he was appointed midshipman on May 28, 1908. He was just beginning his career as Cook was trying to navigate his way home from the North Pole.

The course was initially a five-year one, with one year at sea, three years of academic work, and a final year at sea. But by the time Byrd enrolled it had become four years based in the campus, with extended cruises to provide the experience before the mast. He did well in class, and participated in sports and other activities outside. He still had the burning drive to excel, and choose sports that allowed him to appear in the best light. Being slightly small, he was drawn to gymnastics. He excelled at the discipline, which requires high levels of strength, agility, and discipline, becoming captain of the college team. He trained regularly, perfecting complex routines that were beyond his team mates.

The Rings were an apparatus he enjoyed. The gymnast grasps the two hanging rings in his hands and performs a number of balances and stretches in the air, holding the poses while the judges mark for technique and complexity. Byrd had prepared a routine that was testing, and was trying to put the elements together into a smooth whole before a competition. But one day, as he trained, there was a mishap.

He grasped the rings well, and swung his feet up into the air, to do the first of three consecutive somersaults. The first two were executed flawlessly, but as Byrd briefly released the rings to change his grip during the upswing at the start of the third somersault, one of the rings swung out of alignment. Byrd grasped one ring firmly, but fumbled the second. His body immediately began to fall. One hand still grasped one of the rings, and as he fell he rotated. Had there been time he would have been able to position his body for the fall. But he came crashing down on one leg. There was a sickening crack, and he crumpled to the floor. His team mates rushed over; it was obvious that he was seriously hurt. He lay on the ground, his face ashen.

The injury was serious; the ankle had dislocated, and two bones had broken. It took months to heal properly, and left him with a permanent limp. His days as a gymnast were over. Today the broken bones in his foot could have been reset with routine but expensive surgery. Back then that was not an option; the break was set as best as possible, and time did its work to knit together the torn ligaments. Byrd dedicated himself to exercising in an effort to overcome the restrictions the damaged foot put on him. But on a sea mission as part of his training, he fell and the ankle broke again. This time he was taken to Washington for surgery, and a pin was inserted in his foot. But the bones never knitted properly, and he would have a permanent limp for the rest of his life.

On June 8, 1912, he graduated from the Academy and was commissioned as an ensign in the Navy. He was a junior officer, responsible for the flag on board, and his first ship was the USS *Missouri*. From there he was transferred to the USS *Dolphin*, a gun boat. Physically he was not a typical officer. He was very short, at the limit of the acceptable height. And he limped. But he carried himself with an aloof dignity, a legacy of his First Family heritage. And he was a good organizer. His gifts compensated for his shortcomings, at least in peace time. In 1915 he married his childhood sweetheart Marie Ames, and settled into life in the military

But clouds of war had been looming over the world. Europe had plunged into madness in 1914, and America knew there was a high possibility they would be drawn into the conflict. And any officer not capable of achieving an A1 ranking in their annual physical was useless to a Navy at war. In peacetime Byrd's foot had been nothing but an inconvenience, now it was more of a problem. In 1916 Byrd was retired from active duty on medical grounds, at his own request. Though he was physically very fit, he was frail, and his body gave out under pressure. The leg had rebroken more than once, and he knew the end was in sight. But the Navy was good to Byrd in retirement; he was promoted to the rank of lieutenant (junior grade) and assigned to the Rhode Island Naval Militia as instructor and inspector.

Even this could not soften the devastating blow. War is every young man's chance to make his mark in the military, and Byrd was sitting it out, due to a silly sports injury. He did a good job establishing the Rhode Island Militia, then was transferred to Washington, where he rode a desk at the bureau of Naval Personnel. It was a bleak period in his life. He was happily married, and attending all the right parties. But he knew he was walking in circles. There would be no chance of preferment for a crippled officer. He applied numerous times for a return to active duty, being turned down each time. He used every connection he had, but to no avail.

Then he got an idea. If he couldn't have a traditional naval career, he could have a new type of career. Airplanes were a modern innovation. Since their invention in 1903, they had come a long way. In 1909 Louis Blériot had crossed the English Channel, and now the flimsy craft were being used regularly in the war in Europe. America would have to prepare for the new technology, and Byrd was determined to be at the forefront of the revolution. He began to take flying lessons. Being a former gymnast helped; he coped well with the turbulence and strange motion of flight on the primitive craft of the day. In August 1917 he was granted his pilot's licence.

In 1918 he was transferred to Pensacola in Florida for specialist pilot training. Many of the officers moved their wives and families down, but not Byrd. An old-fashioned Southern gent, he believed women had no place near a military base. To the end of his days he retained an attitude toward women that veered from chauvinistic to downright misogynist.

Pensacola was a harsh environment; the very first day he arrived, a plane plunged into the ground, killing both its occupants. Deaths and serious injuries were a common occurrence. Byrd thrived on the danger and the octane-charged atmosphere. One of the men he became close to tried, as a lark, to switch seats with his copilot while in the air. They lost control and plunged to their deaths. The aviator left a young wife. The event was treated as routine by everyone.

In April 1918, at the end of six weeks of intensive training, Byrd qualified as Naval Aviator 608. He trained for another month to qualify as a seaplane pilot, then became one of the instructors at the base, remaining in Florida for a year. His love of aviation grew the more he flew, but his ambitions also began to grow. He saw the potential of air travel, and hatched an ambitious plan to make the first transatlantic crossing. However, others in the services were already working on that idea, and he stepped on toes when he made his suggestion. Perhaps as a result of this, he was transferred to Nova Scotia in Canada, to establish an airbase to look out for German submarines. He became involved on the fringes of the transatlantic flight mission, but never became one of the main players.

The war ended late that year, and by Christmas 1918 Byrd was back in Washington. Although he could not talk his way onto the transatlantic mission, he did invent and develop a number of tools for navigation. One of these, the sun sextant, allowed the pilot to use a bubble of liquid to create an artificial horizon and take positions. He developed his network in the capital, becoming an influential man. Part of his work involved helping set up an aviation bureau for the Navy. But for some reason he did not get a senior position in the new bureau. Perhaps he was too junior an officer, or perhaps it was because he was officially retired, and only back on active duty because of the war.

For the next few years Byrd strode the corridors of power, based in Washington. From a good family, well married, handsome, and confident, he thrived in the environment. But so did many a young man. Now he had a young family, and he needed to find some way of standing out from the crowd. He tried to set himself up in business, but could not find backers. He seemed stuck in the bottom echelons of the naval bureaucracy. Then he heard an interesting rumor late in 1923: Roald Amundsen was planning on flying to the North Pole. This resonated strongly with Byrd. He had dreamed of the Pole as a child. Amundsen was one of his heroes, and he knew all about his exploits in the South Pole. Americans love a winner, and they did not come more successful than the Norwegian explorer.

Byrd immediately wrote to his superiors volunteering to be part of the aerial expedition. He had been involved in the planning stages of a transatlantic attempt which saw US airmen successfully cross the ocean in relays, via Newfoundland and Greenland. He also had experience in Nova Scotia, and claimed to have spent eight months studying the problems of flying in polar regions. The Navy ignored his request. For the next two years he languished, a junior bureaucrat in the military. He was highly regarded, competent, brave, and ambitious. As was everyone.

Then, in 1923, the Navy announced a plan to fly around the world. Byrd seized the opportunity, and suggested they should also explore the feasibility of reaching the North Pole by air. Times had changed and the Navy were receptive. Byrd was appointed on the seven man presidentially approved commission. Their initial plan was to use an airship rather than a plane, but when their craft was damaged in moorings by high winds, the President himself stopped the project. It was a blow to the Navy, and the Army then came to the fore, achieving the round-the-world flight later in 1924. Now the Navy needed a coup to take back the initiative.

Veteran polar explorer Donald MacMillan, who had been north with Peary in 1909, proposed an exploration of the arctic regions using a combination of traditional methods and aviation, and the idea began to get qualified support in the Navy. In January 1925 Byrd floated the idea of a transpolar flight, and this time he got influential backing. The plan was to bring an airship (a hydrogen-filled dirigible) to Etah in northern Greenland, then fly north. An airship is a lighter than air vessel which floats like a hot air balloon. But it is shaped like a giant cigar and has powerful engines. It can fly vast distances on relatively little fuel, and can carry heavy loads. A cache of supplies would be laid on the ice 150 miles from the Pole as a precaution. They would have fuel for a twenty-five-hundred-mile journey, exploring the region around the Pole, and from the Pole to Alaska, all from the air. But when the National Geographic Society turned down his request for a grant of $40,000 to cover the costs of an airship, the plan began to flounder. It was at this point Byrd began to consider the possibility of using a plane.

For a long time the Navy wavered between backing MacMillan and backing Byrd. In the end they decided to go with the veteran. But Byrd was to lead the air section of the expedition, which was under the overall command of MacMillan. It was not an ideal situation. The fact that the two men had been rivals to lead the expedition meant that there was tension between them from the start. They never overcame that, and on a personal level MacMillan disliked the younger man. The expedition lasted from June to October 1925. It was a frustrating time for Byrd. He managed to get three small planes, but during the planning he was painfully aware that Amundsen was ready for another attempt at flying to the Pole. That would complicate things. Byrd's plans were, by necessity, less ambitious. No matter how well he did, he would end up on the shadow of the Viking.

41

AMUNDSEN MAKES FURTHER FLIGHTS

Amundsen had been a hero to the world. His early expeditions had been characterized by a meticulous attention to detail and great planning. After his first failure as a teenager, he had learned that failing to prepare is preparing to fail. Yet his *Maud* expedition had been a disaster from start to finish. Two men had died at the end of the first season, attempting to sledge from Siberia to civilization with news of the trip. Amundsen had broken an arm, been mauled by a polar bear, and nearly died of carbon monoxide poisoning in that first season. The expedition had ended in failure and bankruptcy.

In disgrace, Amundsen left Norway, with no plans to return. In late 1924 he moved to America, planning on settling in Wainwright, Alaska, in the hut where he had prepared for the disastrous polar flight. Fifty-three years old, he was right back where he started, but without the vigor of youth. He stopped in New York, and stayed quietly in the Waldorf Astoria for a few weeks. His peace was disturbed by calls from creditors, and bills being passed under his door. A proud man, he did not try to avoid the calls, but lifted the phone to face the music whenever it trilled.

On October 8 the phone rang again, and again he reached to pick it up, his heart sinking. But this time it was not a creditor. The caller introduced himself as Lincoln Ellsworth, and explained that he had met Amundsen several years earlier, during the war. He was interested in exploration, and was willing to finance an expedition. The forty-four-year-old engineer had already led two expeditions to South America, and his funds were unlimited. He was the only son of a millionaire. Amundsen invited him up to his room, and the two men quickly got down to business.

Ellsworth had applied to sail on the *Maud* in 1918, but had been turned down. Now he was coming to the party with a fat wallet, so he got a fuller hearing. The two men got on well, and Amundsen came to life under the hero worship of the younger man. They met several times, then agreed to terms. It would be a joint venture. Ellsworth would supply the money, and Amundsen would lead. The following May they would fly from Spitzbergen to the North Pole.

The Napoleon of the North was on the march again.

With a war chest of $95,000, Amundsen was able to purchase the planes that Hammer had ordered the previous year. They settled on just two planes, each with a crew of three. He traveled to Italy to inspect the planes, then in March arrived back in Norway. The new trip had fired the imagination of newspaper readers worldwide and he was once again the hero, feted wherever he went. When he arrived in Oslo he got off the train a stop early, to avoid the huge crowds that shadowed his every move. It was like the old days once more. He had a real chance of redemption. But he couldn't avoid everyone, and was soon suffering the effects of too much good food and wine. In fact, he turned up at one official function well under the weather, with his shirt collar back in his hotel room.

Ellsworth joined him at the end of the month, in time for the grand dinner hosted by the Norwegian Aeronautical Association, complete with a cake in the form of a plane circling the Pole. The following day they took the train to Bergen and a steamship to Tromsø, where the aircraft had already been shipped. Then they sailed on to the island of Spitzbergen, where they began assembling the planes in sub-zero temperatures.

Amundsen explained his plan to the team. Two planes would take off from Spitzbergen and fly to the Pole, landing there to take observations. Then one plane would return to Spitzbergen, while the other flew on to Alaska. It was a crazy plan; everyone urged him to reconsider. The planes should stay together, as flight in such extreme latitudes was a new and highly dangerous pursuit. Eventually he backed down. Then one of the pilots mentioned that there was an airship for sale in Italy for $100,000. Amundsen was immediately interested. He had believed airships were too expensive for his expedition, but this one seemed affordable. Ellsworth agreed, and would have loved to have purchased the airship immediately. But it was a large chunk of change. He would have to talk to his father when they returned from the Pole. This was exciting; with funding, they suddenly had a two-year plan; fly to the Pole and back the first year, then the following season fly in the airship, and drift around the high polar seas, discovering any new land that was left.

On May 21 they were ready for take-off. The local coal miners were given the day off to watch the lunatics launch themselves into the air. It was a big day on the large but sparsely inhabited island. From their base at Kings Bay to the Pole and back was a round trip of 1,500 miles—in an open cockpit with no heating. The six aviators were as wide as they were tall, they wore so many layers of clothing that morning.

Amundsen's plane took off first, lumbering across the ice like a drunken elephant before finally managing to climb into the air. The second plane, with Ellsworth on board, took off immediately afterwards. It was a rocky start, and under the pressure the second plane sprung a small leak in the gas line. But despite this they flew on for several hours, at a steady seventy-five miles an hour. As they had no radios on board (they had not arrived in time) they had to keep each other in sight at all times.

After eight hours Amundsen estimated that they were close to the Pole. The ground beneath them looked smooth enough to chance a landing, so he asked the pilot, Hjalmar Riiser-Larsen, to bring the plane down. Although a qualified pilot himself, Amundsen was in the navigator's chair. As they descended, they could see that the ground was a lot rougher than they anticipated. The ice was torn across by pressure ridges, with gashes of open water and mini-bergs piercing upwards. As they were about to bring the plane back up, one of the engines began to splutter, and the craft lurched to the side. The pilot reacted quickly, bringing them down onto an open channel of slushy water, and managing to stop before they smashed into an ice berg.

The other plane spotted the first plane going in for a landing, and flew on for a few minutes, looking for a safe place to set down. They managed to land on a wide lagoon of slush, semi-frozen sea ice. But the plane had come in too fast, and smashed into an ice floe. It was a hard bang, and the plane began to fill with water. The three occupants jumped out onto the thick snow. They could see one engine was mangled, and the interior was filling with water. They would not fly home.

They were hopeful that the first plane had landed safely. If it had not, and had flown on, they were in deathly trouble. It was a worrying time. They made themselves as comfortable as they could, and waited out the evening. The following day they trekked to a high point and scanned the horizon, eventually finding Amundsen's plane three miles off. They waved a flag, and got a wave in response. Unfortunately no one knew semaphore or Morse code, so communications was as rudimentary as a cheery wave. Both groups spent that second day assessing the damage and seeing whether they could salvage their aircraft. On the third day, Ellsworth ordered his group to try and reach Amundsen: their plane would never take off again.

Though only three miles, it was a brutal journey, across ice barely thick enough to hold their weight. At one point all three men plunged into the sea, and they nearly lost their mechanic. Ellsworth managed to haul the semi-conscious aviator from the water in time. But they were eventually reunited with their companions, and the six men dried off and tried to warm up with hot chocolate.

"Here we were, six hundred miles from civilization, landed upon the ice with airplanes equipped for landing upon water, with the engine of one of the planes utterly out of commission, and with provisions adequate for full nourishment for only about three weeks," Amundsen noted.

Back on Spitzbergen the support team waited anxiously. They were expecting the two planes to return the day after they left, carrying news of triumph. But the following day passed, with no news. Then the next day . . . It was obvious the expedition was in deep trouble. Newspapers began speculating about the fate of the Last Viking and his crew. If they had crashed on the ice, could they ski to Greenland? Or were they dead already?

Amundsen was news again.

Ships began to search north of Spitzbergen, looking for signs of wreckage. If the planes had come down shortly into their journey there was some chance of rescue. But if they were close to the Pole, that chance fell away rapidly. After three weeks, and no sign of debris, the searches were called off. It was widely accepted that Amundsen had perished on the ice.

Luckily, the stranded men did have one thing going for them. Amundsen was one of the most experienced polar explorers in the world, a man used to leading in adversity. He quickly organized the men, giving everyone their own tasks to carry out. Their first task was to right the plane, which was leaning heavily on one side, in a way that made it possible to move. With three men it had been impossible to straighten it; with six it was just a matter of a few hours hard work. Then they began clearing a runway through the ice. This was grueling work, as they had no tools. The runway had to be cleared using one axe, and a few knives attached to ski poles. Lumps of ice were hacked off and kicked to the side. Days and weeks passed in ceaseless toil.

The group had not been anticipating problems, and had not been prepared for several weeks on the ice. Not only did they not have essential survival equipment, they only had food for a short period. Amundsen rationed the food so that it would last twenty-five days. That was his cut-off point. On June 15 they would either take off, or give up the effort and make a dash across the ice for Greenland. He knew this would be a disastrous retreat, a repeat of Cook's year of wandering on his return from the Pole. But the difference was that they had no equipment—no tents, no sledges, no weapons for hunting the scarce game they might encounter. It would be a rout. They really needed to clear the runway, and everyone knew it.

When it looked long enough, they attempted to take off. But the pilot, Leif Dietrichson, had to abandon the attempt, and they went back to digging and clearing. Rations were reduced, and the men weakened. Breakfast was a mug of hot chocolate and three crackers. Lunch was a cup of soup, and dinner was more hot chocolate and crackers. More than three weeks passed. Day by day it looked as if no progress was being made, but by the end they had a runway one hundred yards longer than they expected to need. Plenty of margin for error. Dense fog obscured the ground on June 15, but they did not have the luxury of delay. The six men bundled into a plane designed for three. To save weight, every non-essential—their gun, scientific instruments, a canoe, spare clothing, and the camera—was tossed onto the ice.

For the flight, Riiser-Larsen was back in the pilot's seat, with Amundsen beside him as navigator. The other four were crushed into the small space behind. The ice creaked ominously, and the plane creaked under the strain, as the propellers slowly dragged it down the makeshift path through the ice. The men held their breaths as the ridge at the end of the runway came closer and closer. But at the last minute the nose rose, and the pontoons lifted from the ice. The plane cleared the ridge and slowly began to gain altitude. A weak cheer rose from behind him, and Amundsen grinned. They were away.

Navigation was tough, with the compass useless so near the magnetic Pole, and fog obscuring the ground beneath them. They knew they had enough fuel left to bring three men home, but with the extra weight the plane was burning through gas. Would there be enough to get them home? With only half an hour of fuel left, they spotted the peaks of Spitzbergen in the distance. Bars of chocolate were passed around in celebration.

It was short-lived. As they approached the island, the lateral steering mechanism, which had been giving trouble throughout the flight, gave out completely. Unable to steer, Riiser-Larsen told the men to brace themselves: they were ditching into the sea. He managed to find a small lead of open water, and landed successfully. They were in Hinlopen Strait, many miles and many mountains away from their base in Kings Bay. They faced days of struggle—then Amundsen spotted a sail in the distance. It was a sealing ship, but the sealers had not seen the emergency landing. The men shouted, but were unable to attract the attention of the ship, which was rapidly disappearing over the horizon.

The men bundled back into the plane, and Riiser-Larsen fired up the engines, now running on fumes. They didn't try to take off. They shot across the water, bumping on the small waves, chasing after the sealer. The sailors eventually spotted their unusual pursuer, and stopped. When the plane slid to a halt beside the ship, the sailors looked down incredulously. They saw six thin men, badly dressed, unkempt, and shaggy. They looked like tramps. The oldest man had a familiar look.

Finally it dawned on one of the sailors. This was the famous explorer in all the newspapers, the man who had flown north nearly a month previously. He was once again the most famous man in Norway, and a national hero.

"You are all supposed to be dead," the sailor said.

42

THE RACE IS ON

Byrd's fears were confirmed: before they set out, all the news focused on Amundsen and his difficulties. The MacMillan expedition was relegated to the position of a sideshow. And what publicity it generated was for its leader, not for the leader of the air section. By the time they packed the planes aboard their ship, The *Peary*, for the trip to Greenland, the fate of the Norwegian party was still unknown. Byrd and MacMillan were summoned to Washington and asked whether the Americans could help with a possible search and rescue. Both men were doubtful but willing.

The plan was to land at Etah, Greenland, where both Cook and Peary had spent time, and from there to fly across to Cape Columbia at the north of Ellesmere Island. They would land on the generally snow-free beach at the Cape, and off-load men and supplies, setting up a weather station and reconnaissance base. From there, Byrd would lead sorties to explore the polar region between Alaska and the Pole. They were not aiming specifically to fly over the Pole, and knew some of their resources could be taken up searching for the missing explorers.

But just before they set out, word arrived that Amundsen had succeeded in rescuing himself and was safe on Spitzbergen. The news of the daring rescue excited people, and the excitement became infectious. When the *Peary* and its sister ship, the *Bowdoin*, left Maine's Sheepscot River on June 20, the whole state seemed to be on the shore, waving flags. On August 1, after a crossing beset with difficulties and tensions, the two ships finally docked in Etah. As Byrd looked at the bleak rocky hills, the distant snow-capped interior, and the choppy water of the bay, festooned with broken ice floes, his pulse must have quickened. He was finally about to embark on his life's work.

From the start, things didn't go smoothly. They quickly discovered that taking off and landing on water cost a huge amount of fuel, reducing the operating range of the planes from seven hundred miles to five hundred miles. And the summer was a particularly bad one, with few clear days. When they flew over the interior of Ellesmere Island they could see how rugged and uneven the land was; bases would be confined exclusively to the coast.

They did try on a number of occasions, making successful landings on the far side of Smith Sound. But finding suitable landing areas was difficult. You had to find a fjord with clear water, or a stretch of beach where the ice was not up to the sand. The difficulty with fjords were the katabatic winds: strong winds sweeping down from the cold heights of the interior and blowing with gale force directly off land. The aircraft barely had the power to handle those gusts. And the waters could be very choppy. A plane could be landed sometimes, but not docked safely.

On one flight Byrd successfully deposited a supply of fuel and food, then took off for a second supply run. When he returned to the depot, he found that the open lead of water he had landed on a few hours earlier had already frozen over, and he flew on for a further sixty miles without finding another suitable landing spot. So that depot, and the precious fuel, had to be abandoned. It was typical of his luck.

One evening, one of the planes began taking in water. As the crew struggled to get it on deck before it was completely swamped, the fuselage suffered a crack. So they were down to two planes. Near the end of the month a second plane caught fire, and had to be cut adrift of its mooring behind the *Peary*, so as not to endanger the big ship. Now they were down to one aircraft; and MacMillan gave the order that no flights across Smith Sound were to be undertaken without the back-up of a second plane. Effectively, the air exploration aspect of the expedition had come to an end.

It was not a complete failure. Byrd and his men had covered six thousand miles by air, and had been given rare glimpses into the interior of Ellesmere Island and Greenland itself. Byrd was able to confirm that the interior of Greenland, the dense ice sheet, rose to a height of at least eleven thousand feet, which was higher than anyone had suspected. They had redrawn the map, at least to an extent. They had failed to establish their bases on the far side of Smith Sound, though. Their plan had been to try and set up a base on Cape Columbia, and from there to fly well out over the polar sea. All this work was abandoned.

From Byrd's perspective the only positive to emerge from the expedition was that he flew often with an airman, Floyd Bennett, who would become an important ally in future ventures. Two years younger than Byrd, Bennett was a native of upstate New York and an auto mechanic before he joined the Navy in 1917 to become a pilot. Bennett was a quiet, hard-working man, with a flair for running repairs that was very useful in harsh conditions. He was also a better pilot than Byrd, so often Byrd would take the navigation seat.

It was an ideal arrangement, as Byrd was a skilled navigator and a good flight planner. Their skills blended together perfectly, making them the perfect team in the air. It helped that they trusted each other, and liked each other. Your safety in the air depends on the reliability of your partner, and in Bennett, Byrd had found the perfect pilot.

By September the expedition was over, and the *Peary* and *Bowdoin* were sailing south along the coast of Greenland, ready to return to America. They had one working plane left. When they returned—to a hero's welcome—MacMillan delivered his assessment of the flight portion of the expedition. It was devastating, and probably influenced in part by his dislike of Byrd. He told the Navy, and the National Geographic Society, that the planes had performed satisfactorily, and the men who used them had been very good, but heavier than air craft would take no significant part in the future of Arctic exploration. They were not suited for the terrain and conditions. Future efforts should be directed toward airships.

It was the last message Byrd wanted his superiors to hear. He was convinced that only bad luck and a poor summer had hampered the planes—that, and an expedition leader reluctant to take risks and use them to the fullest possible extent. But Byrd had learned a valuable lesson. If he was to succeed as an explorer, he would need to be the man calling the shots. On his next expedition, he would be the leader.

While MacMillan was milking the exposure from yet another trip north, Byrd began working his contacts. He also wrote an article for the *National Geographic*, and hit the lecture circuit, a favorite fund-raiser of budding explorers. Amundsen was on the same mission, touring the mid-west and taking time out to visit old friend Frederick Cook in Leavenworth Prison. Both were men on missions. Their early attempts to reach the Pole by air had been disasters, but disasters tinged with enough promise to keep the explorers in the race.

Byrd struggled to get the lectures right, often running on ahead of the shaky movie images the projector was showing behind him, or falling behind them.

"I am, as you know, not used to talking to movies," he sheepishly explained to one sponsor. But the public still loved the drama of it all. On the final day of January 1925, he went public with his grand plans for the coming season, announcing that he was going to the Arctic in the spring, for an independent attempt to explore the polar regions from the air.

"We are now trying to reach a decision as to whether an airship or a specially designed plane gives the best assurance of a successful outcome of the venture," he told the *New York Times*.

Whichever he decided upon, he knew that it was not a simple case of setting up camp and heading north. This would not be an expedition, but a race. As he struggled to raise funds, Amundsen was doing the same. Presumably they would both be ready to set off in the spring. There was no margin for error. His opponent had been in a race like this before, and had reached the South Pole ahead of the front runner, Scott. He was a serious opponent, and Byrd was rightly worried. He secured extended leave from the Navy (an echo of Peary), and began searching for a plane.

Initially he was going to use an experimental three-engine plane that Ford was working on, but it was destroyed in a fire before the company could consider his request for it. So he turned to a Dutch company, Fokker, who had a three-engine plane that was suitable. This created a problem. He was a friend of Edsel Ford, son of the entrepreneur Henry Ford. Edsel was president of the Ford company, and Byrd had hoped he would be a major sponsor of the trip. Ford were experimenting with aircraft, and hoping to become major players in the new industry. Luckily Edsel saw the bigger picture. If they sponsored a successful polar flight, even in a rival company's craft, it would increase the general interest in aviation, which would indirectly benefit them. Grateful for the sponsorship, Byrd came up with the ingenious idea of calling the plane *Josephine Ford*, after Edsel's daughter. So the word "Ford" was blazoned across the craft.

Once Ford was on board, other sponsors quickly followed, including the Rockefeller family. Before long he had raised over $100,000. Byrd also sold the motion film rights to Pathé News for $2,500 and the rights to use the film himself for lectures afterwards. He did not realize it at the time, but this was a very good deal. Amundsen had also sold his movie rights to Pathé in a similar deal—but got no advance payment.

The Norwegian had been busy since his return from Spitzbergen the previous season. Amundsen and Ellsworth had been thought to be dead. But they discovered that it was another who had died in their absence: Ellsworth's father. The old man had passed away while they were struggling on the ice. Lincoln Ellsworth was no longer the heir to millions; he was a millionaire himself. Decisions no longer had to be run by his disapproving father. Now he called the shots.

The first thing he did, after the obligatory few weeks of celebration in Norway, was contact Colonel Umberto Nobile in Italy, asking him to meet with the explorers to discuss the airship he had designed. Nobile was both an engineer and an aviator, and had designed the airship for the Italian military. It was a semi-rigid dirigible. This meant that there was a solid keel to which the envelope of hydrogen, which provided lift, was attached. The craft maintained its characteristic cigar shape through pressure of the gas.

Nobile came north, meeting with Amundsen, Ellsworth, and Riiser-Larsen at the explorer's home in Uranienborg in mid-July. The Italian was a senior officer in Benito Mussolini's air force, and was a vain and ambitious man. He insisted on being part of the expedition. He even offered the airship for free, if it could be a joint Italian-Norwegian expedition, flying under the Italian flag. Amundsen rejected this offer. He wanted to buy the airship and hire Nobile as the pilot, no more. After a second meeting in Rome, the deal was struck. They bought the airship for £15,000 ($1.3 million today)—a lot less than they had been prepared to pay. Nobile was the chief pilot. But they had to agree to a crew of five Italian mechanics. Amundsen agreed, but insisted the dirigible be renamed *Norge* (Norway) just so no one was in any doubt whose expedition this was.

He chose Ellsworth as a companion, as well as his pilot Riiser-Larsen, and Oscar Wisting, one of his companions from the South Pole trip of more than a decade previously. He wanted to make sure that the crew included plenty of Norwegians and Americans, to reflect the true origins of the expedition. But Nobile's ego became an increasingly big problem as time passed. He viewed himself as an equal partner in the enterprise, not just as a hired pilot. And he portrayed to the world—backed by the might of the Italian government—that this was a joint enterprise. It frustrated and infuriated Amundsen. As the time neared for the hand-over of the airship, the Italians became more and more unreasonable, demanding huge sums for insurance and trying to take over the expedition.

But on March 29 the dirigible took off from Rome—to huge fanfare—and began its silent drift toward Spitzbergen. Relieved, Amundsen and Ellsworth took the train to Oslo, from where they would make their own way to the island. The airship would be stored and prepared in a huge hanger in Kings Bay, and would be ready for take-off in early May, aiming to fly over the Pole and land in Alaska, completing the first flight right across the top of the world.

Byrd was well aware of his rival's plans; they were reported widely in papers across Europe and America. But his own plans were also progressing well. He was confident that he would also be in Spitzbergen in early May, ready for his own take-off. Then it was a straight race: who could get off the ground sooner? Byrd had one advantage; his plane traveled a lot faster than Amundsen's semi-rigid airship.

To ensure victory Byrd decided on the simplest possible plan; a straight flight to the Pole, then back again. Floyd Bennett would be in the pilot's seat. The rest of the team were also experts, including George Noville of the Vacuum Oil Company, who would be in charge of fuel. Two new inventions were brought along for navigation; a sun compass, and an earth induction compass, a complex electronic device that would let them know if they drifted off their set course. They would also use a bubble sextant as well as a wind indicator. Drift caused by cross winds would seriously throw off their navigational calculations, so they needed to know the extent of the wind at all times.

Finally, on Monday, April 5, 1926, the USS *Chantier* pulled out of Brooklyn Navy Yard, with a crew of fifty, made up of Navy men and Marines on leave, and civilians along for the jaunt. Byrd was positively giddy as he watched the crowds glide by on the quays. It was all so close—cross the Atlantic, set up a temporary aerodrome, and the race was on. Amundsen, as he knew, had already set out from Rome. For nearly three weeks he fretted, as the ship slowly crossed the sea, finally reaching Norway and working up the coast. Where was Amundsen? Did his rival have a headstart?

On April 29 *Chantier* sailed into Kings Bay, where he found a frosty reception from the tiny population of Norwegian coal miners. The island had only been inhabited for twenty years, and facilities were poor. But the big problem was that Amundsen had beaten him to the spot. And Amundsen was Norwegian, almost a local.

There was no help from the locals when it came to off-loading the plane. They stood in sullen groups, watching. Amundsen walked from his headquarters to the top of a hill, watched for a few minutes, then turned his back on the Americans. Relations between Amundsen's party and the American party began frosty, and remained frosty. Amundsen's men threw every possible obstacle in the way of the Americans. They were understandably worried. They might have been there first, but they knew that a three-engine Fokker traveled a good deal faster than an airship. The race was on, and they no longer liked the odds.

Shortly after arriving, Byrd tried to do the decent thing by visiting Amundsen. But he was told the Norwegian was not in the expedition headquarters. He returned later that evening, full of trepidation. This time Amundsen was in, and the meeting was less tense than he expected. Amundsen drew himself to his full height, towering over his short American rival, and shook hands, saying: "Glad you're here safe, Commander. Welcome to Spitzbergen."

Then he spread some maps and charts on the table, and the two men bent over them. This was what drew them together: their love of exploration. With their common interest dominating the conversation, the meeting went well. At the end, Amundsen suggested that a smooth flat area in front of the Norwegian camp was the best take-off site for the Fokker. Byrd was surprised. He asked Amundsen if he would not be uncomfortable having a rival so close.

Amundsen smiled, saying they were not rivals, but companions on a great venture to explore the Polar Regions, one using a heavier than air craft, one using a lighter than air craft. They had different objectives; Byrd wanted the Pole, while Amundsen wanted the transpolar flight. It was the same thing he had said to Byrd when they had met in New York six weeks earlier.

"We are partners in this venture together."

The man had charisma.

The race was still on, but now some of the sting had been taken out of the rivalry, at least among the leaders.

43

WINGS NEAR THE POLE

There are sections to a race. The first section is getting to the starting mark. Byrd managed to have his aircraft ready by May 9, earlier than the Norwegians imagined was possible. They still had a few more days work to do before they were ready to fly. It was a little after midnight, and the flat site outside their hangar was suddenly buzzing with activity. As they sleepily assembled, they could see the Americans preparing their machine for take-off. Amundsen came out, rubbing the sleep from his eyes.

Flight was a full quarter of a century old, but getting a plane into the air still took care and time. Everything had to be checked and double-checked, and an element of luck was needed. A leak or a faulty wire could cause the plane to respect the laws of gravity and plunge from the sky in a flaming fireball. The Americans were double-checking everything.

Byrd knew the value of preparation better than most. He had flown during the war, and had seen enough colleagues come to grief on flimsy and unforgiving machines. But he had his share of luck; he knew that too. Back when he was fighting for his place in the new naval aviation establishment, he had successfully planned the first transatlantic flight, sending a team of aviators from America to Europe. The Pilgrim

Fathers had come from Plymouth. He had sent his aviators back there. They had left Rockaway Beach in New Jersey, ambling in a great circle across the Arctic, stopping regularly to refuel, before arriving at the English town twenty-three days later.

That had been in 1919, the year after the war, and his luck had held, just. Two of the three planes had failed to make the crossing, but one had got through. Today he needed his luck more than ever. Only one plane was making this historic flight, and if anything happened, he would end up stranded on shifting polar ice, hundreds of miles from any possibility of rescue.

Almost without being aware of it he touched the breast pocket of his flying jacket. He was not a superstitious man, but neither did he believe in taking chances. Through the thick fabric he could feel the round disc of the small religious medal a friend had given him. The medal belonged to his friend's fiancée, so it meant a lot when he had presented it to Byrd. He could also feel the small horseshoe a blacksmith had made for him. But the third trinket was the most important. Dangling on a string outside the pocket was a small coin, tarnished with age. This coin had been a talisman for an earlier explorer. Robert Peary had brought it to the Pole and back again in 1909. Now the coin belonged to Byrd, and he hoped to repeat the journey.

Would the trinkets really help? He knew they couldn't hinder, and perhaps that was enough.

It had been a challenge to be ready before Amundsen. The Norwegian had been beaten to the Pole twenty years earlier and had fallen short in 1925, but now he was back for another crack at the prize. And his chances were good. Was Amundsen making the right choice this year? Byrd nervously fingered his talismans again. Airships were as prone to mechanical failures as planes. He had to trust his plan. And they had to do it today; he knew his rivals were almost ready to make their attempt.

The triple-engine Fokker was heavily laden as the engine caught and the propeller began to spin. It shuddered, then lurched forward along the frozen ground of the airstrip. Slowly it inched forward, then faster. Floyd Bennett was in the pilot's seat, checking the ground ahead and keeping an eye on the instruments. Byrd, as the copilot and navigator, was not needed yet. He looked out the window as his team of mechanics, supporters, and ground crew—naval men like himself, many of them—ran along beside the plane, falling behind as it gained speed. The huge international press corps had been caught off guard by the midnight start. Only one man managed to get a movie camera whirring, and he was too late to get anything useful in the dull light. In the distance Byrd could see the rough snow mound at the end of the runway.

As Amundsen ruefully noted in *My Life as an Explorer*: "We bade him God speed, and gave him a cheer when he started."

This was the first hurdle. The plane was heavy. Byrd was taking no chances. They had a rubber inflatable boat, reindeer-skin, polar-bear and seal fur clothes, boots and gloves, a stove, three guns, ammunition, knives and axes, even smoke bombs to scare off polar bears. They were carrying a full medical kit, and food for ten weeks. This was made up of the foul pemmican (a mix of chopped-up meat, fat, sugar, and raisins), chocolate, bread, tea, malted milk, powdered chocolate, butter, sugar, and cream cheese. It was not a healthy diet, but it was full of energy. If they were forced down, like Amundsen, they were equipped to walk to Greenland.

The fuselage of the plane also held a sledge, for carrying the provisions. The sledge was hand-made, and had been presented to them by Amundsen. He was a fierce competitor, but he never let that rivalry cross over into bitterness. If they beat him—and Byrd was determined they would—he knew that Amundsen would be a gentleman about it.

Despite the weight, the plane cleared the ground and crossed over the mound of broken snow into the sky. Through his window Byrd could see men throwing their hats into the air and cheering wildly. The great adventure had begun.

The first part of the trip was simple. As navigator, Byrd relied on dead reckoning. He knew all the landmarks around King's Bay, where they had built their airstrip. They quickly climbed to two thousand feet, giving them magnificent views of the rugged glaciers and snow-covered mountains of the interior of the island. Within an hour they were clear of Spitzbergen and flying out over the polar sea. Byrd was surprised at how quickly they reached the pack ice; it was much nearer the land than he expected. To the east it almost reached the land.

"We looked ahead at the sea ice gleaming in the rays of the midnight sun—a fascinating scene whose lure had drawn famous men into its clutches, never to return," he later wrote. "It was with a feeling of exhilaration that we felt that for the first time in history two mites of men could gaze upon its charms, and discover its secrets, out of reach of those sharp claws."

But he was aware of the dangers: "All the airmen explorers who had preceded us in an attempt to reach the Pole by aviation had met with disaster or near disaster . . ."

Once they were over the sea familiar landmarks faded into the horizon behind them. Now they had to rely on their instruments to navigate. Their compass was useless so near the Pole; it would draw them to the magnetic Pole, east of Greenland. They needed to find true north, and for that they were relying on a solar compass. The solar compass had been invented by William Burt in 1836, and was a little more difficult to use than a conventional compass, but a lot more accurate. The device consisted of three discs. One was set to the correct time; one was set to the current latitude; the third was set to the height of the sun. From these three measurements a reading of true north was obtainable.

Byrd was taking no chances; he had brought two solar compasses. One was a portable one, which he kept in the cockpit of the plane. The second was mounted on a trapdoor at the top of the navigator's section of the craft. Now that they were over the ice, Byrd's first task was to get a good bearing for the rest of the flight. He looked back and took a sighting on a mountain range in the dim distance, on Spitzbergen. Then he used the solar compass, and compared the two readings. They matched; other things going their way, he knew now he could find the Pole.

The next few hours were busy. The instruments had to be checked regularly, and Bennett, though a skilled flyer, had a tendency to let the plane drift to the right, which Byrd had to be vigilant to check. They took turns at the controls, swapping regularly to ensure they both remained fresh. It was bitterly cold; they had to wear gloves, and they kept on their aviator's leather helmets, which provided some warmth. Byrd had brought three pairs of gloves. When he was not at the instruments he could put on the thick mittens. But most of the time he had to wear one of the thinner pairs. Occasionally, when he was taking a reading at the open trapdoor above his head, he had to remove his gloves and work with his bare fingers. Altitude, latitude, and wind chill made that a painful experience.

"We had three sets of gloves which I constantly changed to fit the job in hand, and sometimes removed entirely for short periods to write or figure on the chart. I froze my face and one of my hands in taking sights with the instruments from the trapdoors. But I noticed these frostbites at once and was more careful thereafter. Ordinarily a frostbite need not be dangerous if detected in time and if the blood is rubbed back immediately into the affected parts," he recalled.

In addition to the solar compass, Byrd took readings on the sextant, scribbling notes in the flight log to keep a record of where they were. The featureless waste beneath them made those records essential. An hour or more into the flight the two airmen were confident that they were heading in the right direction, and traveling with sufficient speed to make their destination and return safely. They began to relax.

"I turned my attention to the great ice pack, which I had wondered about ever since I was a youngster at school," said Byrd. "We were flying at about two thousand feet and I could see at least fifty miles in every direction. The ice pack beneath was criss-crossed with pressure ridges, but here and there were stretches that appeared long and smooth enough to land on. However from two thousand feet the pack ice is extraordinarily deceptive.

"The pressure ridges that looked so insignificant from the plane varied from a few feet to fifty or sixty feet in height, while the average thickness of the ice was about forty feet. A flash of sympathy came over me for the brave men who had in years past struggled northward over that cruel mass."

Worryingly, there were plenty of open leads of water beneath them. An emergency landing would be difficult. Dismissing that worrying thought from his mind, Byrd began to study the wind conditions. If the great circle over the Pole were to become a commercial route his observations would be of vital interest. He noted that the flight was smooth; there was no turbulence to speak of. He was not surprised. He had guessed that the flat seascape and stable low temperature would make air pockets and updrafts uncommon.

A couple of hours into the flight, Byrd took over the controls once more, steering with one hand while taking a compass reading with the other. Bennett took the chance to stretch his legs. Then he picked up a five gallon drum of gasoline and poured it into the tank. The tank had to be topped up regularly. After every refill Bennett tossed the empty tin out the trapdoor to the ice beneath. Every bit of saved weight, no matter how trivial, might be important.

The hours passed in a flurry of monotonous but frantic activity. Both men took turns at the wheel. Byrd continued his readings, and his gentle nudging of Bennett to fly straight. Bennett continued to top up the gasoline, tossing the tins out each time. The ice swept under them, and they rubbed their fingers to keep the blood flowing. Could it really be that simple? They were within an hour of the Pole.

"The sun was still shining brightly. Surely fate was good to us. To the right, somewhere, the rays of the midnight sun shone down on the scenes of Nansen's heroic struggle to reach the goal that we were approaching with the ease of an eagle at the rate of nearly one hundred miles an hour. To our left lay Peary's oft-traveled trail," he mused.

Then, in an instant, it all changed. Optimism changed to panic, and they could see their dream snatched from them. The victory would go to Amundsen. They might not survive this day.

The starboard engine was leaking oil, and it was a bad leak. Byrd spotted it first, and he tapped Bennett on the shoulder. The other man looked out the window. He knew the implications. The noise of the plane made it impossible to talk, so he hastily scribbled a note and handed it to Byrd: "That motor will stop."

He was probably right; most leaks were serious problems. The engine would lose pressure, then it would stop spinning. And both men knew that the Fokker would not be able to limp back to Spitzbergen on one engine. If the engine went, they were doomed to a long walk home.

Bennett was confident he could fix the leak. He needed to set the plane down. He gestured to Byrd, but the older man was worried. They were too far north to risk it. If Bennett couldn't fix the problem, they faced a very long walk. They were a thousand miles from anywhere. They would have to haul their sledge and provisions across hundreds of miles before they got far enough south to be able to supplement their supplies with live game. They could be months on the pack ice. At all costs they needed to avoid that. Reluctantly he shook his head. They would not set the plane down on the ice.

Now he faced the problem that Frederick Cook had faced twenty-one years earlier: how far was far enough? Common sense told him to turn around and fly south, gaining as much ground as he could before the engine failed. An hour of flying, a hundred miles, could mean weeks less on the ice if things went as wrong as he suspected they could. Yet he was so near his goal . . . and Amundsen was in Spitzbergen, ready to take off. Ambition fought with the human instinct for self-preservation.

No one knows which side of Byrd's nature won that titanic struggle. At best we can make an educated guess from the surviving evidence. There is the official account, published in Byrd's book *Skyward* (1928), and there are his candid admissions to friends, off the record. There are also his navigational records. There are worrying discrepancies.

The official version is that Byrd took the decision to fly on, hoping that the leak would not result in a loss of pressure in the engine. He wrote: "I kept my eyes glued on that oil leak and the oil-pressure indicator. Should the pressure drop, we would lose the motor immediately. It fascinated me. There was no doubt in my mind that the oil pressure would drop any moment. But the prize was actually in sight. We could not turn back.

"At 9.02am, 9 May 1926, Greenwich Mean Time, our calculations showed us to be at the Pole! The dream of a lifetime had at last been realized."

He claimed that they lingered at the Pole, flying over the spot they had identified, taking readings to confirm their achievement. Then they flew a few miles away, and did a big circle, encompassing the Pole. "We thus made a non-stop flight around the world in a very few minutes."

Then they turned south.

But many experts believe that this official version is not the truth. Would an experienced airman really risk death just to claim a geographical prize already claimed by explorers twenty years earlier? Some experts, such as Norwegian-American aviator Bernt Balchen, felt that the Fokker did not have the power to maintain the speeds claimed by Byrd. Interestingly, Bennett never contested the critics. And some sources claimed that in private conversations both Byrd and Bennett admitted that they had turned south short of the Pole.

For years it was just speculation. Then, damningly, the navigational diary of the flight became public in 1996. Up to then the only record available to scholars was the typewritten official report written on June 22 (six weeks after the flight) and presented to the National Geographic Society. Now that record could be compared to the diary, and discrepancies were immediately obvious. The diary had erased, but still legible, sextant readings that differed from those on the typed report. An expert analysis of the diary revealed what probably happened.

Byrd got most of the way to his destination, but when the leak struck he turned around and flew home. He did not reach the Pole.

Somewhere on that long return journey, as both men monitored the oil pressure indicator and stared at the leak out the starboard window, a tacit understanding was reached. The question of "how far is far enough" had been answered. They were in the air several hours. They had gone far enough.

"At 9.15am we headed for Spitzbergen. But, to our astonishment, a miracle was happening. That motor was still running."

It may be true that they turned at 9:15 a.m., but it is more probable that they turned an hour earlier. Byrd claimed that a tail wind pushed their speed from eight-five to one hundred miles per hour, which allowed them make rapid progress south. The engine held. As the tense hours passed, the feeling began to grow that they just might make it back to base without having to ditch on the ice.

"We were aiming for Grey Point, Spitzbergen, and finally when we saw it dead ahead, we knew that we had been able to keep on our course! That we were exactly where we had thought we were," Byrd wrote.

"It was a wonderful relief not to have to navigate any more. We came into Kings Bay flying at about four thousand feet. The tiny village was a welcome sight. It seemed but a few moments until we were in the arms of our comrades, who carried us with wild joy down the snow runway they had worked so hard to make."

The Norwegians were soon aware of the return of the Americans. "I was at dinner," recalled Amundsen. "Someone said that if Byrd was to have the good fortune to get back, it was about this time he was return-ing. The words were hardly out of his mouth when we heard the hum of the motor. We leapt from our chairs and left our unfinished dinner. We led the dash up to the place where he would land."

In fact, Byrd was not on time; he was several hours early, because he had turned back at least an hour short of the Pole. Because he was not expected for another few hours, Byrd's crew were also at dinner on board their ship; Amundsen and the Norwegians were the ones waiting on the ice when Byrd's plane taxied to a halt. The smiling Norwegian was the first to step forward and offer congratulations. After a hearty handshake, he called for nine Norwegian cheers. Then he followed the two Americans back to their ship.

Byrd's shipmates from the *Chantier* were delighted to welcome home the conquering heroes. They were eager to push Byrd into the cable room of the ship, so that he could share his news with the whole nation. Amidst all the jubilation Byrd could still see two men—Roald Amundsen and his financial backer Lincoln Ellsworth. Both men were putting brave faces on it, smiling and joining in the celebrations as best they could. Byrd's success made their flight, scheduled for three days" time, meaningless. Byrd thought they were "good sports" for showing up. He shook his rivals by the hand, accepting their congratulations.

Would they have been such good sports if they had known how far he had really gone that day? Like the question of "how far is far enough," we can only speculate.

44

THE POLE AT LAST— THOROUGHLY AT PEACE WITH ALL THE WORLD

Amundsen had thought he was a few days away from being ready for take-off. But in fact he was only hours away. The day after Byrd returned from his polar flight, the Norge was declared ready. They decided to take off at 1:00 a.m. on May 11. The reason for the early start was that they were in a zone of twenty-four-hour daylight, so there was sufficient light. And the air temperature was at its lowest at that time, meaning the buoyancy of the gas in the dirigible would be at its greatest.

Amundsen woke at midnight, but then one of his men came with the news that a wind had sprung up, and the take-off had to be delayed. Amundsen went back to bed. At 6:00 a.m., he woke again. Now conditions were perfect. He had his breakfast, then walked up to the hangar with Ellsworth.

They found a scene of total confusion, with Nobile running around like a headless chicken. He said it was far too late to take off; the sun was shining on the top of the dirigible and the gas was losing buoyancy. Not knowing what was happening, Amundsen and Ellsworth stepped on board. Chaos reigned. Then suddenly a calmness descended, and the final checks were done. Moments later a shout went up: "We're off!"

Riiser-Larsen had taken charge. He had told the excitable Italian that he accepted responsibility for what would happen, and ordered take-off. The cine images taken show Riiser-Larsen giving orders and Nobile standing to one side, looking blank. Though a talented engineer, he was not a man for a crisis.

The take-off of an airship is nothing like that of an aeroplane. It is far gentler. They popped into the air, like a cork released underwater, and the ground crew released the ropes that tethered them. Then they began to drift upwards through the clear blue skies of early morning. As they gained altitude the three engines, housed in three large gondolas under the main cigar of the dirigible, began to turn, and the airship quickly gained speed, reaching its cruising speed of fifty miles per hour in minutes.

Byrd and Bennett turned out to see the take-off, and quickly fired up the *Josephine Ford*, flying alongside the *Norge* for the first half hour, until the airship cleared Spitzbergen and began to float over the pack ice. Then the *Josephine Ford* dipped its wings in salute and returned to base.

It was 10:00 a.m. when the *Norge* finally got underway, later than they had planned. But as they were in a region of twenty-four-hour light, that hardly mattered. An airship drifts along like a swan gliding over the still water of a lake. But just as a swan is furiously beating its legs beneath the surface, an airship is a hub of frantic activity. The *Norge* had four gondolas hanging under the hydrogen balloon that kept them afloat. Three of the gondolas housed the engines, while the fourth, the biggest, was up front for the pilot and crew. Two men manned each engine, while there were a dozen crew in the front gondola. Everyone had their task. Nobile was nominally the pilot, in charge of the flight (under the direction, but not the interference, of expedition leader Amundsen). Riiser-Larsen was the navigator, while Ellsworth was busy taking magnetic readings as part of the expedition's science remit. Amundsen was the only man without a specific task. His job was to observe the ground underneath, and be an explorer. Would they find new land?

At a cruising speed of fifty miles per hour—and faster with a tail wind—they covered ground fast. There were occasional mini-crises, as described by Amundsen in *My Life as an Explorer*. According to his account, on at least three occasions Nobile became distracted from his surroundings and allowed the airship to drift dangerously near the ground. On one occasion Riiser-Larsen roughly pushed him aside and took the wheel, bringing the nose of the craft up just before the engines scraped the ice.

"I said nothing. I would have said nothing if we had crashed, for I adhered throughout the voyage strictly to my status of commander and left the operation of the ship absolutely to Nobile as skipper, to whom, by right of the sea and the right of the air, it belonged. Riiser-Larsen, however, did not hold so strictly to the code. It was fortunate for us that he did not, else none of us would have come back to tell the tale," he recorded laconically.

After about fifteen hours of flight, the *Norge* was very close to their target. All the navigators began taking furious readings. At 1:30 a.m. on May 12, Riiser-Larsen announced: "Ready the flags. Now we are there."

Amundsen looked out the window of the gondola, at the ground several hundred feet beneath him. There was nothing to distinguish this bleak spot from any other spot on the thin crust of ice covering the deeply crevassed and pock-marked polar sea. There was no remnant to suggest that Cook had been there two decades previously, or Peary; no sign that Byrd might have flown by only a few days previously. For all the world it looked like virgin ice. Which it was, if only he had known.

Nobile roared an order, and the three giant engines cut out. The dirigible drifted along on its momentum, before air resistance slowed it down to a mere waft. The rudders were adjusted, and it drifted in a tight circle, the ground a mere three hundred feet beneath them.

Oscar Wisting joined Amundsen at the window, and stood by his commander. They had been together at the bottom of the world, the first men to stand at that spot. Now they were at the top of the world, the first men to have reached both places. Words were not needed. They just smiled at each other, and shook hands. Job done. They had reached the Big Nail.

After a few minutes of silent contemplation, Amundsen came to life. He fetched his Norwegian flag—tiny, to conserve weight—and opened the window. The flag was attached to a sharp metal pole, and he released it, watching it fall to the ground and landing, the flag fluttering in the slight breeze. The Norwegian flag had been planted at the Pole. Next, Ellsworth came forward and repeated the procedure, dropping the American Stars and Stripes. The flag that Cook and Peary had both failed to get there was finally fluttering over the most northerly spot on the world.

Then the solemnity of the moment descended into farce. Nobile came forward with a big chest, which he had concealed on the airship. He opened it and removed an enormous Italian flag, big as a blanket. He shoved it through the window, then proceeded to toss a pile of other smaller flags and pennants after it, filling the sky with the obscure regalia of several Italian organizations.

They became "like a circus wagon in the skies," Amundsen joked.

One of the big flags—which were not weighted down like the Norwegian and American flags—became entangled in the idling propeller of one engine. If the engine had been on, it could have caused major problems for the expedition. Finally it fell to the ground, landing several hundred feet south of the Pole.

The *Norge* spent an hour at the Pole, drifting slowly in circles as the men gazed in wonder, and took the navigational readings that would confirm to the world they had reached their destination. Those readings have stood the most vigorous scrutiny in the intervening years. Cook's observations were discredited quickly. Peary's observations lasted only until his personal papers became available to researchers in the past thirty years, then failed under scrutiny. Byrd's observations were in doubt almost from the moment he landed. But nobody doubts that Amundsen reached the North Pole on May 12, 1926. The man who was the first to the South Pole had also become the first to the North Pole. But he did not know that, as he stood at the window of the gondola.

After an hour the engines were switched on again, and the airship began its journey south. But they were not returning to Spitzbergen. Instead they headed across the polar sea toward Alaska. Several hours later they arrived on the Alaskan coast, and began looking for familiar landmarks. Fog descended and the weather became stormy, and it became a matter of blind chance rather than planning that they located a small town, and pulled off a successful landing. They were in Teller, about ninety miles northwest of Nome. The trip had taken four days, and they had crossed from Spitzbergen right across the Pole and into America. On every level it was a resounding success.

A familiar voice accosted Amundsen, and he turned to see a woman he had met a few years earlier in Nome. Now she ran the hotel in Teller. There was a warm bed waiting for the explorers.

"Of course we had a merry evening," Amundsen concluded. "We were all elated at the success of the expedition. One of our hosts produced cigars and a good bottle of whiskey. This, and an appetizing dinner, put us thoroughly at peace with all the world."

And Amundsen had earned it.

EPILOGUE

ROBERT PEARY

All his life had been a buildup to the Pole. When he failed to reach it in 1909, he knew he was too old and too frail to mount another attempt. So exaggerating his distances on the final few days was his only option, particularly when it became obvious that Cook was claiming to have snatched the prize.

The following year he exercised all his ingenuity and cunning to shape the narrative in his own favor. He succeeded magnificently, breaking the reputation of his rival. In October 1910 he was promoted to the rank of captain in the Navy, a remarkable achievement for a man who spent so little of his career in the service.

But he knew he could not rest on his laurels. His own claims were as doubtful as Cook's, and he could not afford to let them come under scrutiny. He headed off a move in Congress to have his claim to the Pole evaluated by an independent panel of explorers. He headed off many such moves, and consistently refused to make his papers available to researchers. His intransigence made no difference. He was given the Thanks of Congress for discovering the Pole by a special act in March

1911, and later the same month, Congress promoted him to the rank of Rear Admiral in the Navy Civil Engineer Corps. The promotion marked his retirement from the Navy.

Peary retired to a spacious home on Eagle Island, in Casco Bay, Maine, where he lived out his final decade. He received numerous foreign honors, and in 1916 became chairman of the National Aerial Coast Patrol Commission, a private organization which advocated the use of aircraft in detecting enemy warships and submarines. This led directly to the formation of the Naval Reserve aerial coastal patrol units—and paved the way for the later successes of Richard Byrd. He was also involved in the planning of a system of eight air mail routes, which became the basis of the US Postal Service air mail system.

Admiral Peary died in Washington on February 20, 1920. He is buried in Arlington National Cemetery. His companion Matthew Henson returned from the polar expedition and spent the next thirty years working at the US Customs House in New York. He died in in 1955, and was reinterred in Arlington in 1988.

Peary's personal papers, including his diaries and notes from the final polar expedition, were not made available to researchers until 1984. When they were finally analyzed, they revealed nothing to support Peary's claim to have reached the Pole. The verdict of history is clear: he fell a hundred miles short.

ROALD AMUNDSEN

Umberto Nobile did his best to hijack the success of the *Norge* expedition, defying his contract by going on a lecture tour of America, and claiming all the glory for himself and Mussolini. But even a braggart can only go so far on old glory; eventually he decided to mount his own Arctic expedition. This would be an entirely Italian affair. During 1927–1928 he prepared an N-class airship, *Italia*, which was slightly bigger than the *Norge* and could travel at seventy miles per hour. He got it to Spitzbergen in May 1928, and on May 23 took off for the North Pole, repeating the first leg of the journey he had made with Amundsen. Nobile was both pilot and expedition leader.

The following day they reached the Pole, then turned south, heading back to Spitzbergen. But a huge storm broke out. The airship weathered the storm as best it could, but on May 25, still well short of home, the *Italia* crashed onto the ice. They were just twenty miles short of Spitzbergen. Ten of the crew were thrown clear in the crash, while six remained attached to the dirigible, which took off into the air after the smash. Nobile watched helplessly as the six men disappeared into the sky. The dirigible and the six men were never found. One of the ten men thrown clear was killed instantly. That left nine injured men on the ice.

Nobile himself suffered a broken arm, broken leg, shattered rib, and a head injury. Others were equally battered. They managed to salvage some survival items, including the radio and a tent, and one of the six carried away to their deaths threw supplies of food from the air as he was swept up. The nine survivors set up camp on the ice, which was slowly drifting toward nearby islands. After a few days three made a dash across the ice. One, the meteorologist who had failed to see the storm coming, disappeared on that march. There were persistent rumours that he was killed and eaten by the other two.

The incident was an international disaster, and quickly many nations offered to help, including the Soviet Union and the Scandinavian countries close by. Amundsen despised Nobile, but he could not watch a fellow explorer die on the ice and do nothing. By now he was in semi-retirement, touring the world, lecturing, and enjoying being a public hero. He even did a lecture tour of Japan, a completely alien culture to Europeans of that era. But when he heard about Nobile's disappearance, he knew where he had to be.

He did not have an aircraft of his own, but he volunteered to be part of a private French effort to save the missing airmen. On June 18, 1928, he boarded the Latham 47 Flying Boat at Tromsø for the flight toward Spitzbergen. On board were five French men, including two experienced pilots. The plane rose into the gray mist and turned toward the Barents Sea. It was beset by fog for most of the flight, with visibility very poor. At some point, the plane simply disappeared. Some wreckage, including a wing-float and part of a gasoline tank, were eventually recovered. Of Amundsen there was no sign. He had simply vanished in the cold air.

It is believed that the plane crashed into the sea due to poor visibility, and all on board were killed on impact. Roald Amundsen, the last of the Vikings, was fifty-five years old. He had overcome his financial woes, and had established a reputation as the greatest of the modern explorers. He never got the chance to enjoy his golden years. Like his great rival Scott, he died in harness, actively exploring the frozen lands that had given his life meaning.

As the years have passed, Amundsen's reputation has continued to grow. It is now widely accepted that he was the first man to reach both Poles, and his list of other achievements is staggering. He was the noblest of men, fearless and incorruptible.

His partner on the North Pole flight, Lincoln Ellsworth, remained interested in exploration, switching his attention to Antarctica, where he led four expeditions, all air based. He completed the first trans-Antarctic flight in 1935.

As for Umberto Nobile, he was rescued by a Russian ice-breaker after a month on the ice. Eight of the sixteen crew returned to safety. The Italian authorities blamed him for the loss of the *Italia*, and it took him several years to rehabilitate his reputation. He ended up an academic at the University of Naples, and he never returned to the Arctic. He died in 1978, still a legend in his own mind.

FREDERICK COOK

Cook lost his media war decisively, and with it his reputation. The whole of America—and most of the world—accepted Peary's version that he was a knowing fraud. The attention on his polar con caused scrutiny of his earlier achievements, and his conquest of Mount McKinley was wiped off the record books.

This was followed by his imprisonment for mail fraud. He was a model prisoner. He worked as night warden of the prison hospital, as well as on a literacy program. He gave lectures to the other inmates, and wrote uplifting articles in the prison paper, *The New Era*, which were widely reprinted. His behavior behind bars did much to rehabilitate him in the eyes of the American public. In 1926 Roald Amundsen took time out of his lecture tour to visit his old friend. The publicity from that meeting also helped rehabilitate Cook.

On his release in 1930, Cook chose not to go back to his beloved but estranged wife. He felt his disgrace too keenly, and felt his family were better off without him. Though they had been divorced before his imprisonment, they remained close for the rest of their lives, getting together several times a year. Cook found no market for his writings, and ended up moving to Chicago, where he helped out with a friend's ophthalmology practice. His own medical qualification was long out of date.

The last few years of his life were spent shuttling from Chicago to New York and New Jersey, where he stayed with his daughters and a sister. Always a gentleman with a charismatic air, he did win back some support. But his stories of great discoveries in the Arctic and in Alaska were no longer believed by the public.

At the very end of his life, Cook received a Presidential pardon from President Franklin D. Roosevelt. He was delighted. It was some vindication, but not the vindication he wanted. He would have been happier if his claim for the Pole was accepted. A few months later, in early August 1940, Cook suffered a cerebral hemorrhage. He died of complications a few days later, on August 5, and is buried in Forest Lawn Cemetery, Buffalo, New York.

He is now remembered as a talented ethnographer and anthropologist, and a gifted explorer, but also as a deeply flawed man with a penchant for exaggeration which led to claims everyone accepts were fraudulent.

RICHARD BYRD

Like Peary, Byrd knew that if he was to shine in the Navy and build up a career, exploration was his ticket. His 1926 flight close to the North Pole achieved that for him. He became a national hero, and was promoted to the rank of commander. He and Floyd Bennett were both presented with the Medal of Honor.

In 1927 he took part in the race to be the first to do a non-stop transatlantic flight. But the plane he and Bennett were flying crashed, and Bennett was injured. Charles Lindbergh made the first successful crossing on May 21, 1927. With a new pilot (Bernt Balchen), Byrd became the second man to achieve a non-stop transatlantic flight, on June 29.

Bennett eventually recovered from his injuries, but they left him in a weakened state. A year later, on April 25, he was flying a rescue mission for the crew of the *Bremen*, which had crash landed on Greenly Island in the province of Quebec, Canada. He had pneumonia at the time of the flight, and succumbed to his fever in the air. There is a persistent rumour that he admitted to a friend shortly before his death that he and Byrd had not reached the North Pole during their historic flight, but turned back an hour short of their target due to engine problems. This is entirely consistent with what is known of the flight.

Byrd switched his attentions to Antarctica in 1928, leading an expedition with two ships and three planes. They established a base at Little America on the Ross Ice Shelf, and in the second summer, on November 28, 1929, Byrd flew to the South Pole and back again, becoming the first man to do this. His fame at an all-time high, he was promoted to the rank of rear admiral by a special act of Congress, becoming the youngest admiral in the history of the United States Navy. Not bad for a man whose career looked to have been cut short by a gymnastics injury.

Byrd led four more Antarctic expeditions (1933–'35, 1939–'40, 1946–'47, and 1955–'56). His adventures, recounted in his popular books, became the stuff of legend. He spent five months alone during the Antarctic winter, manning a meteorological station on his own, and nearly died of carbon monoxide poisoning due to a poorly ventilated stove. In 1946 he led the largest ever Antarctic expedition, involving four thousand men, and in his last expedition he established a permanent base at McMurdo Sound, which is still in use, as well as bases at The Bay of Whales and at the South Pole itself.

He managed to take time out to serve during the Second World War, mostly as a consultant to the Navy top brass. From 1942 to 1945 he headed important missions in the Pacific, surveying remote island groups and setting up airfields, and he was present at the Japanese surrender in Tokyo Bay on September 2, 1945.

Admiral Byrd passed away peacefully in his sleep at his home in the Beacon Hill neighborhood of Boston on March 11, 1957, and is buried at Arlington National Cemetery.

His later career established him as one of the true greats of Antarctic exploration. His reputation never suffered because of his deception on the North Pole flight of 1926. This is probably because, at the time, he was believed to have been the second or third man to have reached the spot, not the first. So his claim never came in for the intense scrutiny that could ruin reputations.

SELECTED BIBLIOGRAPHY

Books

Amundsen, Roald	My Life as an Explorer
	Roald Amundsen's *Belgica* Diary
	The South Pole: An Account of the Norwegian Antarctic Expedition in the *Fram*, 1910–12, Volume 1 and 2
	The Northwest Passage
Amundsen, R and Ellsworth, L.	The First Flight Across the Polar Sea
Anderson, Bruce	True North: Peary, Cook, and the Race to the Pole
Bart, Sheldon	Race to the Top of the World
Brown, Stephen	The Last Viking: The Life of Roald Amundsen
Bryce, Robert M.	Cook and Peary: The Polar Controversy Resolved
Byrd, Richard	Skyward
	Alone: The Classic Polar Adventure
Cook, F. A.	Through the First Antarctic Night
	To the Top of the Continent
	My Attainment of the Pole
Crane, David	Scott of the Antarctic, a biography
Ellsworth, L.	Beyond Horizons
Fiennes, Ranulph	Captain Scott
Henson, Matthew A.	A Negro at the North Pole
Huntford, Roland	The Last Place on Earth
	Race for the Pole: The Expedition Diaries of Scott and Amundsen
Nobile, Umberto	My Polar Flights
Peary, Robert	The North Pole, Its Discovery in 1909 Under the Auspices of the Peary
Arctic	Club
Ross, Lisle A.	Explorer, the Life of Richard E. Byrd
Scott, Jeremy	Show Me a Hero: The Sin of Robert Peary, the Man Who Lied for Fame
Scott, Robert F.	Scott's Last Expedition
	The Voyage of the Discovery
Wally, Herbert	The Noose of Laurels: The Discovery of the North Pole

Periodicals and Newspapers
Standard Union (Brooklyn)
New York Herald
The New York Times
The Daily Chronicle (London)
The National Geographic
Harper's Magazine

346

INDEX